# THE HOUSE ON HENRY STREET

The House on Henry Street, about 1920. Henry Street Settlement Collection.

# The House on Henry Street

*The Enduring Life of a Lower East Side Settlement*

ELLEN M. SNYDER-GRENIER

*Foreword by* PRESIDENT BILL CLINTON

WASHINGTON MEWS BOOKS
*an Imprint of*
NEW YORK UNIVERSITY PRESS
*New York*

**WASHINGTON MEWS BOOKS**
*an Imprint of*
**NEW YORK UNIVERSITY PRESS**
New York
www.nyupress.org

References to Internet websites (URLs) were accurate at the time of writing. Neither the author nor New York University Press is responsible for URLs that may have expired or changed since the manuscript was prepared.

Library of Congress Cataloging-in-Publication Data
Names: Snyder-Grenier, Ellen M. (Ellen Marie) author.
Title: The house on Henry Street : the enduring life of a Lower East Side settlement /
Ellen M. Snyder-Grenier.
Description: New York : New York University Press, 2020. | Series: Washington mews |
Includes bibliographical references and index.
Identifiers: LCCN 2019043246 | ISBN 9781479801350 (cloth) | ISBN 9781479801374 (ebook) |
ISBN 9781479801381 (ebook)
Subjects: LCSH: Henry Street Settlement (New York, N.Y.) | Poor—New York (State)—
New York.
Classification: LCC HV4196.N6 S59 2020 | DDC 362.5/5763097471—dc23
LC record available at https://lccn.loc.gov/2019043246

New York University Press books are printed on acid-free paper, and their binding materials are chosen for strength and durability. We strive to use environmentally responsible suppliers and materials to the greatest extent possible in publishing our books.

Manufactured in the United States of America

10 9 8 7 6 5 4 3 2 1

Also available as an ebook

# CONTENTS

# FOREWORD

## PRESIDENT BILL CLINTON

THE FIRST TIME I VISITED HENRY STREET SETTLEMENT WAS on a sweltering July afternoon in 1992—just hours before the Democratic National Convention was to convene at Madison Square Garden, a few miles north of the Settlement. The occasion was an outdoor town hall meeting, where I greeted the enthusiastic crowd gathered outside the Settlement's Abrons Arts Center. As I looked around, I saw the best of America—young and old, immigrant and native born—all there because they wanted to create a better future for themselves and their families. And it was clear they cared deeply about their neighborhood, and their nation.

I knew that many came from humble origins, just as I had. It was an engaged group, and I was impressed by their insightful questions. I even referenced one in my acceptance speech for the Democratic nomination for President I delivered the next day. Among the many people I met at Henry Street was Danny Kronenfeld, then the agency's executive director. I was so moved by his dedication to his community that I invited him to the Faces of Hope inaugural luncheon, one of 53 Americans invited to attend. I sat next to him that day, and learned even more about the Settlement.

My encounter with Henry Street in the early 1990s was just a brief moment in its long, full life. The organization was founded in 1893 by Lillian Wald, a 26-year-old nurse whose shock at witnessing the misery and poverty on the Lower East Side prompted her—in a moment she later called her "baptism of fire"—to take action. She moved—or "settled"—into the neighborhood and along with the other nurses who lived at the Settlement delivered health care and more to their impoverished neighbors.

Henry Street Settlement was established on the simple belief that everyone deserves a chance to live his or her best life story, and the more fortunate among us should do what we can to give them that chance. The Settlement continues today to open doors of opportunity for the neighborhood's most vulnerable residents. It is deeply rooted in a community that has been home to wave after wave of new immigrants seeking a better life in America, helping them to realize their full potential to become engaged citizens, to find jobs and apartments, and to access health care, education, and the arts.

Inside this book you'll get a glimpse of Henry Street Settlement's 125 years and counting of serving Lower East Side residents, and all New Yorkers, and see how what they have done—and continue to do each and every day—helps build strong families, strong neighborhoods, and a strong nation. It's been a remarkable journey, and thankfully it's not over yet.

# INTRODUCTION

THE HOUSE ON HENRY STREET STANDS ON THE LOWER EAST Side of Manhattan, a neighborhood of constant change where generations of immigrants and migrants have become Americans and New Yorkers. Built in 1827, the home took on new life in 1895 as a "settlement," part of a Progressive Era movement dedicated to tackling the problems of poverty by "settling" in and serving impoverished communities. From the sturdy brick building, Henry Street Settlement's founder—Lillian Wald—built an enterprise that became one of the nation's most important and renowned social service organizations.

Today, the house at 265 Henry Street is still heart and headquarters of the Settlement, now an expansive network of 18 facilities that delivers a wide range of social services, arts, and health care programs to more than 50,000 New Yorkers each year. It is a special place, mostly because of the countless individuals who have crossed its threshold and found a helping hand and a lifetime connection there, but also because its sweeping history illuminates important stories of the Lower East Side, New York City, and the nation: stories about poverty, and who is worthy of help; immigration, and who is welcomed; human rights, and whose voice is heard; education, and who deserves it; health care, and who has access to it. Equally important, these stories illustrate the power of bridging divides to foster social change.

Henry Street Settlement would spawn the Visiting Nurse Service of New York, the school nurse, special-needs classes, free school lunches, the first municipally sponsored playground in New York City, and the United States Children's Bureau. It would help form the NAACP, forge Social Security legislation, create models for the sweeping antipoverty programs of the 1960s, and foster new approaches to homelessness. It would launch legendary institutions—the Neighborhood Playhouse, the New Federal Theatre, and the Abrons Arts Center—and serve as a classroom, a launching pad, or a laboratory for some of the most acclaimed artists of our times: composer Aaron Copland, painter Jackson Pollock, folk singer Jean Ritchie, choreographer Alwin Nikolais, comedian Jerry Stiller, producer Woodie King Jr., actors Anita Velez-Mitchelle, Ruby Dee, and Denzel Washington, and many more. And its expansive dining room table forged a culture of connection. Welcoming all, it brought together neighbors and newcomers, politicians and policy makers, prime ministers and presidents, sociologists, writers, and activists to share meals and ideas, spar over disagreements, cross boundaries—and, in the process, try to create a better world.

The Settlement was born in 1893. On a wet, cold March day, 26-year-old nurse Lillian Wald was on her way to the bedside of a gravely ill young mother. When she arrived at the woman's squalid tenement home, she was shocked by what she saw—and also by what she'd witnessed on her walk there, through the vibrant but impoverished streets of Manhattan's Lower East Side. Wald decided to act. She first moved to the top floor of a tenement along with a colleague to provide nursing and aid to immigrants, largely from Eastern and Southern Europe, who had come in search of possibility and found relentless poverty. In 1895, the wealthy German Jewish banker and philanthropist Jacob Schiff—inspired by the work of this young dynamo, like him the child of immigrants—purchased for Wald number 265 Henry Street as a permanent headquarters. From the House on Henry Street, Wald built an approach to health care that focused not just on the patient but on the patient's environment. She moved from case to cause, curing sickness and then agitating to end the conditions that produced it. What she initially called the "Nurses' Settlement" became "Henry Street Settlement" and one of the most influential social welfare organizations in American history.

Wald was a voice for those whose voices were not being heard, a powerful female activist at a time when women were increasingly finding their place in a male-dominated public sphere. She was a gifted executive capable of managing a vast, multifaceted organization. She was a savvy networker who had the ears of the powerful and the influential. She was a charismatic connector with a loving demeanor who was able to bridge boundaries of class and culture. Her enterprise—invigorated by the work of other social reformers and human rights activists, the rise of social work, and the professionalization of nursing—put her in the vanguard of the settlement house movement and at the forefront of health care and the fight for social justice, and launched an enduring institution.

The year 2020 marks the 125th year since Lillian Wald walked up the steps of number 265 and into the townhouse with the red brick façade, intent on making a difference in the world. Henry Street Settlement is a remarkable institution because it has survived where so many others have not in a changing nation and a changing New York. It has survived both because of its adaptability as an institution and because of the ingenuity at the core of its mission—the concept of brotherhood, of bringing diverse people together. More darkly, it has survived because the issues it was founded to address—poverty, inequality, racism, income disparity—still persist today.

Henry Street Settlement was flexible, committed to responding to neighbors' needs, and always, as Lillian Wald said it must, "moving with the times." It also had a strong guiding vision: that differences were something to be celebrated, and that by bridging divides—of class, culture, and beliefs—we could create a more just world. It was not necessarily unique; it was the vision that drove most settlements. But it burned especially brightly at the House on Henry Street, founded by the child of immigrants who adopted a stylized version of the Chinese character for "bao," which relates to brotherhood, as its first logo. Today, President and CEO David Garza calls it "neighbor helping neighbor."

This book, written to commemorate the Settlement's 125th anniversary in 2018 and its 125th year at the House on Henry Street in 2020, unfolds in three parts. Part 1 begins with Lillian Wald's awakening and her response to need at a time of rising urbanization, industrialization, and immigration. It charts the rise of Henry Street and its integrative approach to community health, its place in the settlement house movement, and its blueprint for social action. Part 2 explores Henry Street in the years following World War I, when conservatism tamped down activism—only to watch it rise with the Depression, which summoned a larger role for government in treating poverty. Through the depths of the economic downturn, the split of the nursing service from the Settlement's social work in 1944, World War II, and the growing tensions of a postwar world, it looks at how Henry Street navigated a new generation and its issues. Part 3 examines what it means to be a neighbor in a new era guided by the tenets of the War on Poverty; the challenges of rising conservatism; and the meaning, significance, and impact of public funding on settlements and their work. And it looks at the Settlement today, as it reenergizes for the 21st century.

A number of issues and ideas run through all these parts, many of them seesawing through time: about changing attitudes toward poverty and how to address it; about who is worthy of support; about professionalization and the role of gender and ethnicity; and about whether the Settlement's arts programs were geared more for a downtown or an uptown crowd. Many of these issues are unnervingly similar to those that face America at the close of the second decade of the 21st century. You can hear the anti-immigration vitriol of the late 1800s in the cries for a wall on America's southern border in 2019. You can feel the 1930s' disappointment over the failure to pass universal health care in the fights over coverage today. And you can feel the anger over Gilded Age income inequality in today's tensions over the rise of the one percent.

The persistence of these and other issues is one reason why Henry Street's story is as relevant today as it was more than a century ago. So are its guiding principles and enduring lessons, which together make up the blueprint for social justice that Lillian Wald created many years ago and which continues to guide the Settlement today.

**Each of us is whole and worthy.** Even though many saw the immigrant newcomers who arrived at the turn of the 19th century as threats, Henry Street celebrated new arrivals—and those in need—as individuals with their own beliefs, hopes, and dreams to be respected and nourished.

**Poverty is a social issue.** Lillian Wald, like other settlement house leaders, believed that disease and poverty were not individual shortcomings, but social problems that should be confronted by the larger forces of government and society.

**There is power in bridging differences.** By celebrating what Lillian Wald called the "power of association," Henry Street created relationships that were rare in a city divided by class, race, and ethnicity. Even though settlement workers no longer live in the houses where they work, the way the first generation did, the power of people working together in a community still defines Henry Street.

**Neighbors matter.** By living where they worked, early settlement house workers created a new relationship between service providers and their communities. Wald called it being a "neighbor." Today, Henry Street President and CEO David Garza calls it the "transformational power of relationship."

This book, which is rooted in the life of a special house and animated by the many people who have crossed its threshold, is not just about the challenges, but about the best possibilities of urban life and the enduring lessons that are worthy of our attention today.

# 1

## A BAPTISM OF FIRE

### Creating a Blueprint for Social Justice, 1893 to the 1930s

MARCH 1893. IT WAS A COLD, DRIZZLY DAY ON MANHATTAN'S Lower East Side. At the Louis Down-Town Sabbath and Daily School, a 26-year-old nurse named Lillian Wald was teaching a homemaking class to new immigrants when a young girl burst in. She begged Wald to help her mother—one of Wald's students—who lay near death in a nearby tenement. Wald took the girl's hand and the two rushed out to the street. They hurried through the din and congestion of tenement-lined streets, along broken pavement, past heaps of uncollected garbage, until they reached the girl's home.

The two made their way up unlit stairs caked with mud, down a dingy corridor, and into two squalid rooms, where the girl's family of seven and their boarders lived. There, the girl's weakened mother lay on a blood-soaked mattress, hemorrhaging after childbirth, abandoned by her doctor because she could not pay his fee. Now the family had nowhere to turn. The scene was, said Wald, "a shock that was at first benumbing." She made the woman as comfortable as possible. And, within half an hour, she decided to move to the Lower East Side, determined to do something about what she had seen.[1]

So begins the story of Henry Street Settlement: with an awakening and a response. Wald's baptism of fire would grow into a blueprint for action, a distinct blend of social work and activism. Just months after that fateful day, Wald, along with her nursing colleague Mary Brewster, moved to a dynamic but poverty-stricken Lower East Side. There they found lodging, began to serve the community, and created a settlement house—part of a larger Progressive Era movement that saw poverty not as an individual shortcoming but a social, environmental one, triggered by the rapid rise of an urban-industrial economy.

Buoyed by the growing settlement house movement, driven by a sense of social injustice, and guided by a belief in universal brotherhood, Wald got to work. She drew together an effective coalition of nurses, neighbors, funders, board members, allies, supporters, and like-minded, powerful women to create an innovative visiting nurse service. She generated myriad opportunities for cross-cultural association in clubs, classes, and the arts. And she built a powerful platform for creating change locally and nationally.

World War I would erode the Progressive Era optimism that spawned Henry Street. It would bring backlash that strangled the flow of immigrants and ushered in rising conservatism—which held that individuals, not the environment, were to blame for poverty. In this new climate, some started to question settlements' role. And yet poverty, and the need on the Lower East Side, remained constants, both drawing on and testing Wald's blueprint for social justice.

## FACING A PANORAMA OF PROBLEMS

The misery that Lillian Wald saw in a squalid apartment, and the walk through gritty streets to reach it, changed her life and how she saw the world around her. "All the maladjustments of our social and economic relations," she later wrote, "seemed epitomized in this brief journey and what was found at the end of it."[2] Wald had been attending the Women's Medical College in Lower Manhattan to expand her education and, possibly, become a doctor. She quit school and started on a new path, determined to confront, head-on, the pressing problems of poverty.[3]

In the late 1800s, as New York and other American cities became centers for business and industry, the demand for unskilled and semi-skilled labor skyrocketed. This seemingly insatiable thirst drew massive numbers of immigrants, pushed by persecution and lack of economic opportunity at home and pulled to the United States by the prospect of better jobs, housing, and greater freedoms than they had in their home countries. Their journeys were made easier by new, larger, faster steam-ships and their largely restriction-free entry to America.

More than 23 million immigrants arrived in the United States be-tween 1880 and 1919. Most came through New York City, and many stayed in the rising metropolis, long a home to newcomers from around the world. The two largest groups of arrivals were Southern and East-ern Europeans. They included Italians—largely farmers and laborers—fleeing such problems as poverty and discrimination in Italy; about one-third would eventually return home. A vast number were Russian and Polish Jews from small villages, pushed to leave by persecution—including violent, anti-Semitic riots and attacks—and lack of economic opportunity; few of them would ever return home for good.[4] While they brought with them rich cultures, most had few financial resources. There was hope and expectation: "My heart pounded with joy when I saw New York in the distance," wrote one newcomer to *The Jewish Daily Forward* advice column in 1908; "it was like coming out of the darkness. . . ." Said another, "If I had known it would be so bitter for me here, I wouldn't have come. I didn't come here for a fortune, but where is bread?"[5]

As immigrants poured into New York City, most settled on the Lower East Side (fig. 1.1). Said to be one of the most crowded neighborhoods in the world, its circumstances were forged by the intertwined forces of skyrocketing industrialization, rising urbanization, massive immigra-tion, an unregulated market economy, and greed and indifference. In the early 1800s, it had been home to affluent merchants and ship captains,

FIGURE 1.1. On the Lower East Side in 1902, streets are filled with pushcarts, pedestrians, energy, excitement, and hope, as well as poverty and disillusionment. Courtesy of the Library of Congress.

who made their living in the city's burgeoning seaport. By the mid-1800s, though, as the well-to-do slowly moved north, it became a home for immigrants who arrived with fewer means: Irish, escaping famine and British repression, and Germans, fleeing a poor economy, religious persecution, and political oppression. And now, in the late 1800s, the Lower East Side had drawn Eastern and Southern Europeans—but mostly Eastern Europeans, who gave the neighborhood its reputation as the Jewish Lower East Side. It was a community with a palpable sense of energy and excitement. For newcomers, the growing numbers of Jewish synagogues and *Landsmannschaften* (mutual aid societies), Yiddish theaters and music, and the availability of familiar foods—from smoked fish to flavorful knishes— helped make the new neighborhood feel a bit like home.

New freedoms made the neighborhood refreshingly different. Max Weren, who would become a Henry Street club member, arrived in July 1905. The first thing he did was head to Seward Park on the Lower East Side "to see some of my countrymen." Once there, he noticed 50 to 60 people gathered around a speaker's platform and, at the center, a man addressing the crowd. "There was a strike in the Bakers' Union, and he was telling everyone to buy bread with the union label," said Weren. "Suddenly, two strikebreakers jumped in to break up the meeting. A policeman, watching from across the street, ran over and took away the two strikebreakers. Instead of shooting the speaker, he locked up the disturbers!" When he saw that, Weren said, "I made up my mind that this was my country."[6]

This dynamic neighborhood was also impoverished, and its many problems challenged residents' health and wellbeing. The streets were congested, packed with people, carts, and horse-drawn wagons and strewn with manure, garbage, and raw sewage. The most common housing type was the tenement. Typically old and poorly maintained, these narrow, four- to five-story apartments had small, dark, cramped, poorly ventilated rooms, cold in the winter and stifling in the summer. Plumbing (including running water) was rare. Toilets, usually located outside, served many more people than they could handle. Martha Dolinko came to the Lower East Side as a young girl; she remembers how her father took the family to Rutgers Street and East Broadway. "He had an apartment for us—what an apartment! The toilet was in the yard. The sink was a black sink in the hall. Everybody was washing there. There was only cold water running. There were three rooms. If it wasn't enough we slept on the roof . . . or I slept on the fire escape."[7] The "dumbbell tenement" (so named for its floor plan, which was pinched in the middle to accommodate a central air shaft), born out of an 1879 law to improve housing conditions, was a seeming improvement; each room had a window, and the air shaft provided much-needed ventilation. But among other flaws, the dumbbell design made the building a fire hazard. If a tenement caught fire, the central air shaft formed a chimney that drew flames ever upward in the building. Nearly half of the city's fire deaths took place on the Lower East Side.

By night, many tenement rooms became cramped bedrooms for family members and, often, for boarders, taken in to help pay living expenses.[8] A place to sleep might mean a shared bed or a spot on the floor. In his 1890 exposé *How the Other Half Lives*, journalist and reformer Jacob Riis described two small rooms in an Essex Street tenement that housed a couple, their 12 children, and six boarders.[9] By day, many of these crowded homes became workplaces: in an effort to reduce cost, manufacturers farmed out jobs to workers who labored at home. Many adults and children toiled long hours at light industries making such goods as cigars, cigarettes, and artificial flowers.[10]

FIGURE 1.2. Clutching her purse in one hand, a woman carries home a heavy load of clothing in this 1912 photograph. Needle-trade workers often picked up clothing pieces at a sweatshop, then brought them home to assemble. Courtesy of the Library of Congress.

The most common industry in the tenements, though, was sewing for the city's garment industry (fig. 1.2). Almost half of all immigrants toiled in the needle trades, enduring long hours of repetitive work with little hope of advancement. "I am working at neckties now—that is all I know how to do—and I see nothing before me but neckties morning, noon and night, day after day, always neckties, neckties, neckties; oh, it's slave's work!" exclaimed one young girl.[11] "The clock in the workshop does not rest," lamented Morris Rosenfeld in his 1898 poem about a sweatshop. "I work, and work, and work without end. . . . There are no feelings, no thoughts, no reason; the bitter, bloody work kills the noblest, the most beautiful and the best . . . ask me not! I know not, I know not, I am a machine!"[12]

Some claimed that America rewarded hard work, but for many, it was impossible to find a job that paid a living wage. To survive, every family member, including young children, often had to work to make ends meet.

A 1906–7 survey of 1,049 children in New York City tenements found that 558 worked; only 491 attended school. A web of economics, injustice, and inequality meant there was often little hope of escaping the brutal cycle.[13]

In crowded tenements, germs traveled easily. For overworked and exhausted tenants, the lack of sanitation, light, and ventilation—coupled with close quarters—not only cultivated sickness but made it difficult to contain. Tuberculosis, dubbed "the white plague," was common; so was infantile diarrhea, and both were often fatal.[14] "Thousands are sick in the sweat-shops," observed journalist and University Settlement worker Ernest Poole, "thousands are sick at home." With almost no social safety net in place, an illness or injury could push a family from getting by into utter destitution. And in 1893, the year that Wald made her life-changing walk, these abject conditions were exacerbated by the worst economic depression that the United States had ever experienced. By January 1894, roughly 70,000 were unemployed and 20,000 homeless in New York City alone; newspapers carried wrenching stories of misery, hopelessness, and suicide.[15]

By middle-class mores, the idea of a young, non-immigrant, middle-class woman like Lillian Wald moving to the Lower East Side would have been outlandish. Born in Cincinnati, Ohio, in 1867, she was the third of four children of Max D. Wald and Minnie Schwarz Wald, German Jews who had fled the economic turmoil of the 1848 revolutions in Europe. The family moved in 1878 to Rochester, New York, where Wald grew up in a liberal Jewish household that nurtured her universal worldview.[16] Wald would have been expected to one day marry, have children, and manage a household. If she chose to work, it would most likely be as a clerical worker, one of the few positions then open to women.

Wald wanted more. When she was 16, she applied to Vassar College, one of a handful of colleges for women at a time when women were discouraged from pursuing higher education. She was refused because she was too young. Not long after, a chance encounter with a professional nurse who was tending her sick sister, Julia, led her in a new direction. Never before had she met a woman whose occupation allowed her to be out in society, doing good work. Wald decided to become a nurse.[17]

It was a radical choice. Middle-class women like Wald rarely became nurses in the late 1800s; nursing was a new profession that had not yet shed its association with domestic service. Most nurses were white, American-born, aged, and poor. In addition, as a Jew in a time of rampant anti-Semitism, Wald faced restrictive nursing school admission quotas (most programs took place in Christian environments) and widespread discrimination against hiring Jewish nurses—but she was undeterred.[18] In 1889, she applied to the New York Hospital Training School for Nurses in Manhattan,[19] laying out in a letter to hospital official George Ludlum her desire for a life with purpose. Her words are an anthem to the aspirations of late-19th-century women living in a male-dominated society with rigid social expectations—or to anyone who ever felt boxed in by someone else's idea of who they should be.

Dear Sir,

Your letter of 25th has just been received. I scarcely know just what to write you that would give such insight into my character as you would care to have. Self-laudating or affected modesty being equally poor guides to such a knowledge.

I may say that I have had advantages of what might be called a good education, knowing Latin, and able to speak both French and German, besides having the habit since leaving school of devoting some hours each day to a study. My life hitherto has been—I presume—a type of modern American young womanhood, days devoted to society, study and housekeeping duties, such as practical mothers consider essential to a daughter's education.

This does not satisfy me now. I feel the need of serious, definite work, a need perhaps more apparent since the desire to become a professional nurse has had birth. I choose this profession because I feel a natural aptitude for it and because it has for years appeared to me womanly, congenial work, work that I love and which I think I could do well.

Nor do I write this in total ignorance of what is expected of one who devotes her life to it, our family having employed graduates of the New York School.[20]

Wald was accepted into the nursing program and enrolled (fig. 1.3).
After graduating in 1891, she took a position at the New York Juvenile
Asylum in upper Manhattan. Drawn to the job by her love for children,
she found the institution too large, impersonal, and stifling, and left
after one year. Wald decided to attend medical school, and enrolled at
the well-respected Woman's Medical College in New York City. Once
again, she was testing society's boundaries; while medicine was slowly
opening up to women, it was considered a man's profession. While in
medical school, Wald was enlisted to organize a homemaking class for
immigrant women at the Louis Down-Town Sabbath and Daily School,

FIGURE 1.3. Lillian Wald as a student at the New York Hospital Training School for
Nurses in August 1889. Courtesy of the Print Collection, Miriam and Ira D. Wallach
Division of Art, Prints and Photographs, The New York Public Library, Astor, Lenox
and Tilden Foundations.

one of a growing number of organizations created by established, affluent German Jews to help newcomers—who shared their faith but not
their homeland—gain a footing in their new home.[21]

Lillian Wald was teaching at the sabbath school when the young girl
found her on that drizzly March day in 1893 and led her through the
gritty streets of the Lower East Side to her mother's sickbed. After that
"baptism of fire," Wald turned her back on medical school. "Deserted
were the laboratory and the academic work of the college," she said. "I
never returned to them."[22]

## "WE HAVE SEEN AMONG OUR NEIGHBORS MANY HARROWING THINGS": TAKING ACTION

Wald began to formulate a plan to bring home-nursing care to the
impoverished residents of the Lower East Side. In the late 1800s, most
medical treatment took place at home—giving birth, setting broken
bones, treating illnesses, even surgery. While hospitals existed, they were
few and still in their infancy—although they were starting to grow in
number, and, thanks to advances in science, they were starting to emerge
from the widespread perception that they were places of last resort,
where only the poorest and most desperate went to die. For the poor,
a home visit from a doctor was rarely an option, since physicians (and
trained nurses) typically catered to the well-to-do patients who could
afford their fees. That meant that if they were extremely ill, a hospital
was their only option—even though illness, an accident, and in particular
a hospital stay for a breadwinner or caregiver could initiate the breakup
of a low-income family. So for inspiration, Wald looked to British "district" nurses, who traveled into their cities' most poverty-stricken areas to
tend to the poor sick (and then returned home), their work underwritten
by wealthy families who paid for the nurses' board and lodging, a model
that had just begun spreading to the United States.[23]

To breathe life into her nascent plan, Wald enlisted 28-year-old Mary
Maud Brewster, a fellow graduate of the New York Hospital Training

School for Nurses.[24] They would "live in the neighborhood as nurses," said Wald, "identify ourselves with it socially, and, in brief, contribute to it our citizenship."[25] The two would tend to patients in their own homes, with compassion and without judgment. Their service would be nonsectarian and apolitical; it would not be tied to any charity organization or institution; and it would begin with the patient and an "organic relationship with the neighborhood." And it would be hourly, with payment tiered according to a patient's ability to pay (although most patients did, in fact, pay nothing). While they were "visiting nurses," the phrase that best described who they were is the one Wald coined for their integrative, community-focused work: "public health nurses."[26] (Today, they would typically be called community nurses.)

Wald may also have been inspired by Florence Nightingale. The renowned British nurse argued that, in fact, some chronic, serious illnesses were unsuited or inadmissible to general hospitals; that in any event there were not enough hospitals to meet the demand; that home care was less costly; that keeping poverty-stricken patients at home helped to keep their families intact; and that, as social reformers repeatedly asserted, to truly improve the health of low-income patients, the impoverished neighborhoods in which they lived had to be improved.[27]

In describing the birth of public health nursing 20 years after the fact, Wald laid out the factors that originally prompted its need (interestingly, echoing many of the same reasons that renowned British nurse Florence Nightingale had enumerated in a paper she wrote for a conference Wald attended). Wald's description provides a useful snapshot of the situation they faced in 1893. She and Brewster had realized, she said, that

there were large numbers of people who could not, or who sometimes would not, avail themselves of the hospitals; that ninety per cent of the sick people in cities were sick at home . . . and that a humanitarian civilization demanded that something of the nursing care given to those in hospitals should be accorded to sick people in their homes. Economic reasons were revealed, too, namely that the valuable and expensive hospital space should be saved for those to whom the hospital treatment was necessary; obvious social reasons, also, namely that many people, particularly women, could not leave their homes without the danger of imperiling, or sometimes destroying, the home itself.[28]

Four months after Lillian Wald's baptism of fire, she and Mary Brewster moved to the Lower East Side—just as a severe economic depression was edging the already impoverished neighborhood into even more dire straits.[29] They temporarily lodged at the College Settlement on Rivington Street, formed by recent graduates of Smith, Vassar, and Wellesley colleges. "With ready hospitality they took us in," said Wald, "and, during July and August, we were 'residents' in stimulating comradeship with serious women, who were all the fortunate possessors of a saving sense of humor."[30] This brief stay with the settlement women served as their immersive introduction to a new phenomenon: the settlement house movement.

The settlement house movement emerged during the Progressive Era, a period in the late 19th and early 20th centuries when a generation of reformers and radicals in the United States confronted businesses that had grown too big, governments that had grown too corrupt, and cities that were too crowded, too dirty, too exploitative, and too unhealthy for their inhabitants. Progressive Era reformers had new ideas about poverty and how to address it. Earlier reformers had blamed the poor for their poverty, believing that those in need were simply lazy, drunk, or immoral. In contrast, Progressive reformers blamed the environment. And, while their predecessors had tried to alleviate poverty by "improving" the poor themselves, they sought to improve the physical and economic environment that, they believed, caused poverty. They also conducted detailed studies and in-depth research, trusting that in research lay solutions.[31]

The first settlement house opened in 1884 in London, England, where Church of England curate Samuel Barnett and his wife, Henrietta, created Toynbee Hall. Convinced that lasting social change would not come about through the piecemeal, individualized approaches of their time, the Barnetts chose a new tactic: they brought together volunteers to live and work in the poverty-stricken East End of London. There, by intimately facing urban ills, they strove to create workable solutions that could be adopted locally and nationally.[32] The term "settlement" described the practice of living in a community or neighborhood with the people being served—which differentiated these new crusaders from earlier charity workers, who worked in poor neighborhoods but left at the day's end to return to their affluent homes.

Inspired by the Barnetts, others followed suit. In 1886, Amherst College graduate Stanton Coit founded the first settlement house in the United States: the Neighborhood Guild (today the University Settlement) on the Lower East Side. The movement quickly spread. By 1891 there were six settlements in the United States; by 1900, there were 100; and by 1910, there were 400.[33] Like Toynbee Hall, American settlement houses were founded and operated by volunteers. Unlike most British settlements, though, which were church-related, American settlements were largely nonsectarian.[34]

What also distinguished American settlements is that they were largely women-led. Three-fifths of American settlement residents between 1889 and 1914 were female. Ninety percent had been to college, part of the early generation of American college-educated women. While men joined settlement houses, they tended to leave within a few years; women stayed (although this dynamic would later shift). Most settlement women were Christian, although some were not (Lillian Wald was one of a number of Jewish heads of settlements); and while most were white, some were people of color, who because of (and in spite of) segregation formed their own institutions. In New York City alone, for example, Victoria Earle Matthews founded the White Rose Home for White Rose Mission in 1897 on Manhattan's Upper East Side to serve southern Black migrants and West Indian immigrants; in Brooklyn, Dr. Verina Morton Jones, one of the first Black female doctors in the United States, established Lincoln Settlement Association along with white civil rights activist Mary White Ovington, and incorporated it in 1914.[35]

Settlement work provided women with an opportunity to do good, interesting, and politically important work in an atmosphere of intellectual excitement within a support network of like-minded women. Just as importantly, it gave them a local, national, and even international platform for the issues they cared about, and a greater opportunity to create change in a world and a power structure that was overwhelmingly dominated by men. Through the settlement house movement, Lillian Wald was able to forge and tap into important female networks, such as women's clubs and civic organizations, to fight for shared causes. Because the movement coincided with women's "freer admission to public and professional life," Wald felt that women's sense of responsibility for social concerns was distinctive.[36]

Among the most influential social welfare organizations of the time, settlement houses became major players in almost all of the Progressive Era's reforms.[37] That is not to say they didn't have detractors. Some saw them as nests of condescension toward their immigrant neighbors, and their workers as dilettantes. A July 31, 1910, *New York Times* article extolled the virtues of settlement house women who tried to address the inequities of the "City of the intolerably rich and the intolerably poor." But it also acknowledged that they suffered from a public perception that a typical settlement worker was "a person of exceptional leisure who chose to live in an ill-smelling district and who had rather an unmannerly habit of making unsolicited visits upon his—or usually, her—less fortunate neighbors—to exert upon the poor a vaguely elevating influence."[38] The editors of the conservative *Hebrew Standard* in 1910 argued that settlements were "hardly worth the great amount of money spent in maintaining a horde of professional 'uplifters' whose highest ambition, as a rule, is to prate and write glibly about the 'ghetto people.'"[39]

Both perspectives described extremes. While settlements did in fact share commonalities, they were not all alike. Some historians have painted them broadly as assimilationists who sought to socially control immigrants in order to make them into their own middle-class likeness at the expense of the newcomers' own cultures. While some were assimilationist, pushing immigrants to abandon their pasts, others were not; their goal was to help new arrivals—like Eastern European Jews, who intended to stay and wanted to move up—to become integrated into American society without giving up their cultures (Henry Street was in this category). Some focused on religion, hoping to sway newcomers to Christianity; most did not. And some were very activist (such as Hull-House, Chicago Commons, and Henry Street); most were not so radical.

Living on Manhattan's Lower East Side, Wald and Brewster experienced settlement and neighborhood life firsthand. One hot night, their room was so stifling that Wald could not sleep. As she went to the window for some air, she looked outside. Beneath her, she said, "life was in full course":

> Some of the push-cart venders still sold their wares. Sitting on the curb directly under my window, with her feet in the gutter, was a woman, drooping from exhaustion, a baby at her breast. The fire-escapes, considered the most desirable sleeping-places, were crowded with the youngest and the oldest; children were asleep on the sidewalks, on the steps of the houses and in the empty push-carts; some of the more venturesome men and women with mattress or pillow staggered toward the riverfront or the parks.

It was 2 a.m.[40]

Operating a settlement cost money, and neither Wald nor Brewster had the independent means to support their work (unlike, for example, Jane Addams, who initially used a small inheritance to fund Hull-House's operations).[41] And so while living at the College Settlement, on the advice of a mutual acquaintance, Wald contacted Betty Loeb, wife of Solomon Loeb, who had accumulated wealth and influence as an investment banker and partner in the Manhattan firm of Kuhn, Loeb & Company.[42] Loeb and her family were part of a group of elite German Jews who supported a variety of causes that catered to newly arriving

Jewish immigrants. By the time of Wald's arrival, they had helped establish a number of philanthropic and educational institutions in New York City—including the Louis Down-Town Sabbath and Daily School on Henry Street, where Wald had been teaching when the daughter of an ailing student sought her help.[43]

While these established individuals shared the religion of new arrivals, they differed from Eastern European newcomers both culturally and economically. Many were second-generation German Jews and had made their fortunes as bankers and merchants in the mid-1800s. When they reached out to Eastern European Jews living in poverty, it was often with a mixture of supportiveness along with a desire to protect their own reputations as Jews. (There were many perspectives on this, however. Felix M. Warburg, one of Wald's most ardent supporters, hated what he described as the "silly layer cake," its "bottom layer being the so-called Russian Jew and the top layer the so-called German Jew." Nothing, said Warburg, "is so ridiculous as this attempt to make geographical distinction between Jew and Jew.")

Wald, who was herself Jewish but did not singularly identify with her faith, enjoyed the support of a number of New York City's most prominent German Jews—chief among them the Loeb, Schiff, Warburg, Lehman, Lewisohn, and Morgenthau families—and all were central to her efforts.[44] Wald visited Betty Loeb at her townhouse on East 38th Street, with its marble-topped tables, heavy drapes, and expensive oil paintings and family portraits, and shared her plan.[45] Loeb described Wald as "an extraordinary young woman," adding that she was unsure if she was "a genius, or whether she is mad." But she wanted to give the passionate young nurse a chance.[46] She introduced Wald to her son-in-law, Jacob Schiff. Schiff, who lived in Manhattan, was the most prominent German Jewish businessman of his time (fig. 1.4). He was a titan in the world of finance, a leader in the Jewish community, an outspoken voice against anti-Semitism, and an extremely generous philanthropist with a wide span of interests, including education for Jews and for African Americans.[47]

FIGURE 1.4. Wald's devoted benefactor, Jacob Schiff, with his wife, Therese Loeb Schiff, about 1915. Funding from the immensely wealthy businessman made Henry Street possible. Courtesy of the Library of Congress.

Wald now had the most prominent, powerful German Jewish businessman of his time at her back. Jacob Schiff embraced Wald and became her benefactor, confidant, and mentor. His inscription in the Settlement's guest book in 1909 suggests how much he respected her: "I have never been as proud, never been as happy concerning anything that has come into my life," he wrote, "than the cooperation it has been my good fortune and privilege to render the self-sacrificing, constructive work done in the Henry Street Nurses Settlement under the intelligent and efficient guidance of Miss Lillian D. Wald, God bless her!"[48] He shared her values, and they learned from each other. Because Schiff insisted on detailed reports about Wald's work, and she wrote him frequently, they left behind a rich archival record of their relationship, as well as a valuable glimpse into the personal values and attributes that made Wald so good at what she did. She was positive, caring, and compassionate; she had a heightened sense of empathy; and she had an uncanny ability to interpret ideas and issues from one class, one ethnic group, one side, to the other. In her private letters to Schiff and in her public writing and speeches, she drew on the personal (real stories about real people with real names and real challenges) and the universal (ideas that anyone could relate to—family, home, aspirations for one's children) to make human connections and shine a light on larger issues. In contrast to newspaper and magazine stories that made immigrants into faceless hordes, she elevated individual stories of dignity and hope, of suffering—"we have seen among our neighbors many harrowing things," she wrote Schiff in 1893[49]—and of rising above suffering. We "see much loveliness of heroism and traits not apparent to the man or woman, who know our neighbors as beggars," she shared, describing how a

young Russian who longs to be a mechanical engineer and who has been dangerously near starving but who would take no charity, was compelled one day last September to take twenty-five cents for carfare to answer an advertisement for work. He did not succeed there but he now sells newspapers and last Sunday afternoon, having saved that much he called to return the money with thanks.[50]

At the end of the summer of 1893, Wald and Brewster began searching for new quarters. "Our work is not identical with the work of the College Settlement," Wald wrote to Schiff, "and now that their regular winter work begins, the rooms that we occupy should be used for workers, who can give their time wholly to the specific work of the house, which is as you know chiefly club work."[51] They found rooms on the top floor of a nearby tenement on Jefferson Street.[52] The view from their windows included a sweatshop below them, where the two watched "figures bent over the whirring foot-power machines." Never, said Wald, "did we go to bed so late or rise so early that we saw the machines at rest."[53] With the move to Jefferson Street, the two nurses formed what Wald called "precious" and "intimate relationships" with their neighbors. "The mere fact of living in the tenement brought undreamed-of opportunities for widening our knowledge and extending our human relationships," wrote Wald. Conversely, she said, "That we were Americans was wonderful to our fellow-tenants," who were all immigrants from Russia or Romania (with the exception of the "janitress," Mrs. McRae, who was Irish).[54]

The two women's initial goal was to build trust. As fellow nurse Lavinia Dock (who would soon join their endeavor) put it, they wanted to "make their own impression as friendly souls before whom all the confidence and problems of living might be safely opened. Their nursing was, of course, their open sesame."[55] Or as Wald said, "From what we call the 'settlement point of view,' we believe that the patients should know the nurse as a social being rather than as an official visitor."[56]

As word of Wald and Brewster spread, neighbors in need found their way to the Jefferson Street tenement. "Workers in philanthropy, clergymen, orthodox rabbis, the unemployed, anxious parents, girls in distress, troublesome boys," all came, wrote Wald. The difficulties they faced, she said, were "not peculiar to any set of people, but intensified in the case of our neighbors' poverty, unfamiliarity with laws and customs, the lack of privacy, and the frequent dependence of the elders upon the children."[57] The problems they sought help for were rooted in both neighborhood conditions and the complexities of modern, urban life. Wald and Brewster provided not only nursing care but small loans, food, job referrals, carfare, emotional support, and more, building the foundation for all that was to come—work that was holistic and responsive, a unique blend of nursing, social work, and activism.

With growing demand for the nurses' services, it soon became clear that they needed more room. And that is when Jacob Schiff purchased 265 Henry Street for their rapidly growing enterprise.[58] Fittingly, the building was located next door to the Louis Down-Town Sabbath and Daily School, where Wald had been teaching when a plea for help changed her life's course.

## THE SETTLEMENT'S FORMAL WORK BEGINS

The house on Henry Street was built in 1827, when the area was prosperous and the neighborhood was home to members of the well-heeled merchant class and those who made their living from the shipyards of nearby South Street Seaport and Corlears Hook. With their stately entrances and rich architectural details, the area's houses were in many ways monuments to New York City's rise to commercial greatness as a port and the wealth it had generated. By the time Wald and Brewster arrived, though, the well-to-do had moved northward. In their wake came newly arriving Irish and German immigrants of lesser financial means, who moved into the old homes, now subdivided by landlords to accommodate the demand for housing and reap profits. When Wald and Brewster moved into 265 Henry Street in 1895 (their belongings moved by unemployed men from their old block who refused payment), they found a house that, unlike many others of the same time period, had retained many of its original details. It is not hard to imagine the two pausing, as they entered through the handsome front door with its leaded glass side lights, to admire the details—seeing not so much these vestiges of the past, but what the home could become (fig. 1.5). For now, with a building of their own, the "formal organization of our work," as Wald called it, began.[59]

Within walking distance of the house were stores, synagogues, and Catholic churches. Just blocks away was Rutgers (later Straus) Square, a hub of political activity for immigrant Jews, a place to talk, debate, gather, and demonstrate. A typical Saturday night might look like the one that transpired in 1892, when, as the Marxist weekly *Di arbiter tsaytung* reported, thousands of Jewish workers, many marching with unions and Socialist Party clubs, assembled for a procession that took them to Union Square, carrying signs with such slogans as "The Best Strike Is through the Ballot Box," "We Demand the Abolition of Wage Slavery," and "Down with the Sweating System," greeted by loud shouts of "hurrah" as they streamed uptown.[60]

FIGURE 1.5. The House on Henry Street, about 1920: animated, as it always would be, by the life of the neighborhood. Henry Street Settlement Collection.

Just two doors up from the Settlement, at 269 Henry Street, was the firehouse occupied by Engine Co. No. 15, built in 1883 on the site of an earlier firehouse, home to Americus Engine Co. No. 6, of which William M. "Boss" Tweed was a founder. Tweed was perhaps best known as the head of Tammany Hall, the Democratic political machine that ran much of city politics. (In a complicated way, Tammany Hall, like the Settlement, ministered to the needs of new immigrants, but Wald opposed it for the corruption that undergirded it.) When Wald and Brewster arrived in 1895, fire trucks still sped out through the ornate cast-iron façade, bells clanging, as they raced to battle city blazes.

The house at 265 Henry Street would become a home, a hub, a neighborhood center, a connector, and a nexus for liberal thought and action. For now, it was a townhouse in need of remodeling. The women converted the ground floor into public spaces: a dispensary, where they could treat neighbors with simple complaints; meeting rooms; and a bathroom.[61] Upstairs were the more formal rooms, including a dining room, and above them, Wald's and Brewster's bedrooms. Wald used her second-floor sitting room, with its expansive wooden porch, as a kind of public/private interspace, where she could, as she did one evening, have a quiet talk with a young neighborhood woman. The woman, said to be leading an "immoral" lifestyle, had come seeking advice; there, the sense of calm and quiet "helped to create," said Wald, "an atmosphere that led easily to confidence."[62] The resident nurses who joined Wald and Brewster lived in the small rooms originally built to lodge the servants employed by the house's well-to-do owner.

Outside, Wald and Brewster created a playground for local children. Samuel Schneeweiss, a neighborhood youngster, recalled how the "nurse ladies" became "special attractions for the swarm of children in the neighborhood" when they moved into number 265. Wald, he said, became "excited about the possibilities of turning the back yard into a playground that would take the youngsters off the hot crowded streets." After making arrangements with the sabbath school next door and their neighbor to the rear, the nurses joined three yards into one expansive playground.[63] It boasted brightly colored flower beds, a sand pile covered by a striped awning, swings, parallel bars, and baby hammocks. Its use ebbed and flowed during the day, said Wald:

> In the morning under the pergola an informal kindergarten was conducted, and in the afternoon attendants directed play and taught the use of gymnastic apparatus. Later in the day the mothers and older children came, and a little hurdy-gurdy occasionally marked the rhythm of dance. . . . At night the baby hammocks and chairs were stored away and Japanese lanterns illuminated the playground, which then welcomed the young people who, after their day's work, took pleasure in each other's society and in singing familiar songs.

Wald called it a "heaven of delight." So enticing was the spot, she said, that once children learned that any child charged with babysitting a younger brother or sister had priority access to the playground, a rivalry would emerge over who was to hold the family baby. "When (as rarely happened) there was none in the family," said Wald, "a baby was borrowed."[64]

Warm, inviting, and welcoming, the house on Henry Street was more than just a house; it was a home. Settlement women like Wald drew on a Victorian ideal of middle-class women presiding over their homes as wives and mothers with care, moral uplift, and nurturing, redefining it for their modern endeavor, rejecting maternalism's limiting aspects and owning its best and most useful parts.[65] Alice Lewisohn, who with her sister, Irene, would help create the Settlement's arts programs, described Wald, Hull-House settlement's Jane Addams, and activist Florence Kelley as "rare statesmen of a new order, for they functioned through a sense of relationship—could one say as Great Mothers?—instead of through the rigidity of a patriarchal system."[66] Through the language of home and family, Wald acted out her desire to think about the city and its people in new ways (fig. 1.6). Class and ethnic and cultural backgrounds would not be barriers at Henry Street, even if they were barriers in the city and society.

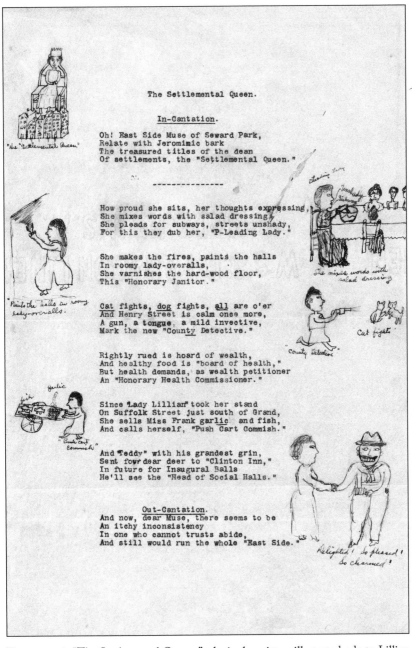

The Settlemental Queen.

In-Cantation.

Oh! East Side Muse of Seward Park,
Relate with Jeromimic bark
The treasured titles of the dean
Of settlements, the "Settlemental Queen."

----------------

How proud she sits, her thoughts expressing,
She mixes words with salad dressing,
She pleads for subways, streets unshady,
For this they dub her, "P-Leading Lady."

She makes the fires, paints the halls
In roomy lady-overalls,
She varnishes the hard-wood floor,
This "Honorary Janitor."

Cat fights, dog fights, all are o'er
And Henry Street is calm once more,
A gun, a tongue, a mild invective,
Mark the new "County Detective."

Rightly rued is hoard of wealth,
And healthy food is "board of health,"
But health demands, as wealth petitioner
An "Honorary Health Commissioner."

Since "Lady Lillian" took her stand
On Suffolk Street just south of Grand,
She sells Miss Frank garlic and fish,
And calls herself, "Push Cart Commish."

And "Teddy" with his grandest grin,
Sent four dear deer to "Clinton Inn,"
In future for Inaugural Balls
He'll see the "Head of Social Halls."

Out-Cantation.
And now, dear Muse, there seems to be
An itchy inconsistency
In one who cannot trusts abide,
And still would run the whole "East Side."

FIGURE 1.6. "The Settlemental Queen," a lovingly written, illustrated ode to Lillian Wald, likely created by one of her fellow nurses. It depicts Wald as host, mother figure, and activist. It also shows that she was not afraid to get her hands dirty—as in the second drawing from the top left, where she "paints the halls in roomy lady-overalls." Courtesy of Lillian Wald Papers, Rare Book & Manuscript Library, Columbia University in the City of New York.

FIGURE 1.7. Members of "the Family"—Henry Street's first residents. Back row: Jane Hitchcock, Sue Foote, Jeanne Travis. Middle row: Mary Magoun Brown, Lavinia Dock, Lillian Wald, Yssabella G. Waters, Henrietta van Cleft. Front row: neighborhood children Sammy Brofsky and Florrie Long. Courtesy of the Visiting Nurse Service of New York Records, Archives & Special Collections, Columbia University Health Sciences Library.

Wald said of the Settlement at large, "we are all one family," and she dubbed the unrelated women who lived with her "the Family"—with a capital "F" (fig. 1.7). The moniker suggests her efforts to adapt the veneration of family and motherhood to the work she wanted to do, on her own terms. By 1898, the Family included 11 members, nine of them trained public health nurses.[67] Among them were Jane Hitchcock, Wald's fellow graduate from the New York Hospital Training School for Nurses, who came to Henry Street as a nurse in 1896 and rose to supervisor,[68] and nurse and dedicated suffragist Lavinia Dock, who joined Wald in 1896 at age 38, helped develop the field of public health nursing, and was Wald's closest friend for 20 years.[69] Mary Brewster, who helped Wald found the Settlement, suffered from poor health; married in 1898, she soon after left the Settlement. She died in 1901, at the age of 37, of heart disease and other ailments.[70]

This modern family, born out of the settlement house movement, quickly expanded. Friendships with the nurses, activists, and other women who joined them sustained Wald, who as the Settlement's "headworker" served the demanding role of a CEO, and provided an all-important support network. For example, Florence Kelley, the child of activist abolitionists who had grown up to become a lawyer and social and political reformer, came to Henry Street from Chicago's Hull-House settlement, and stayed for almost 30 years;[71] well-known homemaking advisor Mabel Hyde Kittredge lived at the Settlement in the early 1900s; and lawyer Helen Arthur, who became involved in the Settlement's theater program, spent the summer of 1906 at Henry Street as a resident.[72] In Kittredge's papers, now in an archival collection, is a tongue-in-cheek poem, likely written in 1904, which suggests that they were more than fine with the predominantly female environment. Its first stanza goes like this:

THE CALLER

Busy! Who said I was busy?
   Walk right in? of course you can
Here's the parlor: dine in next room.
   Yes, all women. No, no men.
Yes, we like it—Pray excuse me
   But I think the door bell rang.

From letters found among her personal papers, Wald is known to have had romantic relationships with Kittredge and Arthur, both affluent, upper-class women. From the letters, the depth of their relationships is clear; both provided support to Wald, and she trusted them deeply. However, Wald worked nonstop, and it is clear that neither woman could ever have quite as much of her as they would have liked. Kittredge was especially up front about her feelings. For example, in a 1904 letter to Wald, she writes, "I haven't got to give you entirely to humanity. I am human too . . ." then semi-apologizes for her neediness in a brief P.S.: "This is the reaction from being a dressed up swell all the afternoon at a big, dull wedding." And in another, clearly resentful of the Lower East Side immigrants who drew almost all of Wald's attention, she apologizes profusely for referring to the newcomers as "your" people, not "our" people.[73]

## "BAO" AND THE FOUR BRANCHES OF USEFULNESS

Lillian Wald had a vision of a city and nation as an expanded family, one that would be defined by an inclusive and generous citizenship. On a 1910 visit to Japan to rest and to explore international humanitarian issues, she saw a symbol that encapsulated this vision: the Chinese character "bao," which related to brotherhood. Wald broadened it to mean "universal brotherhood" and adopted a stylized version of it as the symbol and logo for the Settlement.[74]

Wald believed in what she called the necessity of "association," of stepping across the social boundaries of industrial America to connect with those who were marginalized or merely different. This belief drove the Settlement (and its widening circle of influence) in all aspects of its work—work that Henry Street Supervisory Nurse Jane Hitchcock described in a 1907 article as their "four branches of usefulness": nursing; social work (clubs, classes, kindergarten, gym activities); country work (summer camp, outdoor activities, and their convalescent homes); and civic work (fights for clean streets, "better schools, more parks, improved housing conditions," and more).[75]

### The First Branch

The first "branch" and the Settlement's heart was its visiting nurse service—which made it dramatically different from other settlement houses, not only because of its focus, but because of how it functioned.

Whereas other settlements invited their neighbors *in*, Henry Street both invited neighbors in *and* connected with them in their homes, on their turf, in an exchange based on their needs, that addressed not just their illnesses but the environments in which they lived and worked and the circumstances of their daily lives. As Henry Street nurses traveled through the city, healing, practicing preventive care, and teaching their neighbors about modern hygiene, they—and by extension the Settlement—came to know their neighbors in ways that typical settlement houses could not (figs. 1.8, 1.9, and 1.10).

The nature of this unique relationship with city dwellers living in poverty comes into focus through a day-in-the-life description of a Henry Street nurse, published in the July 21, 1907, *New York Times*. Early in the morning, the nurse begins her rounds by climbing over several vessels

FIGURE 1.8. A Henry Street public health nurse crosses tenement rooftops to reach her patients in this photograph from around 1910. With so many house calls to make, the shortcut made the most efficient use of her time. Courtesy of the Visiting Nurse Service of New York Records, Archives & Special Collections, Columbia University Health Sciences Library/Jessie Tarbox Beals.

FIGURE 1.9. To help meet the needs of residents in nearby Chinatown, Henry Street hired nurse Zing Ling Tair, who visits a child in this photograph from about 1927. Henry Street Settlement Collection.[76]

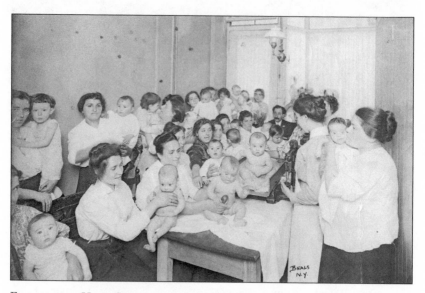

FIGURE 1.10. Henry Street nurses traveled throughout the city; they also conducted preventive care clinics at Settlement branches, like this well-baby class. Courtesy of the Visiting Nurse Service of New York Records, Archives & Special Collections, Columbia University Health Sciences Library/Jessie Tarbox Beals.

to reach a pneumonia patient who lives on a canal boat. From there, she goes on to bathe a newborn baby and its mother, "a poor creature left utterly destitute by her husband's recent death." Then, she makes a visit that is part medical, part social, to an elderly man with leg problems, whose "chief hankering seemed to be for a little intelligent gossip." After attending to both his "physical and mental" needs, she visits a "charming old Irish-woman, almost crippled but not a case for a hospital." With the nurse's help, the woman is able to manage and to maintain a home for herself and her only son.

It's not yet noon when the nurse visits a family of Italian immigrants for a case described as "a peculiarly sad one." Although a dying man and his wife cannot "bear to be separated during the last few weeks," the wife and their daughter continue to sew garments, fearing they would lose their jobs if they fell behind on the piecework. There is little the nurse can do, though, beyond making the failing man comfortable. After lunch, the nurse returns to check in on her pneumonia patient. Then she travels to see a young girl recuperating from an illness, purchasing flowers on her way to cheer up the child's home. Once there, she takes the time to explain a change in medicine to the relieved mother, who, she worries, "would have kept on dosing the child until the end of her days with the medicine that had helped her during the crisis."

Afterwards, the nurse returns to the mother and baby, and, again, to the pneumonia patient on the canal boat (and telephones to request a night nurse to help him through his ordeal). Her work isn't finished, though. "On the way home," notes the article, "the nurse had the happy inspiration of hiring a woman to do the sewing of the Italian man's wife that she might spend all her time with her dying husband and yet not lose her place and be without a livelihood when she found herself alone."

Such visits sometimes precipitated a deeper connection with the Settlement. When teenaged immigrant Rose Gollup (later Cohen), a sweatshop worker, fell ill, her mother called Henry Street for help. Gollup recalled wakening from sleep to see a Henry Street nurse sitting beside her.

Neither in looks nor in dress had I ever seen any one like her in our neighbourhood. She was also beautiful and distinguished.

"How do you feel?" she asked me. Her lips smiled but her eyes remained almost sad. She spoke to mother in German, gave her a card and went away. I spelled out the printed name on the card, Lillian D. Wald, 265 Henry Street.

Later, Gollup wrote in her journal:

Miss Wald comes to our house, and a new world opens for us. We recommend to her all our neighbours who are in need. The children join clubs in the Nurses' Settlement and I spend a great deal of time there. Miss Wald and Miss Brewster treat me with affectionate kindness. I am being fed up. I am to be sent to the country for health, for education.[77]

The Henry Street Visiting Nurse Service, which would expand into a vast network, grew rapidly. With the Lower East Side (and number 265) as its home base, Wald created branches in other struggling neighborhoods throughout the city, including one "adopted" outpost, Hamilton House, which served the health needs of newly arrived Italian immigrants. By 1907, the Settlement had 30 trained nurses at Henry Street with five in executive positions, overseeing operations at the branches and at the convalescent homes they were now running. The remaining 25 worked directly with visiting nursing, and included 23 staff nurses, a supervisor, and an assistant supervisor. Of that 25, 10 staff nurses and the two supervisors lived at number 265; the other 13 lived, noted Jane Hitchcock, "in other settlement houses scattered throughout the city, or in flats of their own, but always in the neighborhood of the people whom they wish to serve."[78]

Wald, like her friend and fellow settlement head Jane Addams, purposefully sought equality for people of color.[79] And so as the visiting nurse service expanded to meet the needs of immigrant New Yorkers, it also expanded its outreach to the city's Black residents. New York City had an African American population with deep roots as descendants of the free and enslaved people who had helped build the city into a thriving metropolis. Beginning in the 1910s, the Black population swelled with the arrival of newcomers from the rural South who came as part of the Great Migration, seeking opportunity in the city's thriving industries. The North held promise of a better life than the Jim Crow South, but newcomers and oldtimers alike, despite growing political participation, were largely relegated by whites to second-class citizenship, given separate quarters in hospitals, told to sit in theater balconies, and denied service at white-owned businesses.[80] As Addams observed, "not only in the South, but everywhere in America, a strong race antagonism is asserting itself."[81]

In 1906, Lillian Wald heard of the work of New York City's Jessie Sleet, the first Black public health nurse in the United States, and contacted her to see if she could refer a Black nurse for Henry Street. Sleet recommended Elizabeth Tyler, who had come to New York to pursue postgraduate training.[82] (Henry Street did not segregate services, but the city was largely segregated, and Wald worked within the constraints of her time—even as she tried to shatter them.)

Wald hired Tyler in a move that likely shocked most white-run settlements, which did not hire people of color—and encouraged Black nurses, who had to overcome huge hurdles to do what they wanted to do: become professionals and help others. Since Henry Street had no Black patients at the time, Tyler hit the pavement, seeking out those in need of medical help, where they lived, in ingenious ways—asking tenement house janitors, for example, if they were aware of any African American tenants who might need care. Tyler was so successful that in the spring of 1906, Henry Street hired Edith Carter to work with her.[83] Carter was an 1898 graduate of the Freedmen's Hospital School of Nursing, established by the federal government to train African American nurses to help formerly enslaved people of color in and around Washington, DC.[84]

With Lillian Wald's backing, the support of wealthy benefactor and philanthropist Mary Stillman Harkness, and Carter's help, Elizabeth

Tyler established the Stillman House Branch of the Henry Street Settlement for Colored People in a storefront on Manhattan's Upper West Side, in a neighborhood then called San Juan Hill. By the late 1800s—and before Harlem became the hub of Black city life—San Juan Hill was home to the city's largest Black community. Like the Lower East Side, the neighborhood was a vibrant one, with rich social and religious institutions. It was also, like the Lower East Side, poverty stricken. Good health care was unaffordable, and shoddy, windowless, overcrowded tenement homes made it difficult to limit contagious illnesses. Systemic, unrelenting racism contributed to and compounded these problems: in line with citywide and national statistics that showed people of color were disproportionately impacted by disease, in San Juan Hill, the mortality rate for Black people was far higher than that of whites, and was on the rise.[85]

Tyler and Carter lived in the area so that families could easily find them, and proactively searched out those in need by speaking with ministers, doctors, and clinic workers; each week, they checked in with their supervisor at Henry Street to report their progress. Like its parent organization, Stillman House conducted research on local living conditions and offered a wide variety of clubs and classes, including music, cooking, sewing, and city history. A 1913 article in the *New York Age* described the settlement's main features: four ground-floor rooms, all multipurpose, with the largest alternatively used as a classroom, a gymnasium, and an assembly hall. The most striking feature, though, said the article, was the fact that classes were integrated. "No color line is drawn and we have the unique spectacle of a school established primarily for Negro children" also serving white neighborhood children (primarily Jews, Germans, and Italians). Through Wald's efforts, San Juan Hill gained a much-needed resource, and she gained a reputation as a trusted advocate for the rights of people of color.[86]

In 1914, Elizabeth Tyler moved on to a new position in Philadelphia; Edith Carter stayed, working for Henry Street for 28 years and becoming the face of the Settlement in the community. "To the people in this area Miss Carter *is* Henry Street," said Dorothy Cooper, Carter's supervisor. "She is a welcome friend to all who live there and to walk through this district with her makes you wonder how she ever gets to the homes to visit cases, for she is stopped every other step to give advice to some mother, talk to a child, or to pass the time of day with some old friend who is so glad to see her nurse."[87] By 1918, Stillman House had expanded—it joined with two other neighborhood organizations, the Walton Kindergarten and the Lincoln Day Nursery, and moved to larger quarters—and changed its name to Lincoln House. Buoyed by its success, Henry Street also opened a branch in North Harlem (fig. 1.11; nurse Marian Pettiford is identified in Darlene Clark Hine's *Black Women in the Nursing Profession*[88]), by the 1920s the center of Black New York cultural, residential, and commercial life.[89]

In addition to establishing nursing branches throughout the city, Wald expanded the reach of public health through collaboration and education. In early 1909, she was at a charity event where she met Lee K. Frankel. Frankel was an industrial social worker hired by Metropolitan Life Insurance Vice President Haley Fiske to help realize his belief that insurance could be a means to improve the life of the underprivileged. Traditionally MetLife, like other insurance companies, had sold policies to middle- and upper-class customers. But in 1879, it had begun selling small policies to the working poor; they were typically used as burial insurance. Each week, as agents called on customers to collect their premiums, they learned of any illness in the family. Healthy families were a Progressive Era goal; for insurance companies, they were also an economic asset: lower mortality rates meant fewer payouts. Together, Wald and Frankel decided to launch an experimental partnership. If an agent saw a family in need, he would report it to the Settlement and pay for a nursing visit. This alliance between public health and private industry was a win-win for both entities.

After a brief, successful trial in New York City, the project mushroomed, and two years later, MetLife had affiliations with 350 visiting nurse associations. Other insurance companies, seeing the benefits,

FIGURE 1.11. In this photograph taken around 1926, nurse Marian Pettiford stands in front of the Settlement's branch in North Harlem, where she was assistant supervisor. Courtesy of the Visiting Nurse Service of New York Records, Archives & Special Collections, Columbia University Health Sciences Library.

followed suit. Programs like the MetLife partnership and others in New York City and beyond, coupled with the rise of public health nursing as a field, generated a demand for more trained nurses. Wald helped meet the need with postgraduate training and field experience. She helped create both the Department of Nursing and Health at Columbia University's Teachers College (which was affiliated with the Settlement)[90] and the National Organization of Public Health Nurses, formed in 1912 to provide public health, develop standards, and serve as a clearinghouse for information.[91]

## The Second and Third Branches

Henry Street's second and third branches were "social work" and "country work." Both branches had similar ultimate goals: to forge an "interplay of association" that would bring diverse people together. Under the category of "social work" were classes in music (fig. 1.12), pottery, woodwork, and knitting, as well as exercise-related activities and a kindergarten. In sheer numbers of participants, clubs led the pack (fig. 1.13). They provided a more "closely knit existence" than classes, city planner Arthur Holden asserted in his 1922 book, *The Settlement Idea: A Vision of Social Justice.* Because clubs were composed of people bound by common interests, it was hoped that they could help bridge cultural divides as participants built lasting friendships.[92] Henry Street's first club was the American Heroes, so named because its members, 11- and 12-year-old boys, studied great Americans of the past. It was established in 1895—the same year that Wald and Mary Brewster moved into 265 Henry Street—and its members grew up to be among Wald's most loyal supporters. They eventually created the Settlement's long-running alumni group, the Old-timers, which held reunions and raised funds for Henry Street.

FIGURE 1.12. A music class in the Settlement's dining room, 1915. Henry Street Settlement Collection/A. Tennyson Beals.

FIGURE 1.13. A Henry Street boys' club, 1907. Many children maintained lifelong connections to Henry Street because of the sense of family and belonging they experienced in its clubs. Courtesy of the Social Welfare History Archives, University of Minnesota Libraries.

Articles in the November 1912 issue of *The Settlement Journal*, a newsletter published by Henry Street's clubs and written by club members, suggest the variety and vitality of these organizations. The season's first meeting of the Men's Club (the Settlement's senior organization) was "a fiery one," reported the newsletter, with "heated discussions during the meeting." For the Senior Girls' Club lecture series on civics, Belle Israels Moskowitz was slated to speak. The social reformer had recently spearheaded a drive to regulate commercial dance halls, whose boozy atmospheres were seen as a threat to the young women who patronized them (Moskowitz would go on to become the most powerful woman in New York State, and then federal, politics in the 1920s and 1930s). The newsletter reported that the Mothers' Neighbors Club had "decided to cooperate with the city department in bettering the conditions in the neighborhood and has committees on the look-out for bad tenements, unsanitary conditions and dirty streets." (Wald admonished club organizer Karl Hesley for the name he gave the club; "You know my sentiments" she said, "about the right of a woman to be something besides a mother.") The Acorn Club was researching the history of the neighborhood; a meeting of the Drama Club, "always more or less exciting," drew would-be heroes, heroines, and villains. Newsletter editor Abraham Davis noted that while there was a time when members of the LaFayette Club "were as excluded, haughty and as uncommunicative as a Standard Oil Baron," a forced stint of stage duty had remedied that; now, he proclaimed, "No dance is complete without them." All of the senior clubs, as well as a vast array of junior clubs, had some kind of activity every day of the week from afternoon until 9:30 at night.[93]

Clubs fostered a sense of family, as one of Henry Street's earliest members, Jacob R. Patent, recalled. He and his single mother came from Minsk, Russia, to the Lower East Side in 1907, where they lived in two rooms with two windows, no heat, no running water, and a communal toilet in the yard. "My mother went to work, and I was left with a key around my neck, I must have been about four years old at the time," Patent recollected. In winter, unable to afford a coat, his mother bundled him in sweaters; unable to afford shoes, in fifth grade his mother took him to a charity shop in hopes of finding a free pair. They didn't have any children's shoes, but they did have a small pair of women's shoes with low heels. "So mother took them," Patent said, "and we tried to put a dye on it, it was some sort of a purple color, I wore them to school . . . and if the teacher called me to the blackboard, I'd try to hide my feet behind each other. I did suffer emotionally for a while, to wear those shoes, to give you an idea of the poverty we were in."

Patent was an only child, and Henry Street's clubs, with Wald as their beloved matriarch, became his family. When Wald visited, he said, "we almost choked her with our affections! She was known as Mother Henry." Abraham Davis had similar recollections. He remembered the 1903 meeting where Wald dropped into a boys' club he had just joined. Davis recounted her words and their lasting impact. "There were no speeches," he said; "we merely talked."

I still remember her beautiful smile and the warm affection in her quiet voice as she told us, our club leader and the group to which he belonged were her children and we who followed them were her grandchildren; all of us, she said, were members of one large family, with common interests, common problems and common responsibilities. . . . Miss Wald put the young people in their most natural setting—the family. . . . We felt no loyalty to bricks and mortar and we had no impression of the existence of an institution unless it was the institution of the communal family. . . . Her interest in labor early stimulated our desire to know what trade unions really were and how they functioned. She imbued us with her desire for good government which led us to participate in political campaigns long before we could vote. . . . We learned from her that democracy was a social unit; that race was unimportant but that people were, and that democracy was an evolving process, and that improvement did not come as a result of lip service but out of active doing, out of work. Lillian Wald truly molded a family life at Henry Street in its broadest aspects.[94]

In summertime, "country work"—the Settlement's third branch—extended the work of clubs from the steamy Lower East Side to the New York State countryside (fig. 1.14). School was out, and the camps emerged along with the turn-of-the-century rise of the summer camp movement, which held that nature could both inspire and instruct children who might otherwise be tempted by the idleness of summertime city life.[95] Camp Henry, for boys (established at Lake Secor in Putnam County in 1908), and Echo Hill Farm, for girls (established a year later at Yorktown Heights), gave generations of Henry Streeters fun and lasting memories.

To Miriam Hirsch, who came to the Settlement in 1905, when she was 10, dancing, sewing, and drama classes were fabulous—but summer camp was in a league of its own, especially when Lillian Wald was there. Wald would come for the weekend, Hirsch recalled, and "it was she who taught me my first botany lesson, as she took us for a hike into the woods. . . . She also participated in our outdoor picnics and sang with

FIGURE 1.14. Lining up to board a bus to Henry Street's summer camp, around 1920. Courtesy of the Visiting Nurse Service of New York Records, Archives & Special Collections, Columbia University Health Sciences Library.

us around our bonfires. She worked for the heart of humanity and was loved, honored, and cherished by everyone." Alice Hartsuyker, who lived on the Lower East Side and went to Echo Hill in the 1930s, recalled the rustic buildings, the smell of pine needles, making daisy chains, and eating at the dining hall, Angel Inn. The food was "wholesome and fresh," she said, but she and her fellow campers "may not have appreciated that, used as we were to pungent, highly flavored cuisines of our neighborhood, where Jewish, Italian and Chinese foods were part of our diet." Hartsuyker remembered returning home happy (and speckled with mosquito bites), "grateful to those who made it possible."[96] In addition to the camps, "country work" also included the nursing services Henry Street provided at three convalescent homes, located at Valley Cottage, Grand-View-on-the-Hudson, and Echo Hill.[97]

## The Fourth Branch

The Settlement's fourth branch was "civic work"—essentially social and political activism—what Jane Hitchcock described as "fights for (clean) streets, better schools, more parks, improved housing conditions, etc." The work of this branch brought together settlement house leaders, government workers, elected officials, community members, lawyers, suffragists, labor leaders, and others to forge change in the neighborhood, the city, the state, the nation, and even the world. The issues, always, emerged out of neighbors' concerns and their homes, workplaces, and lives. The heart of this branch was 265 Henry Street; "all the currents of [Lower] East Side life run through it and across it," observed Lavinia Dock in 1900.[98]

These currents swirled around the Settlement's spacious dining room table, because that is where Lillian Wald gathered together visitors of all views and experiences to dine—and prove that barriers "between honest-thinking men and women of different nationalities or different classes" were absurd. "Human interest and passion for human progress break down barriers centuries old," reckoned Wald; they formed, she said, "a tie that binds closer than any conventional relationship."[99]

At the head of the dinner table was Wald. Besides being a brilliant social activist, she was an outstanding host, and she deftly managed both roles at the dinner table. "Lively spirits sparred across the table, and presiding at its head, Lillian Wald played not one part, but innumerably changing characters," recalled Alice Lewisohn. "In her role as hostess, her hands seemed to work automatically as she mixed the crisp green leaves in the salad bowl, while she clarified some problem about unions, interlarding her conversation with whimsical stories."[100] Frances Perkins, the sociologist and workers' rights advocate who would go on to become the US secretary of labor, described the scene as Wald skillfully

turned the conversation to life in the city of New York, the working people, where they lived, how they lived, the general living conditions of the area around Henry Street, why you had to have settlements. She would draw out of each one of us in a tactful way something about what we had been seeing. "Now, Frances, what did you see? I know you've been making that investigation into cellar bakeries with Raymond Fosdick. I haven't heard you say what you found." Then it was my turn to deliver what I had recently seen of the living and working conditions of the people of the great city. One person after another would comment. Tenement house inspectors were there, as were people who knew about factories and factory life and arrangements. That was the kind of thing that went on.[101]

With Wald as host, the Settlement's dining room became an international hub for social justice. "The visitors at Henry Street came in unending streams," recalled Settlement volunteer (and later board member) Rita Wallach Morgenthau; "the fish market peddlers from under the bridge would come to state a grievance—the garment workers to discuss hours and wages or to try to adjust differences between themselves and their employers." Wald welcomed these and other citizens of the Lower East Side, as well as the social reformers of the day who came to share ideas.[102]

Renowned settlement leader Jane Addams came to dinner at Henry Street. So too did Boston's Helena Dudley, head of Denison House, who in 1909 wrote in Wald's guest book, "Love the brotherhood!" (In 1928, another Denison House social worker—Amelia Earhart, fresh on the heels of a pioneering transatlantic flight—signed the same book.)[103] Suffragists—writer and feminist Charlotte Perkins Gilman and Emmeline Pankhurst, the militant leader of the British suffragette movement—came. There were national and world leaders, revolutionaries, and activists: W. E. B. Du Bois, sociologist, writer, and civil rights activist; Ramsay MacDonald, a founder of Great Britain's Labour Party and later its prime minister, who brought with him the ideas of the labor activists, socialist leaders, and radical intellectuals in his orbit; and Russian revolutionary Catherine Breshkovsky, who brought with her ideas about political solutions to inequality, oppression, and poverty in her country. There were labor organizers, lawmakers, political figures, funders, board members, and many others, from the neighborhood and around the world.

Consider, for example, the guest list for a dinner party Wald held in the late 1890s. Around the table was a cast drawn from the ranks of people who were making New York City a center for culture and social reform: Richard Watson Gilder, poet, civic leader, and editor of the famed *Century Monthly Magazine*; William Dean Howells, the critic and author whose novels captured America's growing social divide; Felix Adler, American educator and founder of the Ethical Culture Society; Seth Low, munici-pal reformer, president of Columbia University, and later mayor of New York City; Graham Wallas, the British educator, social psychologist, and socialist; Teddy Roosevelt, New York City police commissioner (Wald said her first recollection of him was when he visited one blustery winter night, "laughing uproariously" after a humorous exchange with a peddler outside); and journalist Jacob Riis, who had brought the impoverished Lower East Side to the world with his 1890 bestseller, *How the Other Half Lives*.[104] (On another visit in 1912, Riis would write of Wald in her guest book, "The heart of New York, and the wise head, are here."[105])

Wald leveraged this growing network to create change, for after all, as Wald had said, her goal was not only to nurse the sick but to address the underlying social problems that contributed to poor public health. Case became cause. Trouble became action.[106] Like other Progressive Era social reformers, Lillian Wald believed that poverty should be con-fronted by the larger forces of government and society. At City Hall, the State House, and the White House, Wald attacked the challenges of the Lower East Side, focusing on issues of equality and equity, and bringing power to those who did not have it. Passionate and persistent, she joined committees, prodded politicians, spoke publicly, and nagged the power-ful. Most often, she was fighting for the rights of the marginalized—immigrants, workers, children, women, and Black Americans—whose issues and challenges were often interconnected.

### FIGHTING FOR THE RIGHTS OF IMMIGRANTS

As immigrants poured into the United States at the turn of the century, many Americans eyed them with hostility and suspicion (fig. 1.15). Some

VOL. 17 NO. 440    MARCH 22 1890.    PRICE 10 CENTS

*Judge*

ENTERED AT THE POST OFFICE AT NEW YORK AS SECOND-CLASS MATTER.    COPYRIGHT 1890 BY THE JUDGE PUBLISHING CO.

THE PROPOSED EMIGRANT DUMPING SITE.

STATUE OF LIBERTY—"Mr. Windom, if you are going to make this island a garbage heap, I am going back to France."

FIGURE 1.15. The Statue of Liberty recoils as Europeans arrive in New York Harbor aboard two "garbage ships" and are "dumped" at her feet. This 1890 political cartoon captures the views of Americans who opposed immigration and saw newcomers as the cause of urban problems. Courtesy of Cornell University–PJ Mode Collection of Persuasive Cartography.

uneasy workers saw them as competition; some Protestant religious leaders saw them as a threat to a Christian majority. Those who saw the late 19th-century rise of cities as a threat to town and farm life now watched cities mushroom, and decided to blame their new immigrant residents for the accompanying urban ills: congestion, machine politics, and crime. Increasingly, newcomers were conflated with contagious diseases.[107]

Some settlement houses sought to assimilate immigrants by erasing their ethnic and cultural differences, thus maintaining an "American" way of life. While Wald believed in integrating newcomers into American life, she embraced immigrants—whom she saw as "a steady stream of new life and new blood to the nation"—and their cultures.[108] Wald was herself the child and grandchild of German immigrants, and had early on adopted her belief in universalism and the idea that classes must depend on each other with a sense of "mutuality."[109] For Wald, differences were something to be celebrated. An outspoken champion for newcomers, in a speech she gave at Manhattan's Free Synagogue as part of its 1907–8 lectures series she shared her perspective:

I find that there is one question that seems to be the Bromide of new acquaintances whenever they learn that I have lived in tenement house neighborhoods and that is always, "What *shall* we do to keep those *hordes* from over-whelming us" and I have yet to meet the American who has lived close enough to know on social terms these hordes that has not protested against the attitude of the community in general to them, their measuring of them for gain—the indifference to them as people.

"The element of the absurd," Wald went on to say, "does creep into the tenacious desire to hold to the original type" (meaning white, Anglo-Saxon Protestants) when in fact, as she pointed out, "the real strength of the country has come from its great mingling of types."[110] Symbolically, when immigrant neighbors gifted Wald with brass samovars—traditional Russian tea urns—she gave them pride of place at the

Settlement: in the formal dining room, where so many people, from all walks of life, gathered to exchange views (and where they are still on view today).[111]

Wald frequently enlisted for help the people whose relationships she had nourished around the dining room table. In 1908, she invited New York Governor Charles Evans Hughes to the Settlement for dinner with colleagues who she felt could speak authoritatively on constructive social measures and policies that would help new immigrants adjust to life in America—and sent him home after dinner with his arms full of maps and documents to review. Out of that encounter, several months later, the legislature authorized a commission to investigate immigrant labor in New York. Named to the commission, Wald and social worker Frances Kellor traveled the state to investigate working conditions; their report led to the formation of the New York Bureau of Industries and Immigration of the Department of Labor.[112] And when a government test for literacy was proposed—which would essentially block the arrival of immigrants from Southern and Eastern Europe, and keep out Chinese and nonwhite newcomers—Wald confronted President William Howard Taft about it: "We speak from a continuous and intimate acquaintance with the immigrant population, covering a period of twenty years," she said, "and with a knowledge of the historic values that the immigrant has contributed to the making of the United States."[113]

## FIGHTING FOR THE RIGHTS OF WORKERS

Wald had observed firsthand the brutal conditions endured by sweatshop workers; she had witnessed the powerlessness of individuals at a time when employees, most of them not unionized, could be fired at will; and she saw herself as a working woman and a comrade. She became a lobbyist, a strike supporter, an investigator, a union organizer, and a valued interpreter to both sides, especially those who might see labor unions as the enemy.[114] Wald was amused by the reaction this sometimes triggered. "In my earlier days on the East Side," she said, "labor unions were as feared as Socialists were later and as Communists are to-day. I remember telling a dinner of comfortable people—bankers, industrialists, a lawyer or two—about one of these heroic labor leaders. Every knife and fork stopped when I mentioned casually that I knew and respected a 'walking delegate.'"[115] Yet she managed to open and even change minds, making the Settlement what she called "the neutral ground where both sides might meet."[116] One of the minds she opened was that of her benefactor, Jacob Schiff. Wald made sure that Schiff, a conservative businessman, personally met with workers around Henry Street's dining room table. Once, when he was talking with a Jewish tailor, a heated discussion about a strike concluded amicably with Schiff's arm across the tailor's back and both men swapping phrases in Hebrew.[117]

And, at a time when more than 20 percent of women over the age of 16 were in the labor force,[118] Lillian Wald fought against damaging stereotypes and for gender equality. In a 1906 article, she shared the perspective that informed her views. Despite the large numbers of women at work in the rising industrial economy, she said,

> as a nation we superstitiously hug the belief that our women are at home and our children at school. As a whole the community is reluctant to face the situation frankly and seriously, that women no longer spin and weave and card, no longer make the butter and the cheese, scarcely sew and put the preserves at home, but accomplish these same industries in the factories, in open competition with men, and except in the relatively few instances of trade organization, in competition with each other.[119]

In 1903, Wald helped create the National Women's Trade Union League, the first national association dedicated to organizing women workers and an advocate for an eight-hour work day.[120] When hazardous working conditions fanned a small fire into an inferno, killing 145 workers at Greenwich Village's Triangle shirtwaist factory in 1911, league members conducted a four-year investigation of factory conditions that helped establish new regulations.[121] And in July 1910, during the New York City cloakmakers' strike—when tens of thousands of garment workers backed by the International Ladies Garment Workers' Union struck for their rights—Wald offered Henry Street's delightful backyard, with its winding wisteria, as a meeting place.[122]

FIGHTING FOR THE RIGHTS OF CHILDREN

At the turn of the century, children were seen as the most "blameless" members of society and therefore the most deserving of aid. Their plight in the new urban-industrial world was a common cause for Progressive Era reformers. Wald was among them. Believing that the "welfare of the child is the welfare of the nation," she forged change on the playground, in the school, and in the workplace.[123]

She had only to walk out her front door to see the lack of spaces for children to play; it was the reason the Settlement had created a backyard playground in 1895. Believing that playing was a child's right and "an integral part of his claim upon the state,"[124] in 1898 Wald collaborated with New York City Parks Commissioner Charles Stover to found the Outdoor Recreation League, an advocacy group that funded playgrounds in undeveloped parks. The league built Seward Park, the first permanent, municipally built playground in the United States—which was a resounding success.[125] When it opened in October 1903, just a few blocks from the Settlement, 20,000 gleeful children swarmed the gates and rushed in.[126]

A place to play, Wald held, was a civic responsibility; so too was an education. She saw learning as an equalizer; the public school, a "stronghold of our democracy."[127] She had seen children who had been left behind, who came to school hungry, who had missed classroom time because of easily treatable medical conditions—and introduced special-needs classes, the free school lunch, and the school nurse.

Seeing that some children were challenged by traditional learning, or had mental health issues, Wald enlisted Elizabeth Farrell, an educator at nearby Public School No. 1 who had been developing teaching methods for children with special needs, to help. With the permission of the Board of Education (which, fortuitously, included Henry Street board member Felix Warburg), Farrell, with the Settlement's help developing theory and curriculum, created the city's first class for "ungraded pupils" at PS 1, where she used innovative methods to meet each child's abilities. For a class of boys, for example, she described how she used nontraditional supplies: "instead of books, they had tin cans, instead of spellers they had picture puzzles to solve, instead of penmanship lessons, they had water-color paints and brushes, instead of arithmetic and the multiplication table, they had wood and tools, and things with which to build and make." The groundbreaking initiative led the New York City public schools to create a separate department for special-needs students in 1908, and by 1915, 3,000 children were in classes with specially trained teachers who adapted the school work to the unique needs of their students. Farrell's work with Henry Street was the foundation for special education programs throughout the United States.[128]

Then, knowing that children living in poverty often came to school hungry, in 1908 Wald pushed for school lunches—lunches that would be free, to avoid stigmatizing those too poor to pay for them. "It is a serious loss to the individual child to have 'free food kitchen' associated with the school," she said. "His most precious gift, if foreign born, is the absence of class distinction in the public school."[129] Next was the push for the school nurse. Concerned about the high rate of school absenteeism due to illness, the New York City Board of Education sought Wald's advice. Inspired by England's use of school nurses, Wald responded by offering the free services of a Settlement nurse, Lina Rogers, for one month as an experiment. Rogers visited daily, treating conditions that were typically cause to send a child home, such as skin infections, conjunctivitis, and ringworm. For those students who *had* been sent home, Rogers provided the treatment that allowed them to return to class.[130] As one grateful mother wrote, "We are very much obliged to you for . . . not sending Sadie home. I am busy working in the store from early morning to late in the night. I will put this salve on her head every night till it is cured." The successful trial led to a citywide practice of medical inspection in the schools that spread nationally and continues today.[131]

Wald also took her concerns about children's welfare to the national stage. She had seen the bootblacks bent over patrons' shoes morning until night and the children assembling artificial flowers from parts for pittances in cramped tenements, missing out on their education and their childhood. For in the workplace of the new industrial age, child labor—less expensive than adult labor, and therefore attractive to many employers—was widely prevalent; according to an 1890 US Census report, almost one out of every five children ages 10 to 15 was employed.[132] Children needed a voice, and over breakfast at Henry Street in 1903, Wald and Florence Kelley conceived of a way to help give it to them. As they chatted over coffee, they came up with the idea for a federal agency that would promote and advocate for child health and welfare. With only a skeleton of an idea, Wald said, the two wrote to one of their frequent dinner guests—Theodore Roosevelt, now president of the United States—requesting an audience. His telegraph in response was unhesitating: "Come to Washington."[133] On the day the two women visited the White House, wrote Wald, "the Secretary of Agriculture had gone South to ascertain what danger to the community lurked in the appearance of the boll weevil. This gave point to our argument that nothing that might have happened to the children of the nation could have called forth governmental inquiry." As for Roosevelt, the two left with his endorsement; the president, Wald said, thought their idea was "bully."[134]

It would be years before their idea came to fruition; in the meantime Wald continued to agitate against child labor. In 1904, she helped organize the National Child Labor Committee (NCLC) with a board of directors composed of prominent leaders and supporters of social welfare in her circle: funders Felix Adler, Paul Warburg, and Jacob Schiff; Florence Kelley, Jane Addams, Rabbi Stephen S. Wise, economist Edward Devine, minister and Chicago Commons settlement house founder Graham Taylor, and others. The committee promoted the rights of children, conducted studies of child labor, and mounted campaigns to attract support and sway public opinion. One of their most successful tactics was to hire investigative photographer Lewis Hine to document child-labor

abuses; Hine assumed various roles—a Bible salesman was one—to in-
veigle his way into workplaces and capture the most compelling portraits
he could.[135] Wald had always believed that if people knew of abuses, they
would do something, and through Hine's emotionally wrenching photographs, their cause moved forward, bringing public opinion to their side.
In large part because of the NCLC's work in building public awareness,
in 1912 the US Children's Bureau became a reality (and continues to play
a key role in issues around children and families today).[136] Wald, elated,
called it "a symbol of the most hopeful aspect of America."[137]

### FIGHTING FOR THE RIGHTS OF WOMEN

In an era when women lacked the vote and equality, Wald joined coali-
tions of settlement house leaders and activists to fight for suffrage.[138]
While she preferred cooperation and conciliation over militant action,[139]
she nevertheless backed her more radical colleagues—like Lavinia Dock,
the spirited, impassioned nurse who left her job as superintendent of
nurses at Johns Hopkins Hospital to join the Settlement in 1896. Dock
had walked picket lines in support of female workers; she had fought
for women's access to birth control; and, as a member of the most radical wing of the women's suffrage movement, she had served jail time in
the brutal Women's Workhouse in Occoquan, Virginia, for her beliefs.[140]
In 1913, just two months after Washington, DC, crowds spit on suffragists protesting Woodrow Wilson's presidential inauguration, Dock
organized Henry Street's Lower East Side neighbors to join a massive pro-suffrage parade in New York City. They were among the more
than 10,000 women and men who advanced down Fifth Avenue—
Manhattan's most prestigious thoroughfare—on May 10, banners and
flags held high, in front of half a million spectators who packed the
sidewalks and spilled into the streets.[141] Wald painted an evocative
scene of Dock's work mobilizing

> Russians, Italians, Irish, and native-born, all the nationalities of our
> cosmopolitan community, for the campaign. When the suffrage parade

marched down Fifth Avenue in 1913, back of the settlement banner, with its symbol of universal brotherhood, there walked a goodly company carrying flags with the suffrage demand in ten languages. The cosmopolitanism of our district was marked by the Sephardic Jewish girl who bore aloft the Turkish appeal. The Chinese banner was made by a Chinese physician and a Chinese missionary.[142]

There was power in their voices: when in 1917 an amendment to the New York State constitution passed, giving women the vote, it was with conspicuous support from the borough of Manhattan—in particular from the districts that the Settlement served, where pro-suffrage votes were notably higher than those for the borough as a whole.[143] In 1920, the 19th Amendment to the US Constitution was ratified, giving all American women the right to vote.

FIGHTING FOR THE RIGHTS OF BLACK AMERICANS

Increasingly, Henry Street Settlement gained a reputation for its work in and with New York City's Black communities, and Wald for her efforts to bridge racial divides. She was trusted: when a case of alleged police brutality against a Black child emerged in San Juan Hill, a resident asked Wald to intercede; Wald responded by urging the New York City Police Commissioner to look into the matter.[144] As the modern civil rights movement took form in the early 1900s, backed by northern Blacks and whites who fought to bring full citizenship to Black Americans, Wald was a vocal advocate.[145] She helped found the National Association for the Advancement of Colored People (NAACP)—which would become the nation's premier civil-rights organization—when she signed "The Call."

In February 1909, appalled at the level of racially motivated violence, an interracial group of activists met to respond, among them W. E. B. Du Bois, anti-lynching crusader and social activist Ida B. Wells-Barnett, civil rights activist Mary Church Terrell, journalists Oswald Garrison Villard and Mary White Ovington, reformers Jane Addams and Florence

Kelley—and Wald.[146] On February 12, 1909, the centennial of Abraham Lincoln's birth, the group issued the "Call for the Lincoln Emancipation Conference in 1909," to be held in New York City in the spring. An invitation-only meeting at the United Charities Building on East 22nd Street was to be followed by an open meeting at the 900-seat Great Hall of the Cooper Union for the Advancement of Science and Art.[147]

Lillian Wald offered the Settlement's dining room for an opening reception. "At the time of the first convention of the organization, formed to further better race relations in this country," Wald said,

> the occasion promised to be almost too serious unless some social provision were made. I suggested a party at the House, but even the organizing committee was fearful.
>
> "Oh, no!" they protested. "It won't do! As soon as white and colored people sit down and eat together there begin to be newspaper stories about social equality."
>
> "But two hundred members of the conference couldn't sit down," I submitted. "Our house is too small. Everybody would have to stand up for supper."
>
> "Then it would be all right," they said with relief, and the party was successful.[148]

Deliberations began the next day, and the formal organization of the NAACP followed in 1910, with Wald as one of its board of directors.

As the head of one of the most renowned and influential social service organizations in the nation and by now an internationally recognized figure, Wald continued to put her weight behind the NAACP, which had established its national office in New York City. In 1915, she joined its coalition to protest the release of D. W. Griffith's silent drama, *The Birth of a Nation*, for its racist, repugnant portrayal of African Americans and glowing, glorified depiction of the Ku Klux Klan. To persuade New York City Mayor John P. Mitchel to ban the film, the NAACP planned to organize a march down Broadway from Union Square to his office. But the police effectively blocked the group's strategy by insisting that such marches could take place only on Saturdays or holidays. In response, the NAACP decided to assemble a high-powered group to meet with the mayor. On May 30, Lillian Wald, reformer and rabbi Stephen S. Wise, W. E. B. Du Bois, and Oswald Garrison Villard met with the mayor, with 500 others in attendance, including African American businessmen, clergy, and professionals. While they were unsuccessful—Mitchel would agree only to cut out the film's worst scenes—their actions spoke not only to the level of injustice faced by African Americans, but to Wald's willingness to join with others to publicly confront it at the highest levels.[149]

## TAKING STOCK AT 20: THE 1913 PAGEANT

The city had paved Henry Street just for the occasion. Above the thoroughfare, a glimmering canopy of incandescent lights, donated by the Edison Company, created what one observer called a "multi-colored heaven." Spectators hung over the building roofs and crowded onto fire escapes as 10,000 others packed the street to watch the Settlement's pageant, mounted in honor of its 20th anniversary.[150] Nearby, at All Saints Church—festooned with flags and bunting—500 participants, drawn from Henry Street's club members and leaders, its gymnasium, dancing and choral classes, its residents, and more, waited patiently in the warm June air for the peal of the church bell at 8 o'clock that would signal the start of their march toward number 265. In a gesture that symbolized the central role of the community, all wore costumes made with the help of neighborhood women and public-school children. In fact, noted one observer, everything but the lights "had been made by the people themselves."

The pageant acted out the Settlement's history within the context of the city's past. Down the street came Native Americans and "White Strangers" who exchanged gifts of wampum and pelts. Each chapter in local history was then acted out sequentially, through the last: "Episode

VI.—1893–1913." Now, the actors presented all of the nationalities that had lived on Henry Street since the mid-1800s—the "Irish, the Scotch, the Germans, the Italians, and the Russians," singing and dancing the songs of their home country.[151] To close out the evening, Henry Street's public health nurses, wearing their starched blue uniforms, joined in and passed by the bandstand where Wald, the mayor, officials, and Settlement friends sat. As they did, the crowd erupted in a cheer for Lillian Wald. The street, said one observer, was "flooded with love."[152]

The pageant had turned the Lower East Side into a public stage that demonstrated to the neighborhood and the nation its values and the best possibilities of life in a diverse New York City neighborhood. Along with the pageant, Henry Street produced a 20th-anniversary report that summarized its accomplishments. From its founding in 1893, it had expanded dramatically. It had branch centers and 92 staff nurses who in 1913 would make almost 200,000 nursing visits and some 6,000 social service visits. It had almost 3,000 club members, and in just one month, December 1912, had recorded a total Settlement attendance of 25,000. Wald was one of the country's best-known nursing professionals and social activists. The Settlement had an international reputation for its work, inspired others, allied itself with public movements, and carried Henry Street's philosophy outward and forward. "Our first conception of the neighborhood unit as a restricted area of a few blocks has expanded," said Wald, "until we find that what we care about in one neighborhood belongs to all."[153]

But Wald was aware that to thrive, the Settlement would have to continue to be responsive and flexible. "If the public will continue to encourage us," she asserted, "we are ready to go on twenty years more, with the same ardor and the same faith, and not with a fixed program, but moving with our times."[154] The need to change with the times became starkly clear when in June 1914 World War I broke out in Europe, and the nation shuddered.

Lillian Wald ardently opposed war; she believed it would exacerbate existing problems, disrupt Henry Street's work with the poor, siphon off already scarce resources, and jeopardize her quest for democracy and social progress. And so she sprang into action. Together with social workers, society women, suffragists, and pacifists—many of them, like Mary K. Simkhovitch, Jane Addams, and Lavinia Dock, part of her network of female reformers—she helped mount the Women's Peace Parade in New York City.[155] The parade, an effective publicity technique borrowed from the women's suffrage movement, took place on August 29, 1914, on Fifth Avenue. Roughly 1,200 anti-war activists, with Wald and her fellow organizers at the head, moved along the street, some dressed in the black of mourning, others in one of suffrage's signature colors—white—as spectators observed a hushed silence that was only broken, reported the *New York Herald*, "by the reverberating, dirge-like roll of the muffled drums."[156]

The following month, Wald, fellow anti-militarist Jane Addams, and Paul U. Kellogg (editor of the *Survey*, a leading social work and reform journal) invited more than thirty people to Henry Street for a full-day roundtable conference about the war.[157] Out of the group—which included Florence Kelley, Max Eastman (writer and editor of the radical socialist journal *The Masses*), economist and sociologist Emily Greene Balch, and Rabbi Wise—emerged a coalition that became the American Union Against Militarism (AUAM), with Wald as its chairperson.[158] The group stood, said Kellogg, "for sanity at home, using the full force of our position as the world's greatest neutral to see if we could bring anything about." It became the nation's leading pacifist organization, with 6,000 members by 1915. Kellogg recalled how Wald's efforts spawned "reprisals, ugly ones, against the nursing and neighborhood work. She stood up to it."[159]

In her dual roles as Settlement leader and head of the AUAM, Wald wrote to President Wilson, encouraging him to call together neutral countries to mediate a solution for peace. "As Head Resident of a social Settlement, organizer of institutions for the care of the sick, interested for many years in measures for the conservation of life," she pleaded in a November 25, 1915, letter, "I beg to add my petition to the many that have been sent you for consideration of some method by which the neutrals may be assembled to consider ways for ending the war."[160] But the group could not convince Wilson to pursue their idea. In September 1917, Wald resigned over frictions in the AUAM. Although she continued to voice her views, she turned her energies more fully to the work of the Settlement.[161]

## ART + ACTIVISM

From the Settlement's earliest days, Lillian Wald had championed the arts as essential to life. She believed in the power of dance, drama, music, and visual art to transcend barriers and give form to old and new identities in America. She lamented the lack of access to the arts for people who were poor.[162] Like many other Progressive reformers and settlement house workers, Wald sought to make the arts accessible to all, not just to the elite or the most gifted, and now, in a country at war, she felt that their healing power was more necessary than ever.

The two individuals who would most help Wald inculcate the arts into the Settlement's life were sisters Irene and Alice Lewisohn, daughters of one of Wald's affluent German Jewish funders, wealthy industrialist Leonard Lewisohn. Alice Lewisohn recalled her first visit to the Settlement in 1901, when she was a teenager. She accompanied her father to dinner, driven downtown in a taxicab that traveled along garbage-strewn avenues, vied for space with street peddlers and pushcarts, and drew the jeers of local children who loudly shouted at them, "Get a horse!" Arriving at the Settlement, father and daughter snaked their way past children playing jacks on the stoop, knocked on the front door, and were welcomed in. Lewisohn described Wald as "vigorous, joyous," her "handsome face" surrounded by dark hair. The Lewisohns' mother had died the year before; with their father's death the following year, the two sisters increasingly came to see Wald as a mother figure. Wald took both under her wing, affectionately dubbing them "Alirene."[163]

In 1905, the sisters began organizing classes, festivals, and dramatic and dance performances at Henry Street. The arts programs were inclusive, focusing on the life of the Settlement's immigrant neighborhood; festivals celebrated neighbors' cultural traditions and an array of global cultures. Typical was a 1910 event created around the theme of "spring," representing it as it would have been perceived by children of different religions and nationalities—Hindu, Greek, and Japanese. In like fashion, a winter festival, alongside a Christmas tree, featured Chinese lanterns and Chanukah lamps. Such productions affirmed immigrants' heritages and their contributions to the arts and public culture.[164]

Henry Street did not have a theater, so performances took place wherever there was space, be it the dining room after hours; the gymnasium it had acquired at 303 Henry Street, where the Lewisohns mounted informal festivals of folk songs and dances; or city streets.[165] Weary of this nomadic existence, in 1915 the sisters decided to fund and build the Neighborhood Playhouse at 466 Grand Street, just blocks from the Settlement's headquarters at 265 Henry Street (and conveyed the building's deed to the Settlement the day before it opened). Irene Lewisohn oversaw dancing and production. Her sister, Alice, oversaw dramatics, and both were helped by Agnes Morgan (who brought skills as an actor, director, and stage manager) and theater manager (and lawyer) Helen Arthur.[166]

When the three-story Georgian building, built of red brick and white marble (fig. 1.16), opened on February 12, 1915, the *New York World* described it as an island of culture in a sea of gaudy commerce:

> Garish millinery shops display their showy goods. Peddlers with push-carts lit by flickering flames, vie with each other in their array of gaudy neckties and bargain shirtwaists. Blazing electric signs herald the thrills of movie shows. And, salient by the force of extreme contrast, a plain little white poster board makes its influence felt. It is lit by two iron lanterns, and reads simply, 'The Neighborhood Playhouse.'[167]

Inside, before the curtains were drawn for the opening night, Lillian Wald spoke about the power of music, drama, and dance. She shared her vision of the arts as a means to bring people together, to celebrate their different traditions, and to speak to the soul:

> It pleases us to think that what will seem best tonight has been woven out of the traditions of our neighborhood, and that the music and the dance and the color are part of the dower brought to New York by the stranger. . . . Above the din of industrialism and the roar of machinery of the city, there rises the hope that a community Playhouse, identified with its neighborhood, may recapture and hold something of the poetry and the idealism that belong to its people—not to cling to meaningless fealties because they are old and solemn, but in order to save from ruthless destruction precious inheritances and also to open wide the door of opportunity for the messages, in drama and picture and story and song, that reflect the moral and social and art convictions of our time.[168]

The Lewisohns chose *Jephtha's Daughter* as their first production. It was fitting in important ways. For one, it honored the cultural backgrounds of the audience, which was mostly Jewish; the dance performance was adapted from a story in the Bible's Book of Judges.[169] Secondly, it was a political statement about the horrors of the Great War then ravaging the fields, towns, and cities of Europe. Before going into battle with the Ammonites, Jephtha, a judge, promises God that if successful, he will offer up a burnt offering of whoever comes from his house to meet him on return. Tragically, the welcomer turns out be his own daughter. That sacrifice, said Wald while speaking at Cooper Union during the show's run, was an "analogy of the barbarity of the sacrifices that are now being made in the name of a god of war."[170]

Reactions to the production were mixed. Some applauded it. "The chorus chants old Hebraic melodies," wrote the *New York World*, and audience members sang along. "The play takes on the aspect of an ancient religious ceremonial. Old men and women are in tears, moved by the sad history of their race."[171] Others criticized the show. Henry Street's Orthodox Jewish neighbors, Alice Lewisohn claimed, felt that

FIGURE 1.16. The Neighborhood Playhouse, which opened in 1915. Performances celebrated local cultures, tackled social issues, spoofed Broadway, and spotlighted new American playwrights. Motion pictures, then a novelty, were also on the bill. Courtesy of the Library of Congress.

the Playhouse had taken too many liberties with its interpretation of the Bible. Radicals disliked the fact that the Bible was chosen as a source over such Russian writers as Leonid Andreyev or Maksim Gorky. More conservatively minded audience members disapproved of the dancers' bare feet. "Still another chorus," said Lewisohn, "raised its voice in behalf of strictly American culture, protesting that only poor material and no good could come from this East-Side venture."[172]

Conflict erupted when the Playhouse decided to mount an anti-war production, *Black 'ell*, in 1916. After a group of militarists saw the play, the Commissioner of Licenses (tasked with revoking a theater's license if he felt a production would "be to the prejudice or disadvantage of the state or nation") decided to bar the last performance.[173] In response, Lillian Wald informed the city's police commissioner that if he did, she would let audience members take their seats—then publicly announce exactly why the curtain was not going to rise. In the end, the commissioner relented and the show went on.[174]

For the most part, though, the Playhouse was a whirl of activity, with classes in acting, dancing, choral work, costume and set design and construction, and more. On weekends, there were productions by the Settlement's Neighborhood Players; midweek productions featured local or "imported" talent. Four evenings a week and on Saturdays, the playhouse presented motion picture shows. By 1916 the playhouse, reported social worker John Collier, had "250 people in its classes and uses actively in one way or another perhaps 700 persons, drawn from the neighborhood and from the clubs of the settlement. The weekly audience is about 3,000, and at night the roof of the Playhouse is used for dancing."[175] As an innovative, experimental "little theater" (one of several that emerged in large cities to offer more reform-oriented, noncommercial performances), its work would garner national acclaim, attracting uptown patrons to its downtown location.[176]

## HOMEFRONT CHALLENGES AND POSTWAR PROBLEMS

On April 2, 1917, after long seeking to stay out of the war overseas, President Woodrow Wilson stood before the US Congress, proclaimed the "world must be made safe for democracy," and asked it to declare war on Germany. Resounding cheers rose in response. Four days later, the United States was at war; more than two million American soldiers would head overseas to fight.[177] On the Lower East Side, there was widespread bewilderment. Many immigrants had come to America from oppressed countries to avoid compulsory service and seek opportunity in a free country. "They had not dreamed," said Wald, "that a great, modern, intelligent nation could become involved in war."[178]

Wald dedicated herself and the resources of Henry Street to supporting and helping those affected by the conflict. Henry Street nurses backed their Red Cross colleagues when they marched alongside them down Fifth Avenue on October 4, 1917, with some 300,000 spectators watching; as they paraded, cheers rose for them, too.[179] "We carried no war standards," said Wald; "we were conservers of life."[180] Wald served on the Council of National Defense and headed its committee on home nursing; she allowed the local registration board to use the Settlement for conscription; and collaborated in the wartime work of such agencies as the Food Council, the Red Cross, and the Baby Saving Campaign. She also put her support behind the Mothers' Anti-High Price League, formed by a group of Jewish immigrant women who, worried their children might starve, banded together to protest the city's unaffordable wartime food prices.[181] As Henry Street "boys"—the young people who had joined clubs, acted in theater performances, and in summertime, swam at Camp Henry—were drafted, Wald comforted their families and offered the Settlement for hurried weddings.[182] In addition to managing regular caseloads, Henry Street visiting nurses now also looked over the families of servicemen. And, as Settlement nurses left for the front, leaving the agency shorthanded, some of their remaining colleagues, overworked and exhausted, fell ill. Meanwhile, food and fuel shortages took their toll on the neighborhood; more and more children were undernourished.

Through it all, Wald remained encouraging, seeing in the national crisis an opportunity to serve. At the Settlement's October 16, 1917, board meeting, Wald reminded the assembled group that despite the growing "burdens laid upon our shoulders," they were there because of the Settlement's reputation for responding in times of need. "Trouble has come and we are ready to meet it," Wald said, "and I, for one, am glad that we are not only able to serve our own community but to help far and wide, directly and indirectly."[183]

Problems, though, continued to mount. In December 1917, Wald reported to the board that "Because of the increase of illness in the city—illness due to insufficient heating of the houses—the removal of so many doctors, the high cost of living and the undernourishment of the children, we are practically confronted by a war situation in the city." Demands continued to surpass capacity as the Settlement was increasingly called upon for help. Wald told the board that when she returned home from a two-day business trip, "there were on my desk ninety odd notes, telegraphs and telephone messages awaiting decision."[184]

On November 11, 1918, World War I finally, gratefully, ended. "Victory Day Celebrated by Millions in New York; All Nation Wild with Joy," proclaimed the front page of the *Evening World*. In a holiday "declared by the people themselves," schools, stores, factories, and the Stock Exchange closed; an impromptu celebration erupted in midtown, clogging streets with foot traffic, ecstatic soldiers and sailors (some snaking through the crowd in spontaneous conga lines), and stalled streetcars caught up in the crowds. Just weeks later, as the ebullience subsided, Wald shared with the board that the postwar period of readjustment was bringing new challenges. Among them was the rise of the Spanish flu, a deadly mix of fever, nausea, and diarrhea that was sweeping through the city. No medicine could cure it or the pneumonia that often followed it; the primary treatment was skilled nursing care.[185]

Henry Street's visiting nurses were among the first to respond to the epidemic. Over the course of four days of October alone, they cared for some 500 cases of flu and pneumonia; along one city block of 1,400 residents, 220 were ill. "Our entire staff is nursing influenza and pneumonia cases," Wald reported to New York City Health Commissioner Royal Copeland. "We are doing the best that we can; nobody is hysterical. The supervisors themselves are carrying the [nurse's] bag."[186] Wald described as fairly typical the case of a Harlem family in which the father had pneumonia, the mother had the flu, two of their three children had the measles, and none had received any care until the case was reported to the visiting nurse.[187]

In mid-October, Lillian Wald was named chair of the New York City Nurses' Emergency Council, formed to coordinate the crisis response by hospitals, nursing schools, social work agencies, and religious organizations. With funding from the Red Cross, the council purchased a half-page advertisement in the Sunday newspapers to reach potential volunteers. "A STERN TASK FOR STERN WOMEN" encouraged "not only trained women, but untrained women" to respond to the call of "humanity." When the crisis subsided, Copeland wrote with gratitude to Wald for Henry Street's agile response. "I found your organization alert to the necessities of the emergency," he wrote in December 1918, "and ready day or night to respond to the urgent calls for help."[188]

## THE 1920S: END OF AN ERA OF PROMISE

With the end of World War I came an end to the idealism, optimism, and promise of the Progressive Era, and the rise of affluence, big business, and political conservatism. Concerns about people living in poverty—which had risen dramatically at the turn of the century—now lessened. Responding to a rising fear of foreigners, the government passed new, restrictive immigration laws, and the number of immigrants coming into the United States plummeted.[189] Social reformers now watched as a new political climate took hold, and new administrations in the White House pursued agendas that focused more on individualism and less on the collective good.[190]

With war's end, wartime suppression of dissent evolved into a nationwide red scare. Anti-radical hysteria was based in nativism, fears of Bolshevism and anarchism, and conservative responses to the Russian Revolution.[191] In this climate of fear, the US Military Intelligence Service's Archibald E. Stevenson created a list of individuals suspected of disloyalty for failing to back America's entrance into World War I. Not surprisingly, Lillian Wald was on the list.[192] While she had supported the war effort in all ways except militarily, her anti-war stance was widely known, as were her efforts to defend immigrant "aliens," and, like many reform leaders of the time, she was a socialist. It likely didn't help that for its 25th anniversary, the Settlement had hosted a neighborhood celebration of the 1917 Russian Revolution. All was fodder for her enemies.[193] In 1919, the Lusk Committee, charged with investigating individuals and organizations "who were suspected of promoting the overthrow of the American government in violation of the criminal anarchy articles of the state's Penal Code," targeted Wald for her "seditious activities."[194]

Some funders withdrew their support of Henry Street.[195] One was the wealthy philanthropist Mary Stillman Harkness, who in 1919 told Wald, "For some time I have felt much disturbed concerning the work you are carrying out at Henry Street because of the knowledge that you hold such socialistic ideas. For this reason, I have, at last, reluctantly come to the conclusion that I cannot . . . continue the contributions I have made." When she could not persuade Harkness to reconsider, Wald vented her frustration in a letter to Lavinia Dock: "Confidentially, my political attitude is making some of our generous friends uneasy and one of our largest givers—nearly $15,000 a year—has withdrawn," she said, "because I am 'socialistically inclined'. Poor things; I am sorry for them—they are so scared. It is foolish since, after all, counting things in the large and wide, I am at least one insurance against unreasonable revolution in New York."[196] When Harkness said she would withdraw her contributions as of January 1920, the board backed Wald, passing a motion to endorse freedom of expression and belief to all members of the Settlement.[197]

The rise of a conservative climate was just part of a larger number of changes that were swirling. Settlement work was also changing. The spontaneity of the early years—when volunteers like Lillian Wald and Mary Brewster improvised as they went along—was increasingly replaced by a new professionalism and bureaucratization. Henry Street and other settlements hired trained social workers and nurses educated in university programs (programs that were, in many ways, inspired by Wald's work and vision). As social work emerged as a profession, it focused more on the individual—through casework and psychology—than on collective and social action.[198]

The 1920s also saw rising concerns that settlement work had become redundant. The robust, middle-class reform response to the massive influx of immigrants at the turn of the century meant that a handful of organizations serving the disadvantaged had grown to dozens. In the twenties, other recreational services—such as neighborhood youth centers, YMCAs, high-school programs, and summer camps—became competition for settlements' clubs, gymnasiums, camps, and arts activities. Lillian Wald, by now a seasoned veteran, responded to these concerns about relevance. She realized that settlements, as she put it, "have been before the public long enough to have lost the glamour of moral adventure that was associated with their early days." But that didn't mean they weren't doing valuable, critical work. At an October 1925 board meeting, Wald shared numerous letters she'd received from America and abroad that applauded Henry Street for its "liberalizing influence" in a conservative, intolerant, unsettling political climate. Not just their "branches of usefulness" but the underlying values that girded them—values of equity, equality, of the power of bridging differences—were needed. At a time when "narrow, reactionary forces such as the Ku Klux Klan can develop in our country," Wald asserted, "the 'liberalizing influence' of Henry Street is of inestimable value."[199]

In her November 1927 address to the board, Wald returned to the theme. "The position of Henry Street Settlement is strategic," she said.

> Though it has become in a way a center for the meeting of all nationalities, of all grades, it bears a moral responsibility because of its position in the minds not only of our own neighborhood but of people who come to New York or who find themselves in New York from all quarters of the globe. . . .
>
> Like other educational organizations, one meets the question whether settlements have not passed their day of usefulness; but in the fact of at least three settlements in New York financed to build houses at

enormous cost and the inflowing life and a new generation ready to be
guided by the older people in the movement and the fact that the settlements have adhered to their principles of respect for human beings and
for promoting understanding in human relations, would be the answer.[200]

With rising American consumer prosperity (even if it was a prosperity not shared by all), and with public schools taking on some of the
programs that settlements had pioneered, there was a settlement-wide
shift away from the notion that they were relieving destitution to what
Jane Addams called "raising life to its highest value." For many settlements, the arts now became a key element in the new shift. As Paul U.
Kellogg wrote, the settlements' role in the revival of the arts in American life was a powerful symbol of their resiliency during their "ten years
of sag in the political and economic fields."[201]

For Henry Street, which had always placed a strong emphasis on
the arts, the 1920s were not so much a time of new initiatives—as they
were for settlements with less developed arts offerings—but a time of
change and growth in its existing programs. The Neighborhood Playhouse was an increasingly vital force. It featured new plays by acclaimed
American playwrights (such as Eugene O'Neill's *The First Man*, in the
1921–22 season), extensive programming, and classes in costumes and set
design. Prominent theater critics acknowledged its place in the growing
little theater movement.[202] As the Playhouse grew increasingly successful with an uptown crowd, though, tensions resurfaced over the balance
between amateur and professional, between serving a downtown, local
neighborhood audience and an uptown, upscale one.

Typically, Henry Street plays were performed by amateurs. In 1920,
though, the Playhouse opened the season with paid, professional actors.
While Settlement volunteers, youngsters, and club members continued
to participate, theirs was now a supporting, not a starring, role. The division was made clear by formally reorganizing the company entities into
the professional-amateur Neighborhood Playhouse Acting Company
and the amateur Festival Dancers. Playhouse staff members had conflict-

ing views. Alice and Irene Lewisohn, who had essentially started Henry Street's arts program, were more idealistic; they preferred an "enlightened amateurism." Their Playhouse colleagues, Agnes Morgan and Helen Arthur, preferred a professional setting with more of a focus on making money. Fiscal problems exacerbated the debate, and rising costs and poor financial management forced them to close for the 1922 season.[203]

Tensions eventually came to a head in 1926. Wald, writes historian John P. Harrington, was "skeptical of the financial extravagance and artistic egoism necessary to take a successful production from the neighborhood audience to an uptown, larger, and more profitable one, and she saw production transfer uptown in terms of departure and loss rather than destination and opportunity."[204] In 1927, the Lewisohns left. "After twenty years of experimentation in unusual plays and new forms of drama and lyric drama," stated an April 11 press release, "The Neighborhood Playhouse, feeling that it has come to the end of its present method . . . now announces that, so far as the present organization is concerned, it will cease with the close of the current season." According to the press release, the Playhouse had become a victim of its own growth and success. The "handicaps of location and capacity loomed larger and larger," it said. "The steady march of residential New York to regions further and further north each year made the task of reaching the Neighborhood Playhouse more difficult and time consuming, while the size of the theatre prevented even such a success as [the play] 'The Dybbuk', which played to capacity throughout its long run, from adequately supplementing the endowment."[205] Harrington attributes its demise to a more complex set of factors, including "mission confusion, internal rivalries, poor financial planning, and an unsustainable philanthropic model for a non-commercial theater."[206]

In its successes and failures, the Playhouse had, though, enacted Wald's idea of association by bringing together many different people: longtime Lower East Siders, new immigrants, students, professionals, benefactors, and others.[207] It had also raised the Settlement's public profile. With its closing, the Settlement lost its classes, productions, and

performances. One year later, happily, benefactors Herman Gettner and
Louis Abrons acquired the Playhouse for the Settlement. Reopened
under the name Henry Street Playhouse, it once again offered dance
and dramatics. The Lewisohn sisters, along with Rita Wallach Morgenthau, went on to create the Neighborhood Playhouse School of the
Theatre on East 54th Street in Manhattan, which still operates today.

The departure of the Lewisohns spelled an end to one chapter in
the Settlement's arts history. But a new one was being written with the
creation of the Henry Street Music School. Music classes, long conducted in cramped club rooms, now moved into a dedicated home: a
Pitt Street tenement attached to the back of the Playhouse. "I cannot
claim any right to speak for music," said Lillian Wald at its opening on
November 4, 1928, "other than that of one who knows its value as a profound cultural development and that of all the arts in the world it belongs to the people." To head the program, Wald hired European-born
violinist Heidi Katz, who came with superb credentials. Well-known
musicians—Aaron Copland, George Gershwin, Jascha Heifetz—
soon supported the school and served on its advisory committee, and
prominent funders backed it financially, among them members of the
Warburg family, longtime Settlement supporters; mining magnate and
supporter of social, cultural, and educational causes Adolph Lewisohn
(the uncle of Irene and Alice); violinist and philanthropist Carolyn
Allen Perera; Helen Dinsmore Huntington, the first wife of wealthy
businessman Vincent Astor and a patron of the arts; composer and conductor Walter Damrosch and his wife Margaret Blaine Damrosch; and
publisher William Randolph Hearst and his wife Millicent, a champion
for social causes.[208]

By its second year, the school boasted 160 students in four depart-
ments: instrumental, vocal, dancing, and "the instrument workshop,"
where instructors taught the construction and repair of musical instruments. When the child prodigy violinist Yehudi Menuhin visited prior
to the Music School's 1931 benefit—for which he was to perform at
Carnegie Hall—he was gifted a violin made by Isadore Buyers, one of

the workshop participants.[209] There was an adult chorus, a boys' chorus, and a "colored chorus" taught by the famous African American tenor Taylor Gordon. While the name of the chorus suggests that activities were segregated, that was not the case. As Lillian Wald proudly told Walter White, head of the NAACP, in 1935, Henry Street did not segregate; the chorus of Black men and women had been organized, she said, by choice through a committee that was made up completely of the ministers of local Black churches.[210]

At the Music School, group lessons were open to all students, regardless of talent or ambition, at a nominal cost. But head Heidi Katz, who wanted to provide professional-level training, made requirements for private lessons extremely rigorous.[211] While the first few years of her tenure went smoothly, tensions eventually erupted over her vision for the school and that of Lillian Wald. Their competing concepts encapsulated the kinds of dilemmas that, as historian Shannon L. Green writes, plagued "most settlement music programs at the time: the purpose that music training and music activities should serve within the settlement environment."[212] Wald's primary goal was to provide access to music for the neighborhood's low-income residents. Katz's primary goal was to mold talented children into the music professionals of the future.[213] A budget deficit only fanned the flames of debate. Henry Street struggled annually with the cost of the Music School because it wanted to give access to anyone who wanted it whether they could pay or not. The heart of the controversy was not about money, though; it was about purpose.

For Lillian Wald, the answer was clear. The school was not to be primarily a professional training ground. Rather, she wanted it to provide a means for working-class people to find cultural expression. In the end, writes Green, "at both Henry Street and within the National Federation of Settlements Music Division, the dilemma between conservatory-style training and the group-focused, socially oriented program was never wholly resolved; in both instances a lack of reconciliation and cooperation between the two factions led to a divisive separation with continued hard feelings on both sides for years to come."[214]

In its first 40 years, Lillian Wald had transformed a house into a Settlement; built a vast home nursing service with branches throughout the sprawling metropolis; and created a "family" at Henry Street. She had formed lasting relationships with neighbors, fashioned a network of reformers and supporters to further the cause of social justice, and brought international renown to the Settlement's work. Most importantly, she had forged an enduring blueprint. As the world around Henry Street changed, that blueprint would be its guiding star. And even as questions about relevance persisted, settlements' responses to both the everyday concern and the international crisis would show why they, and Henry Street, were still important to the life of the neighborhood and the nation.[215]

# 2

## MOVING WITH THE TIMES

### Testing the Blueprint in Neighborhood and Nation, 1930s to the Mid-1960s

ON A WARM SUNDAY IN MAY 1943, AS WORLD WAR II RAGED overseas, a crowd of 2,000 gathered at Corlears Hook Park on Manhattan's Lower East Side to celebrate Henry Street's 50th anniversary. Breezes spilled off the East River as attendees, seated on folding chairs, heard Mayor Fiorello La Guardia honor the Settlement for its role in the city and nation, for helping government to recognize that "the right to live well and properly is recognized as one of the responsibilities of the government and not left to the generosity of individuals." The work of the Settlement was contagious, he said, noting that "The whole world is considering the social welfare of its people, the whole world is considering economic security for its people."[1]

Then Helen Hall, who had taken over as head of Henry Street after Lillian Wald's retirement in 1933, addressed the crowd. She spoke of her pride in the sense of brotherhood that had always guided the Settlement; of the importance of neighbors and community; and of the power of association, especially in a world at war. "Today," she said, "statesmen have borrowed the name of neighbor from us to describe what we hope for in a new and peaceful and free world."

Longtime supporter and board member Rita Wallach Morgenthau now rose to speak. She described Henry Street in terms that looked to past and present, putting her finger on the salient characteristic that had helped the organization survive and meet both the intractable and the changing challenges of an impoverished neighborhood. Henry Street, she said, represented "the best that is in American tradition; it remembers the past, but does not let it shackle it; it keeps its freedom to interpret the present and to have vision for the future."[2]

The 50-year milestone was a testament to the resilience of the Settlement and its continued ability to change with the times, as Morgenthau had so movingly described. It was also a reminder of the enduring blueprint that Lillian Wald had created: one that valued the power of association and "the name of neighbor." That blueprint would be tested in the era from the 1930s to the 1960s by an economic downturn, a world war, and the departure of industry from New York City—which took with it the promise of jobs that had sustained earlier newcomers. A second generation of leaders, exemplified by Helen Hall, would face new ideas about social work and continuing questions about settlements' relevance, even as, every day, they helped to meet the overwhelming needs of neighbors living in poverty.

## FOREBODING AMONG OUR NEIGHBORS

On the Lower East Side, what would grow to be the Great Depression began as a gnawing concern. In 1928, Lillian Wald and the Settlement staff met to discuss the growing numbers of people who were coming to Henry Street in search of work.[3] Close to the ground—as they had always been—it was possible to see that all was not well. There was "no sudden avalanche," said Wald, "but a creeping, daily change—shortening hours of work, an increasing number of dismissals, wage cuts, and the uneasiness which none can comprehend unless they have learned to recognize and share it. It permeates a neighborhood like a thickening fog of anxiety and fear . . . months before the stock-market crash, we were made aware of the foreboding among our neighbors."[4]

However unevenly wealth had been distributed in the 1920s, for many it had been a time of prosperity. Now, the 1929 stock market crash triggered a brutal economic downturn. Millions of Americans lost their jobs, their savings, and their homes. As unemployment rose to over 20 percent, fear and despair blanketed the nation. On the Lower

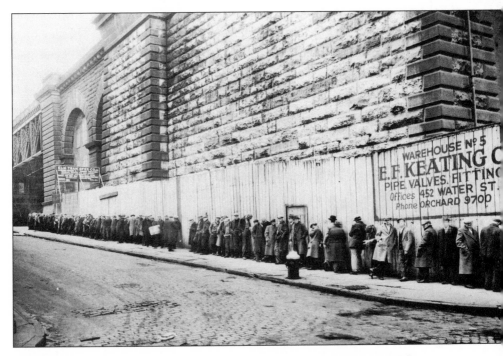

FIGURE 2.1. A bread line forms alongside the Brooklyn Bridge approach during the Depression. Until government filled the vacuum, private charities and churches helped feed hungry, out-of-work New Yorkers. Courtesy of the Library of Congress.

East Side—where the average yearly income per capita was the lowest in Manhattan, and living conditions were poor and declining—the prospect of hard times was especially worrisome[5] (fig. 2.1). Journalist, activist, and Catholic Worker Movement cofounder Dorothy Day, who worked in the neighborhood, recalled how the evictions were so numerous that "you couldn't walk down the street without seeing furniture on the sidewalk."[6] The Depression would make clear that local solutions to poverty would not be enough, and bring about a search for new, national solutions—in which settlements would play a key role.[7]

In 1930, Henry Street conducted a survey to assess the early impact of the economic downturn. "In an attempt to find out what unemployment means on the human side," reported Karl D. Hesley, Henry Street's director of social work, at the November 30 board meeting, "the question was asked,—How has unemployment altered your plans." Hesley then shared some of the responses: "Mother had to go to work"; "Have had to move to cheaper houses"; "Will be forced to accept charity, although I'd rather do anything else first"; "Wife and baby do without needs"; "Many arguments with parents because I (son) can't find job"; "Have had to give up school"; "Have had to borrow money"; "It will mean nowhere to live—on streets soon"; "Used up all savings."[8]

Henry Street had already begun to respond to its neighbors' growing problems. It hired unemployed men to clean and paint at the Settlement and at its summer camp for girls, Echo Hill. It offered neighbors food, rent, loans, and help fighting eviction. Wald, as chairperson of the Lower East Side Community Council Unemployment Committee, offered the professional services of 135 area social agencies to the Mayor's Relief Committee to help reinvestigate and supplement a police survey of people in want. She surveyed young people to determine their specific needs, worked out a plan to cope with what was euphemistically called "enforced leisure time," and created emergency industries for women in settlements.[9] And she wrote articles that put a human face on a national tragedy: "Have you seen the uncontrollable trembling of parents," she wrote in the *Survey*, "who have gone half starved for weeks so that the children may have food? Do you know what it means to try to minister to the sick or the dying or the newly born in an overcrowded home where there is no heat, no food, no clean clothing or bedding, gas and electricity turned off, no furniture worth pawning or selling, an eviction notice tacked on the door?"[10]

With all the Settlement was doing, there was always more to do. Wald came home at night to growing piles of letters asking for assistance, loans, and job leads—like the one sent by Louis Delinsky of 297 Henry Street: "My mother asked me to get in touch with you as she says that you could possibly help our family," he wrote. "I've been looking for work for months now without finding any . . . I am the sole support of the house and have three other children in the house of school age."[11]

As the pleas for help intensified, debate over what to do played out in the city and nation, where methods for public relief proved archaic and inadequate. New York City's many public and private welfare agencies had no unified response, and since the city's charter prohibited cash relief, there were limited ways to help penniless families.[12] President Herbert Hoover argued vehemently against the "dole," insisting that private charity should take care of Americans' problems. On the other side of the debate were those who, like settlement houses, believed that the desperate situation required a robust response from the federal government.[13]

In 1933, in the midst of the crisis (and a year after the nursing service had treated its millionth patient), Lillian Wald's failing health forced her to retire. She had suffered periodic bouts with infections and anemia after a trip to Mexico in 1925, and undergone several operations, all while trying to keep up her typical frenetic schedule. While Wald stayed involved as board president, she now spent most of her time at the country house she'd bought in Westport, Connecticut, years earlier. And in her place, the Henry Street board hired Helen Hall, who had served as director of Philadelphia's University Settlement House since 1922. Tall and stately, Hall was experienced, energetic, confident, fair-minded, and savvy. She would become the leading settlement voice for social reform.[14]

Helen Hall was born in Kansas City in 1892. Her father, Wilford, made surgical instruments, and her mother, Beatrice, was an artist. Like Wald, a specific, illuminating moment had ignited her desire for a life of service. When she was 14, she visited an Armenian family that had escaped a massacre at the hands of the Ottoman Empire. One of the family members was a girl the same age as Hall. Seeing her sick and hungry, surrounded by her undernourished brothers and sisters, Hall became angry at the injustice.[15] She had planned to be a sculptor; now, she said, she "wanted to stop and find out what was done for people who were very poor, and in trouble."[16] Hall decided to become a social worker.

Hall spent a year taking classes at the New York School of Philanthropy (today the Columbia University School of Social Work); although she never completed her degree, she considered herself a social worker. Afterward, she organized a small settlement in Tuckahoe, New York, called Eastchester Neighborhood House; she also worked in the Westchester county welfare office.[17] When World War I broke out, Hall joined the Red Cross and directed efforts for the servicemen of the American Expeditionary Force at base hospitals; later, she organized a girls' club for the YWCA in France, then arranged recreation services for enlisted men in China and the Philippines.

In 1922, back in the United States, Hall was named head of Philadelphia's University Settlement House and became active in the National Federation of Settlements (NFS), formally founded in 1911 by settlement house leaders—including Lillian Wald, Jane Addams, and Mary Simkhovitch—to educate the public about social issues affecting neighborhoods and help settlements with programming and public affairs. When Hall became NFS president in 1933, it helped give her a useful national platform.[18]

Settlement houses in the United States were now in their fifth decade, and their workforces and leadership were changing. Hall represented a new breed, a transition between the founders and professional social workers. She brought a lot to the table. Hall knew, as her predecessors in settlement work did, of the value of published studies as a way to chronicle, analyze, and shine a light on changing social conditions, and wrote prolifically; a 1959 bibliography of her writings lists 65 studies done between 1928 and 1958.[19] She had staunch allies in the field of settlement work, and gained a power partner in 1935 when she married *Survey* editor Paul U. Kellogg, who came to live with her at Henry Street. Hall networked effectively with other settlement house leaders and cultivated influential politicians on behalf of New Deal welfare reforms.[20] And like Lillian Wald, Hall knew the power of a story. By drawing on the real-life struggles of real people, she brought dry, impersonal data to life. She was also wickedly funny. Her "humor and mimicry were part of her national reputation," said Henry Street social workers Ruth and Ralph Tefferteller, and her motivational skills were legendary: "She was never satisfied until convinced that you, too, were as 'beset' as she that something had to be done about a problem affecting human lives," they said. "Helen's by-line from the minute her day began was 'I am beset that we must try to . . .' and then the humor—witty, devastating, beguiling—would follow."[21]

When Henry Street's board appointed Hall as its new—and only second—leader in 1933, New York City's settlement heads reached out to congratulate her. On April 16, Lillian Wald sent a Western Union telegram to her successor: "Easter greetings sent with affectionate good wishes for our joint future service to mankind happy I am in the thought in passing on the prophets [sic] cloak to be anointed." On May 9, Hamilton House headworker Lillian Robbins wrote, "You probably know that we are an adopted member of the Henry Street family, the relationship being a bit indefinite, but nevertheless a very real and vital one. I shall be glad to hear from you when you have established yourself at 265." And on June 5, Greenwich House director Mary Simkhovitch dropped her a line to say "How rejoiced we are in New York that you are going to be one of us! Your presence will add a great deal of distinction to the settlement movement, and besides all that, it will be such fun to see you from time to time."[22]

In August, Hall moved from Philadelphia to the Lower East Side and her new home at number 265. "Henry Street Welcomes Miss Helen Hall as Head Worker of Famous Settlement," announced *The New York Times*. Boys and girls playing games in the street, mothers with their babies sitting on stoops: all congregated around to eagerly welcome her. "Some of them," it said, "insisted upon carrying her luggage into the stately old house with its brass door knocker, reminiscent of the day when it was fashionable to live in Henry Street."

Helen Hall hit the ground running (fig. 2.2). As chair of the Unemployment Committee of the National Federation of Settlements, she had overseen an important 1928–29 study. Undertaken with the collaboration of 104 neighborhood houses (including Henry Street Settlement) in 20 states, 32 cities, and the District of Columbia,[23] it had demon-

FIGURE 2.2. Henry Street head Helen Hall (front, right) with labor leaders and sup-
porters Felice Louria (front, left) and (back row, left to right) Robert S. Lynd, B. F.
McLaurin, and Michael Quill, at the White House in February 1938. This delegation
from the Consumers' National Federation came to submit a four-point program to
President Roosevelt in hopes that he would back a central, federal consumers' agency.
Courtesy of the Library of Congress.

strated rising national despair—and the rising need for Congress to
act by providing national unemployment insurance. (The *Catholic Charity Review* called it "a practical portrayal, in neat, concise and intelligent form, of the injustices of man to man."[24]) Now, in 1933, as head
of Henry Street Settlement, she used those findings, along with all she
had learned from house-to-house visits on the Lower East Side, to put
a human face on the Depression—and convey that portrait to those in
power. "We have seen families driven step by step from self-reliance
to dependence," she reported. "The months of job hunting are made
of small things, little enough each one, but calculated to wear down,

in time, the gayest of spirits."[25] Such studies starkly highlighted the inadequacies of public policy and the need for government intervention. They also made Hall a sought-after expert and would soon put her, and Henry Street, at the center of efforts that would help spawn the modern American federal welfare system.

In 1933, Franklin Delano Roosevelt took office as president of the United States after a landslide victory over Herbert Hoover. He backed a federal-level response to the economic collapse, and was convinced of the need for social insurance to ensure that the crippling destitution would never again come to pass. His "New Deal" was an innovative set of programs designed to promote economic recovery and social reform.[26] On June 8, 1934, Roosevelt outlined his social program in a message to Congress: "Next winter we may well undertake the great task of furthering the security of the citizen and his family through social insurance," he said, avowing that he was "looking for a sound means which I can recommend to provide at once security against several of the great disturbing factors in life—especially those which relate to unemployment and old age." Now, the goals of Progressive Era pioneers like Henry Street were at the forefront of the nation's agenda. "The newer concept of the obligation of the State to the economic security of the industrial worker," commented Wald from her retirement home in 1934, "bids fair to uproot the old American persuasion that success is a matter of individual effort."[27]

To move his plan forward, in June 1934 Roosevelt issued Executive Order No. 6757, which created the Committee on Economic Security (CES). Chaired by Secretary of Labor Frances Perkins, the roster of cabinet-level officials on the committee included Secretary of the Treasury Henry Morgenthau Jr., Attorney General Homer S. Cummings, Secretary of Agriculture Henry A. Wallace, and Federal Emergency Relief Administrator Harry L. Hopkins. (Morgenthau was a former Henry Street resident; other committee members had dined around the table at number 265.[28]) Roosevelt also put in place an advisory council of prominent public representatives to advise the committee, naming Helen Hall to the 23-member group. With input from the advisory council, the CES drafted Social Security legislation and put the federal government into the welfare business on a permanent basis, a step that also put Hall on the cutting edge of welfare reform.[29]

Characteristically modest about her part in the undertaking, Helen Hall later reflected on the critical role settlement houses had played in making Social Security a reality—following a decade in which some had written them off as irrelevant. "The social settlement, here and abroad," she wrote, "has from the beginning been an instrument of social reform, using first-hand knowledge to bring about changes in living conditions." That their studies on unemployment were used, as she said, as "supporting evidence for much of our social security legislation of the Thirties by the late Senator Robert F. Wagner and others," was "most cheering to those who participated in the hard, grinding work of assembling the facts."[30] Settlement social action, tamped down during the conservatism of the 1920s, had now reemerged as a potent force.

When the Social Security Act passed in August 1935, it laid down basic welfare structures that still exist today.[31] It was a watershed moment for social welfare: out of the despair of the Depression had emerged significant reform, much of it based on the work that Henry Street and other settlements and Progressive Era reformers had long championed. The New Deal had put in place a new model for funding: a national, universal public welfare service. While the world would never be the one of universal social services that some New Dealers had envisioned, much had improved.

Hall was unhappy, though, about what the legislation had left out— compulsory (universal) health insurance—an omission that continues to resonate in American life and politics. Writing in her 1971 book, *Unfinished Business in Neighborhood and Nation*, Hall despaired at the lack of progress in a fight that had gone on for so long, without success. She recalled how as early as 1917, "the National Federation of Settlements passed a resolution in favor of some sort of compulsory health insurance." And she reflected on the human cost, recalling the time she was working at the University Settlement House in Philadelphia and overheard a little girl exclaim, "We're God lucky at my house" because her mother fell ill on her father's payday. National health insurance had in fact been on the table during the Depression, but President Roosevelt feared the fight that would come with it could derail his entire Social Security legislation. And so, with so many out of work, unemployment insurance, followed by old-age benefits, took priority, and compulsory health insurance was taken off the table.[32]

Hall never gave up the fight. As head of the National Federation of Settlements, she supported a 1936–37 study of the English health insurance system, which showed that contrary to critics' claims, doctors, patients, and the public at large found it satisfactory. In 1952, she published a report—*When Sickness Strikes a Family*—that used the Lower East Side's needs as a lens through which to view the continuing need for national health insurance. And she protested, sometimes traveling to Washington, DC, with the Settlement's activist seniors to elevate their voices. Because of her continuing efforts, in 1965 she was invited to watch President Lyndon B. Johnson sign the Medicare Bill into law. Hall brought back one of the signing pens and displayed it at Henry Street's Good Companions (its senior center), "where it certainly belongs," she said, "for they had never missed an opportunity to speak, write, parade, or go to Washington for Medicare."[33]

Hall's work on national social security demonstrated her ability to build the kinds of political relationships and bridges that were so necessary to the Settlement's work. In New York City, she worked closely with its energetic reform mayor, Fiorello La Guardia, a Republican who took on his first of three terms in 1934, routed Tammany Hall from power, and embraced Roosevelt's New Deal. Hall often asked La Guardia for help; he often asked her to be on citywide committees that addressed pressing urban issues. Their relationship was close: when she once feared she had offended him with a request, he responded, "How in the world could I ever be 'mad at you.' Not at all. One may be hurt by but never mad at anyone he loves."[34] Hall also had a strong working relationship with the powerful US senator Robert Wagner. Wagner, who became chairman of the Senate Banking and Currency Committee during the New Deal era, helped pass both the Social Security Act and labor legislation that protected the rights of unions and workers.[35] In addition, she continued the warm relationship that Lillian Wald had forged with Edith and Herbert Lehman, both generous supporters of the Settlement. Lehman, who was New York State governor from 1933 until 1942 and then US Senator from 1949 until 1957, believed in government for the people and enacted a "Little New Deal" for New York; while he supported Henry Street financially, Hall supported him in his campaigns for government office.[36]

As head of Henry Street, and then as head of the NFS from 1934 to 1940, Hall also forged supportive relationships with other women leaders in the settlement house world at a time when women were still in the majority. Lillie Peck was a friend; she was a resident at Henry Street and worked alongside Hall as NFS executive secretary for many years. Helen Harris was another close friend. In the late 1930s, she headed New York's National Youth Administration, later became a city administrator, and in 1946 began a long tenure as head of the United Neighborhood Houses of New York. Hall and Harris frequently collaborated on such local issues and concerns as housing, city planning, and settlement house day care.[37]

Whether on the local or national stage, Hall never lost sight of the need to see both the very big picture and the individual human being in front of her, the need to balance national advocacy with neighborhood need—a way of seeing that characterized her skills as a leader and one of the reasons that made Henry Street so successful at its work. As she wrote of the Great Depression,

> in all those years of struggle and makeshifts what we could do was so inadequate and what was needed so overwhelming that while your eyes were on the misery and the bit of immediate help you could give, you continually had to be working on the broader picture.

But if you worked in a settlement, you couldn't put off a mother with a sick baby and an eviction notice by saying that you were working at City Hall to get a more humane way of handling rents. It had to be both and at the same time, and if you couldn't help, you listened, which kept your own awareness up to the minute with plenty of emotional urge behind it.[38]

## RISING PROBLEMS

In a broadcast on radio station WINS in January 1934, Helen Hall described the problems that the Settlement's visiting nurses encountered throughout the city as the Depression wore on: increasing cases of mental illness, malnutrition, starvation, even suicide. Struggling to meet the desperate, growing need, the service also struggled to fund the expanding work. The nurses "are trying to live up to their slogan of 'never refusing a call,'" Hall said, "but this will have to be abandoned unless we raise our emergency fund of $300,000; a drive to obtain this money is now in progress, and the citizens of New York must decide whether the visiting nurses can maintain their tradition—or whether calls from the sick who cannot afford a private nurse will have to go unanswered."[39]

Meanwhile, intensifying its response to local unemployment, Henry Street became an office for the Civil Works Administration (CWA), a New Deal job-creation program. The move drew fire from New York State Congressional Representative Samuel Dickstein, who in June 1934 falsely charged that communists had received CWA jobs through the Settlement's influence. "I'm going to make it my business," he fumed, "to find out how it is that hoodlums who spend their time parading through the streets and waving red flags get these jobs where more deserving citizens fail to get them." (Dickstein, who established what would become the House Committee on Un-American Activities, was later found to be a paid Russian agent. His Soviet code name was "Crook."[40]) Through the WPA's program for artists, instituted by the government in 1935, the Settlement also gained new teachers, enabling them to offer workshops to some 300 adults (fig. 2.3). Henry Street had also benefited from earlier

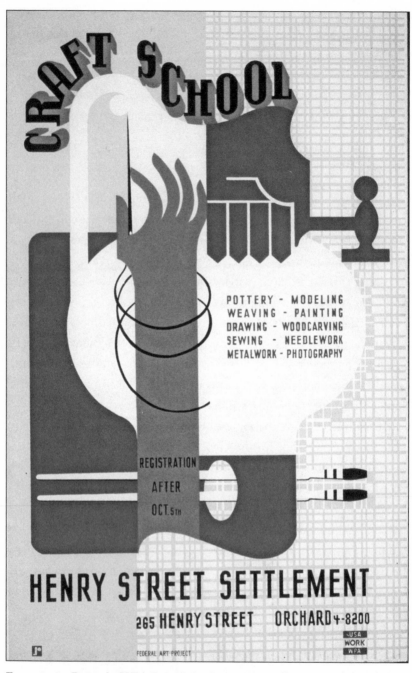

FIGURE 2.3. Poster for WPA Federal Art Project–sponsored art and craft classes offered at Henry Street Settlement, about 1936. Courtesy of the Library of Congress.

funding from New York State's work relief program, which supported free classes—including one in ceramics—which a young, down-and-out artist named Jackson Pollock attended in 1932. Pollock had been encouraged to take the class by Rita Benton, the wife of his good friend artist Thomas Hart Benton (Benton had taught at Henry Street Settlement and, in fact, met his wife there). Pollock became so adept at creating plates and bowls that Rita Benton put them up for sale at a makeshift showroom for fledgling artists, located in the basement of the gallery where her husband showed his work. All of the pieces sold.[41]

When in 1935 Henry Street opened the Workers' Education Center, the Settlement again came under suspicion for communist activities. The center was a WPA-sponsored program designed to offer out-of-work adults education, stimulate conversations around contemporary social and economic issues, and foster a sense of shared responsibility for action, with the goal of helping neighbors determine how they might find solutions to their community's dire problems. Located at 263 Henry Street, it served 150 students, most of them from the Lower East Side: unemployed cooks, clerks, laborers, stonecutters, shipping clerks, garment workers, and more. It was sponsored by Washington relief agencies, but the Settlement's reputation for radicalism—along with the fact that the program was an outgrowth of a summer school that had been under investigation—attracted spies and investigators looking for dirt. Hall wryly observed that at the same time the government was accusing the school of radicalism, "a group of our dramatic players vehemently protested to us that we were too conservative, saying that the plays chosen were neither experimental nor revolutionary"—even while a part of the same group labeled their fellow thespians "'ungrateful Communists' who wanted the leading parts and whose sense of values had gone wrong."[42] It was not the first time charges were leveled at Henry Street, and it would not be the last.

As Hall took up fights that were important to the neighborhood, the city at large, and the nation, two issues dominated her work: consumer advocacy (which would again bring baseless charges of communism) and better housing.

Women's activism had receded after women won the right to vote in 1920. Now, in the 1930s, one of the places it was seeing a resurgence was the consumer movement. Led by strong women who mobilized female consumers around the issue of high prices and price gouging, the movement was big, it was grass roots, and it was effective—and Helen Hall was at its forefront.[43] She was a fierce consumer advocate, and one of her key battles—and one vitally important to her Lower East Side neighbors—was the fight over rising milk prices.[44]

During the Depression, the milk market collapsed. When milk prices became so low that farmers couldn't survive, they struck for higher prices.[45] At a time when so many consumers were struggling, however, any cost increase was devastating—and because milk was the foundation of children's diet, they were the strike's main victims (fig. 2.4). Hall attacked the problem on multiple levels. She called on Mayor Fiorello La Guardia for help. She marched through city streets with a cow. And she testified about the impact of higher prices on the poor.[46] In May 1934, she appeared before the New York State Milk Advisory Committee, where she spoke about a study of 21,559 families, initiated by Henry Street and sponsored citywide by United Neighborhood Houses with the cooperation of Mayor La Guardia and the New York City Public Schools. The study demonstrated that milk consumption among the largest groups of American families was directly influenced by higher milk prices—a fact the milk industry had often disputed.[47]

Hall's testimony before the committee mixed findings of the study with the kind of emotional appeal that she, like Lillian Wald, had perfected. First, the facts. There "has been an increase of approximately 50 percent in malnutrition among school children in New York City since 1927," Hall said. "When recently we made a survey of eleven blocks close to the Henry Street Settlement, we found that 54 percent of the families are earning less than $15 a week. No one could go over these family budgets without knowing that one cent on the cost of milk would have a direct bearing on the health of children." Then, the emotional appeal. Milk, she said, was the best food for a child's diet and there was nothing

FIGURE 2.4. Milk time, 1930s. Whether at the State House or at the Settlement, Henry Street helped children obtain the nourishment they needed as rising prices made it difficult for impoverished families to afford the basics. Henry Street Settlement Collection.

that could take its place. "I am sure there is not a member of this board, who has children, who would not feel a sense of alarm if he knew that tomorrow he would have to give them less milk than they need because he could not afford to buy it," she said. "I am sure, too, that your wives and mothers would react just as the women of our neighborhood do. They, too, would go without food so that their children could have milk."[48]

Hall also addressed consumerism on the national stage. She helped form, and from 1936 to 1941 served as chair of, the Consumers' National Federation (CNF), an affiliation that helped give her access to those with political power; a colleague at the CNF described it as an "open sesame."[49] In what was coming to feel familiar, the work drew charges of communism. In 1939, J. B. Matthews, an investigator for the Special

Committee on Un-American Activities, charged the CNF with having links to a communist front. Hall, as head of the CNF, refuted the unfounded charges. On the contrary, she said, the organization had been created in 1937 to bring together the work of various national consumer groups to make them more effective in their service of what were primarily low-income groups. "So far as we know," she clapped back, "it is not un-American to be poor nor to serve the poor."[50]

Undeterred by the attacks, Hall continued to agitate for consumers— sometimes, very close to home. In 1937, she helped spearhead a credit union at Henry Street, formed by Settlement youngsters, to make credit available to low-income individuals at reasonable interest rates. The impetus came from a neighborhood teenager who sought the help of Henry Street after paying a loan shark an exorbitant $500 in interest on a $25 loan—and was still in debt. Henry Street paid off the loan, and a group of 15 Settlement youngsters banded together to attack the widespread problem by forming a credit union. While then-resident Felix Greene, who worked for the British Broadcasting Company and was familiar with the English cooperative movement, offered his help, the boys took on the bulk of the work. The experiment blossomed into an important neighborhood institution, prized by small businesspeople from all over the city. A 1954 *Reader's Digest* article even highlighted it, extolling how, with "no banking experience, and following a credit policy so liberal it would make a banker blanch, they have not only routed the loan sharks but turned their shoestring into a thriving institution."[51]

In 1893, a walk through the Lower East Side to a squalid tenement had moved Lillian Wald to act. More than 40 years later, Hall returned to the same tenement to expose the lack of progress in creating livable, affordable housing. Testifying in Albany before the joint Senate and Assembly Committees on the Affairs of the City of New York in 1936, Hall reported that "One family still lives in the front, and their wash was hanging wet on the clothes line in the court Miss Wald described. While for over thirty years erection of new multiple dwellings of that obsolete type has been prohibited here, the ban did not run against the continued occupancy of those already standing."[52] Disheartened, Helen Hall spoke out for better housing, and, hoping to shift responsibility to the state, explored the possibilities that lay in government subsidies.

In 1937, the $500 million Wagner-Steagall Housing Act opened a financial window of opportunity. Through it, the federal government would provide subsidies to public housing agencies with the express goal of creating better housing for families with low incomes.[53] When the act passed, Mayor La Guardia appointed builder and civil engineer Alfred Rheinstein to head the City Housing Authority and expand its functions under the new law.[54] Vice-chair of the authority was Greenwich House settlement founder Mary Simkhovitch, an authority on public housing.[55] The housing authority decided it would combine slum clearance with the creation of low-cost housing. It set about finding sites that were 1) suitable for building housing; 2) would result in eradicating the largest stretches of inferior housing; and 3) were accessible to industry and/or mass transit.[56] It's important to note that while the approach was welcomed by many at the time, it eventually led to bulldozing swaths of substandard housing in impoverished neighborhoods and driving out their inhabitants without providing them a new place to live.

For years, conversation had swirled around what to do with a swath of aged, substandard housing along the East River on the Lower East Side, an area known since colonial times as Corlears Hook. When it was proposed as a possible site, Alfred Rheinstein demurred, deeming the land too expensive.[57] A Henry Street–commissioned study proved him wrong—paving the way for blocks of slum clearance and construction of the six-story Vladeck Houses on an 18-acre plot. One section was aided by federal funds and housed 1,531 families; the other was financed by the City of New York and accommodated 240 families. The new housing took the place of 172 buildings, most of them old-law tenements in poor condition.[58] Fittingly, the project was named for Russian socialist and labor leader Baruch Charney Vladeck, who had been manager of *The Jewish Daily Forward*, a member of the New York City Council, and on the first New York City Housing Authority.[59]

FIGURE 2.5. Vladeck Houses, 1941. Built with Settlement backing, Vladeck Houses provided desperately needed affordable housing—and for kids, a place to play. Courtesy of the Library of Congress.

*Vladeck Houses: A Lesson in Neighborhood History*, published by the New York City Housing Authority when the project opened in 1940, enthusiastically described the apartments' modern bathrooms, electric refrigerators, gas stoves, laundry tubs, and more. Notable is how it highlights features that Lillian Wald had fought for as necessary decades before: every room had at least one outside window and running water; outside, there were playgrounds for children, and grassy, tree-filled grounds to bring in light and air (fig. 2.5).[60] For many, it was a dream come true; one tenant called it a "four and a half room paradise!"[61] For Henry Street and all who had fought for the dream—including local residents who'd pressured City Hall—it was long overdue.

After Vladeck Houses opened, Henry Street created innovative *in situ* programs for them, among them the Home Planning Workshop and, later, Good Companions, a program for seniors. At a time when money was especially tight, the workshop gave residents a place to sew their own clothes, make their own home furnishings, repair shoes and appliances, and more. The program, one of the earliest in a public housing facility in New York City, continues today, providing services to community members where they live.[62] And one of its longest-running teachers is one of its most beloved: Ruth Taube, the workshop's nonagenarian director (fig. 2.6). Taube, born and raised on the Lower East

FIGURE 2.6. Ruth Taube, the longtime and beloved director of the Home Planning Workshop, 2018. Henry Street Settlement Collection/David Grossman.

Side in a cold-water tenement, became a workshop instructor in 1966, and through the decades, has taught generations of New Yorkers to knit, sew, and crochet, imparting wisdom with each lesson. "It's always been—from day one when I started in 1966—learn to do for yourself and you won't be in need," Taube says. "Help yourself and you'll be on the right track." Today Ruth is a local celebrity—recognized (and hugged) on the street by many former students—and a national one; in 2009 the Fashion Institute of Technology bestowed on her its President's Award for Lifetime Achievement, putting her in the company of such legendary icons as Anna Wintour and Bill Blass.[63]

## THE ARTS AND SOCIAL ACTION

As part of the Settlement's search for creative ways to address the Depression's multiple challenges, a group of Henry Streeters—the "Sunday Night at Nine" committee—raised the idea of using the Playhouse stage to highlight issues and seek collaborative community input:

> Housing . . . youth . . . credit unions . . . milk . . . labor . . . crime . . . medicine. . . . They are headlines, real problems in our neighborhood, these subjects; we face them every day. But how much do we really understand them, in their broader aspect? There's a theatre in the settlement. Could we put these problems on the stage? And perhaps, in the process of dramatizing them, we could somehow bring them into focus for ourselves and other people; get a clearer idea of what we might do to solve them.[64]

In a 1938 memo to Helen Hall, the committee argued its case. Henry Street workers had noticed, they said, "a need in the community for articulation of social problems." Performance was an ideal medium for satisfying this need, but it needed a little shaking up: it should be collaborative and participatory, and it should make the Playhouse less a performance space and more of a "meeting place." As they put it, "Our audience does not come to watch a play but to participate, literally and practically, in

FIGURE 2.7. A scene from *Dollars and Sense*, one of the Living Newspapers mounted by Henry Street as part of the Federal Theatre program. Here performers mix art and activism as they bring a consumer problem—rising milk prices—to the stage. Henry Street Settlement Collection.

producing it: to choose its subject matter, write it, stage it and criticize the results."The committee had a track record; it had already done several presentations about peace, pure food and drugs, and credit unions (the latter based on the Settlement's new credit union) as part of the "Living Newspapers" series, developed by the WPA Federal Theatre Project to entertain, instruct, and bring attention to national issues (fig. 2.7).

The committee got what it wished. And, in a case of art imitating life, when word got out that one of the scenes was in a poolroom, the regular clientele of the local poolroom/bookie joint crashed the first rehearsal. "The boys came to jeer," the committee members said, but ended up wanting to be part of the production. When the poolroom proprietor came to see where his clientele had gone—and then returned for a dress rehearsal—he snidely remarked, "You guys are not only get-ting up there and making fools of yourselves, but you're wising up the neighborhood." The young actors took it as unintended encouragement, crediting him with providing them "an expression, 'wising up the neigh-borhood,' which might be used as a slogan for our program."[65]

In 1935, Grace Spofford succeeded Heidi Katz as head of the Henry Street Music School.[66] Spofford came to the Settlement from Philadel-phia's prestigious Curtis Institute, where, as dean, she had cultivated an international student body in the belief that it could foster transnational understanding. This philosophy closely allied with the Settlement's, and along with her experience and expertise as a trained musician, made her a good fit for Henry Street. Spofford wanted to create program-ming that felt relevant to the school's Lower East Side neighbors; she also wanted to contribute to the wider field of music education. To ad-vise her, she created a music committee that included, among others, composer Aaron Copland, violinist Jascha Heifetz, and composer and pianist George Gershwin (Gershwin had grown up near Henry Street but had once told Wald he couldn't recall his exact house because his family had moved so often)—each of them professionally celebrated and socially liberal.[67]

For the 1936–37 academic year, Spofford undertook a bold experi-ment: she asked Aaron Copland to create an opera for the school, one that would be suitable for the school's young performers. Copland, who was involved in New Deal circles and left-wing politics and described himself as "sympathetic for the more radical side of things," welcomed the challenge.[68] He set about writing *Second Hurricane*, a two-act, one-hour opera; his friend, dance critic Edwin Denby, would write the li-bretto. The plot revolves around the story of high-school students who try to rescue hurricane victims, become trapped on an island, and, in the process, learn lessons about freedom, courage, and tolerance.

In a July 26, 1936, article in *The New York Times*, critic H. Howard Taubman discussed the work in progress, describing it as an example of daring experimentation, all the more novel considering that opera companies and symphony orchestras rarely undertook experiments. As Taubman put it, "audiences generally prefer the trade and familiar masterpieces, and budgets require audiences." But, he said, "artistic currents flow in many directions in a city like New York and a country like the United States. Movements that may have profound influence sometimes start in obscure corners. And organizations or institutions with limited means have been known to take musical ventures of importance." *Second Hurricane*, he predicted, would be a successful and important experiment.[69]

The opera opened at the Playhouse on April 21, 1937, with performers drawn from 8- to 19-year-olds at the Music School, Henry Street's adult chorus, the Professional Children's School, and nearby Seward Park High School. Copland chose as director a 21-year-old Orson Welles, who was heavily involved in the Federal Theatre and was already well known for his acting and directorial work.[70] While reviews were mixed, Spofford deemed it a success, in part because it had shown that the school was able to successfully marry the world of trained musical experts with the world of untrained community members. In innovative public experiments like *Second Hurricane*, but also in the everyday work of the Music School, they were demonstrating that they were both "a school of quality" and a "demonstrably valid instrument of social welfare."[71] Spofford's approach seemed to have successfully straddled, at least for the time, the longtime tensions over whether their focus should be on amateurs or professionals, on creating art with the neighborhood or for uptowners.[72]

In 1940, an era ended when Henry Street founder Lillian Wald passed away at the age of 73. She died of a cerebral hemorrhage at her Connecticut country home, where her devoted nurse proclaimed that "To her, Henry Street was her only home." At Wald's memorial service, held at Manhattan's Carnegie Hall, tributes from Henry Streeters, doctors, reformers, and political figures reflected the themes that had always guided Wald and the Settlement: inclusivity, connectedness, equality, equity. Charles-Edward Armory Winslow, a renowned figure in public health, said "we did not think of Lillian Wald primarily as a nurse, or as a social worker, or a pioneer in public health, or a citizen or a states-woman," but as all of these. He applauded Wald's contributions to "the healing of the nations" and credited her with forging an ever-widening circle of people who were willing to cross racial boundaries. Reformer and *Survey* editor Paul U. Kellogg marveled at "that quality of hers in not only welcoming people through that door, but in going out from it, going out from it and giving out of it to the far ends of the earth." Mayor La Guardia called Wald "a civic force in the entire United States." And in the US House of Representatives, the Honorable Samuel Dick-stein of New York (who not long before had accused the Settlement of harboring communists), said of the woman who had come to be known as Mother Henry, "The common brotherhood of man is not a phrase to her; she knows people. . . . She administered a budget of $600,000 a year, but the night telephone rang at her bedside until a fellow worker forcibly removed it." But perhaps most poignant were the words spo-ken by Abraham Davis, who met her when she dropped in on his club meeting in 1903. "Miss Wald put the young people in their most natural setting—the family," he said. "She created a sense of communal loyalty, and a consciousness of responsibility for the common welfare of the group which has persisted throughout the years and motivated our par-ticipation in her projects and life of the settlement." Wald was gone, but her outsized spirit would live on.[73]

## THEN CAME THE WAR

In 1939, World War II broke out in Europe. President Franklin D. Roo-sevelt began to funnel billions of federal dollars into defense; wartime industries sprang up around the nation, creating an enormous labor demand. The economic resurgence that followed brought an end to the Depression. But for all the good feelings about the "economic upswing," Hall observed, "we knew that it was the shadow, and then the reality, of war that was bringing it about."[74] On December 7, 1941, a surprise Japa-nese attack on the United States military base at Pearl Harbor decisively

drew America into World War II. "During the Depression, unemployment and hunger, above all else, set its stamp on the neighborhood," said
Helen Hall. "Then came the war, and survival in another sense drew
people together for a common purpose."[75]

A little more than a week after Pearl Harbor, Hall, her husband Paul
U. Kellogg, economists, and planners gathered around Henry Street's
dining room table to discuss postwar planning. The event, which had
been planned before the Japanese attack, now took on deeper urgency.
Attendees included Manhattan Borough President Stanley M. Isaacs;
Lillie Peck, executive secretary of the National Federation of Settlements; and representatives from the Rockefeller and Russell Sage Foundations.[76] The guest of honor was Dr. Luther H. Gulick III, a prominent
social scientist and expert on public administration. Gulick had just re-
searched postwar plans in Great Britain; Kellogg was in the process of
creating a special *Survey* issue on the topic.[77] Together, they planned
ways to foster conversations about the future with a broad swath of
people, including local residents. It "seemed right to us," said Hall, "that
our neighbors should begin to think along with us of a future when the
war would be over. The families in our neighborhood were immediately
immersed in the tensions of the war and we felt it would be helpful if
young and old would start thinking of a world organization to prevent
war."[78] Because of the meeting, the National Federation of Settlements
decided to spearhead the organization of postwar planning conversations around the country.[79]

Even as it fostered discussions about the world after war, Henry
Street had to contend with it in the present. Nursing shortages, which
had emerged even before the United States entered the fray, accelerated
as staff members left to help in the war effort.[80] In March 1942, Henry
Street board chair John M. Schiff—grandson of Jacob Schiff, Henry
Street's first major benefactor—headed off to take up duty with the
Naval Reserve, and in 1944 resigned his board chairmanship.[81] In the
spring of 1942, Helen Hall left to work with the Red Cross in the Pacific
war zone for a year.[82] The Settlement's *Our Boys* newsletter reported on

the Henry Streeters fighting overseas, including "Sgt. Harry Adoff—another East Sider who is being kept busy knocking Nazis out of the sky over Europe," and "Frank Levine, sweating it out in the Pacific."[83] It also shared the young servicemen's longing for home and family. "I have been reading your paper for the past few months and I find that when I read it I float spiritually back to N.Y.," wrote US Army Private First Class Charles J. M'Glincly, "and that is the kind of feeling that keeps up our morale on these lonely islands." US Army Sergeant Peter Trubak wrote that "With each copy of OUR BOYS I keep recalling memories of the fellows and Camp Henry's song: 'The joy I've had in knowing you, will last the whole year through.'"[84]

With the economy shifting to war production, rising shortages of consumer goods triggered nationwide rationing. To help its neighbors deal with the hardship, in 1943 Henry Street created the "Swap Shop," where they could exchange useful items without cost; following Henry Street's example, civilian defense authorities around the country established similar shops.[85] And to help neighbors contend with the rising fear of enemy attacks, Henry Street staged a civilian defense headquarters in one of its older buildings, which volunteers manned. "The white helmets of the Civilian Defense Wardens, hanging in tenement kitchens," said Helen Hall, "were worn by many of the same men with whom we had walked in demonstrations directed toward jobs and relief during the Depression."[86] Under the direction of Jacob Markowitz (a former Henry Street club member and future State Supreme Court judge and Settlement board member) were a dependable corps of "lieutenants" who taught neighbors how to extinguish lights that might be beacons to enemy aircraft or hostile submarines. They also furnished buildings on the Lower East Side with pails of water, pails of sand, axes, and other tools for firefighting in the case of enemy bombings.[87]

The arts at Henry Street were also feeling the effects of war. On one hand, the Music School was thriving, with classes in violin, voice, piano, and more, and the faculty had expanded: in the 1940–41 season, the school boasted among its faculty Russian pianist Isabelle Vengerova,

Iranian-born violinist Ivan Galamian, harpist Lucile Lawrence, and composer Roy Harris, a seminal figure in American concert music. The 1942–43 student roster, at 608, was twice what it had been just six years earlier. Students, who hailed from 26 national backgrounds, had collectively taken 13,313 individual lessons and 15,966 group classes. But there were also challenges. Six faculty and 42 students (including two in the Women's Army Corps) had joined the armed forces, and older students were leaving to take defense jobs. Because of the growing prevalence of juvenile delinquency—a troubling side effect of troublesome times—the school had added a special music workshop for neighborhood children to better engage at-risk youth. And funding was down, with public support diverted to the war effort. To Grace Spofford, such difficulties only heightened her belief in the importance of the arts at Henry Street and throughout the world. Human life "is worth very little if cultural values are eliminated," she said. "This great democracy of ours with its emphasis on human dignity will be strengthened by art, which is the search for truth and beauty—the real meaning of life."[88]

Not surprisingly, given its tradition of elevating social issues through the arts, Henry Street made war a theme in its drama program, which was led by Vassar graduate Esther Porter Lane. Lane came to Henry Street from the Federal Theatre Project,[89] and, in the topical style of its Depression-era Living Newspapers, for the 1943–44 season staged *It's Up to You*, which encouraged wartime rationing. On one level, the Settlement's music and drama programming raised neighborhood awareness of social issues. On another, even more important level, it helped create a sense of belonging for youth in difficult, tension-ridden times. "What [the Music School] did for a generation of people just coming out of the Depression," recalled Henry Street alum Martin Canin, was give "us a start . . . and a sense of . . . some sort of community."[90] For a 15-year-old Jerry Stiller, who would become an acclaimed actor and comedian, it was transformative. One day, Stiller—who lived in nearby public housing—passed the Henry Street Playhouse and decided to look inside. "I entered the lobby carrying my books and could hear a piano playing inside the theater. Nobody stopped me so I opened the door and ambled in," he recalled. "The theater was empty. The stage was bathed in a blue light and someone was playing 'Night and Day.'" As he stood there, "the music and the blue lights enveloped my senses," he said. "I felt a sereneness I had never experienced before. It was like I had been transported into a land that was trouble-free." At the theater, he met Esther Porter Lane, who invited him back to be in a play adapted from James Thurber's children's book *Many Moons*. Stiller was hooked.[91]

Stiller was not alone in his sense of the Playhouse as a special, almost magical place. The arts were part of Henry Street's intentional efforts to create a sense of community, something that felt especially crucial in wartime. As the Playhouse's 1943–44 report noted, "The magic of working together on various stage productions has been able to weld functioning and important-feeling units of Jewish, Italian, Greek, German and Polish-descent children, teen age boys and girls, and older young people."[92]

## WAR'S END, AND BIG CHANGES

Henry Street's ability to move with the times would prove to be as critical as ever as major changes rippled through the Settlement, the city, the nation, and the field of social work. In May 1944, the Settlement's nursing services and social services formally separated. It was not unexpected; the separation had been a topic of board discussion for years, and its main opponent, Lillian Wald, was now gone. That's not to say Wald hadn't seen the writing on the wall, especially in the years surrounding her retirement. As the Settlement's architect, she had always considered nursing and social service work integrated, and prized the interplay between the two. But she also realized it would be difficult for any successor without a foot in the two worlds to succeed at keeping the entities together. The May 25, 1944, *New York Times* reported that the "city-wide work of the Visiting Nurse Service has grown so steadily" and the neighborhood settlement's work has "become so varied" that the only way to efficiently administrate it was to divide it.[93] From its Lower East Side headquarters at 265 Henry

Street, the Settlement now focused solely on social services, and the "Visiting Nurse Service of New York" emerged, in a new headquarters uptown, as an independent organization, today described by its website as "the largest not-for-profit home- and community-based health care organization in the United States, serving the five boroughs of New York City, as well as Nassau, Suffolk, and Westchester Counties."[94]

With the reorganization came, slowly, a new board, which Hall described in her book, *Unfinished Business*. When she arrived at Henry Street in 1933, Hall inherited, she said, "an interested and interesting board" but she felt that the board built after the 1944 separation was unusually active, "made up of people drawn from many different professions and backgrounds—as to my mind it should be," especially given their responsibility to raise funds. The first post-reorganization board president was Newbold Morris, who had been New York City Council president and then parks commissioner; he brought broad knowledge and "especially warm friendliness to our neighbors," she said. Finances—especially complicated during the reorganization—were handled by B. A. Tompkins, the first vice president of Bankers Trust; lawyer Fairfield Dana also helped Henry Street navigate through complicated issues. Hall credits investment-fund executive Winslow Carlton, who later became board chair, with helping to build the new group, and credits his wife, Margaret, for her fundraising acumen. She describes writer, newscaster, and philanthropist Janet Murrow (wife of broadcaster Edward R. Murrow) as an "expert in theater benefits," and calls out the continued devotion of the Warburg and Lehman families. Hall also gratefully acknowledges the former Henry Streeters who grew up in the neighborhood and brought firsthand knowledge of its issues—Benjamin Schoenfein and three lawyers: Jacob Markowitz, William Calise, and Samuel Schneeweiss—all of whom she relied on for behind-the-scenes knowledge. Nicholas Kelley, son of Florence Kelley (the activist who had lived at Henry Street for many years), was a lawyer with one of the city's oldest law firms and, said Hall, "handled these fine things they called bequests for us!"[95]

While Hall drew heavily on her partnership with the board,[96] she also drew on the Settlement's partnership with its neighbors. Hall relied in particular on Henry Street's active "Adult Council," which was made up of elected representatives from all the adult clubs. Headed by its president, Betty Trager, said Hall, they "brought their thinking to bear not only on Henry Street programs but on the social causes they thought we should all press for, and they represented Henry Street at hearings and citywide meetings." And, "as the neighborhood changed," said Hall, "they did their best to draw the new neighbors into the settlement."[97]

On September 2, 1945, World War II came to an end with the formal signing of Imperial Japan's surrender. On the Lower East Side, jubilant residents hung banners on tenements and storefronts, greeting returning servicemen and women with two simple words: "Welcome Home." Many—but by no means all—Americans would now share in the economic boom and unprecedented prosperity that followed war, buoyed by an optimistic belief that most economic and social problems could be solved.[98]

From its earliest years, the arts had played a key role in Henry Street's work. Now, with war's end, that role continued. At the Music School, programs for youngsters were thriving. A young, Kentucky-born Appalachian folk singer named Jean Ritchie, who came to Henry Street with a BA in social work along with impressive skills on guitar and dulcimer, played songs for the 8- to 10-year-olds in her group. The children nicknamed Ritchie (who went on to become a key figure in the folk music movement of the 1950s and '60s) "Kentucky."[99] The Servicemen's Readjustment Act—better known as the GI Bill, which provided a variety of benefits to returning World War II vets, including tuition reimbursement—brought older students to classes.[100]

But Playhouse director Esther Porter Lane fretted over their ability to attract other local adults to programs. About to leave for a new position, she submitted a parting report to Helen Hall and the "future Director of the Playhouse" sharing her unvarnished assessment of the challenges that lay ahead.[101] "It seemed," she said, "to make little difference to the community whether or not the Playhouse was open and functioning." Touching on the longtime issue of whether they were serving local residents or uptown New Yorkers, she wondered if "Perhaps the neighborhood lethargy toward the projects carried on under their very noses would decrease if uptown participants were known to be traveling to the Lower East Side for these same advantages." Lane warned that in "the Post-War World it will be necessary to provide an attractive plan and good publicity campaign in order to get adults to use the Playhouse," and encouraged the Settlement to look beyond the Lower East Side for its audiences.[102]

In what was likely a response to Lane's warning, in 1948 the Settlement hired avant-garde dancer and choreographer Alwin Nikolais to direct the Playhouse and revamp its program (fig. 2.8). Nikolais—tall, intense, with piercing blue eyes—was a longtime dancer and teacher. After serving overseas in World War II, he returned in search of something more meaningful, something bigger and better, for his life.[103] Shortly after arriving at Henry Street, he retired from dancing and turned to choreography, teaching, and creating electronic music. In 1949, dancer Murray Louis joined Nikolais at the Henry Street Playhouse. Louis performed in the new Playhouse Dance Company (later renamed the Nikolais Dance Theater) and became its leading man as well as, in 1951, an associate director to Nikolais; in 1953, he formed his own company.[104] This unique collaboration between these two brilliant artists spawned new heights of creativity, and raised the profile of the program and the Settlement.

"I like to mix my magics," said Nikolais, and Playhouse audiences were mesmerized by his groundbreaking multimedia creations, where dramatic lighting enveloped dancers as they interacted with moving elements.[105] *Masks, Props and Mobiles* in 1953 was Nikolais's first production; other avant-garde performances soon followed, garnering international attention. Renowned dancer, choreographer, and educator Phyllis Lamhut recalls being dazzled by Nikolais. In the fall of 1948, she came to Henry Street to take classes, intent on becoming a ballet dancer.

# PLAYHOUSE SCHOOL OF DANCE

### HENRY STREET SETTLEMENT, 466 GRAND ST., NEW YORK 2, N.Y.

PHONE ORchard 4-1100      ALWIN NIKOLAIS, Director      SEASON 1949-50

Performance photos by DWIGHT GODWIN      Studio Photos by GENE DAUBER

## A PROFESSIONAL SCHOOL EQUIPPED WITH THEATRE AND STUDIOS.

Offering: - MODERN DANCE TECHNIQUE - COMPOSITION - DANCE THEORY - PERCUSSION - WORKSHOP - PERFORMING COMPANY    -    -    Veterans accepted under G. I. BILL. FULL OR PART TIME STUDY    -    -    CLASSES ALSO FOR LAYMEN AND CHILDREN.

**Office Opens Sept. 6th - Registration Begins Sept. 19th - Classes Begin Sept. 26th**

# YOUNG PEOPLES THEATRE

### HENRY STREET SETTLEMENT, 466 GRAND ST., NEW YORK 2, N.Y.

PHONE ORchard 4-1100      LOIS WARNSHUIS, Director      SEASON 1949-50

CLASSES FOR YOUNG PEOPLE 8 TO 20 - ACTING - MODERN DANCE - TAP DANCE "SATURDAY'S AT THREE"    -    -    A PROGRAM FOR CHILDREN TWICE MONTHLY

**Office Opens Sept. 6th - Registration Begins Sept. 12th - Classes Begin Oct. 4th**

FIGURE 2.8. An advertisement for the Playhouse School of Dance, with Alwin Nikolais, director, for the 1949–50 season. Courtesy of the Social Welfare History Archives, University of Minnesota Libraries.

Dancer Gladys Bailyn met her in the hallway with a warning: "Don't be alarmed, there's no more ballet. . . . Don't worry, just go in there, there's a man named Alwin Nikolais." She did. Nikolais interviewed her, only to find out she was underage and therefore ineligible. "I just looked him straight in the eye," said Lamhut, "and I said, 'But I want to dance!' And he said 'You're in.'" Lamhut remembers the training as extraordinary, with classes in "dance technique, improvisation, choreography, notation, percussion, stagecraft, lighting, children's productions, and teaching," adding that Nikolais also emphasized the importance of learning how to teach others. To her mind, none of the many dancers who passed through "would have developed, including Nikolais, if he had not had that wonderful theater."[106]

Even as the art scene blossomed and a sense of normalcy returned after World War II, a deep uneasiness permeated the Lower East Side. Already one of the poorest neighborhoods in the city, it now felt the weight of long-brewing problems that had only been exacerbated by war. Industries that had geared up to meet wartime demands now scaled back or closed, with the last hired—women and people of color—the first to be let go. Returning veterans faced competition with civilians who had entered the wartime workforce and stayed. Unemployment began to rise. And the nature of the Lower East Side population was changing as well.

First- and second-generation immigrants were leaving, headed for other boroughs. Among those left behind were older, largely Jewish residents. The Lower East Side, Hall said, "has been their home since the beginning and they still are tucked away in old-law tenements all around us, and some in the housing developments. . . . For the most part the old folks are unhappy and lonely, and distressed at the changes going on around them."[107] To help, Henry Street created the Good Companions senior program, which in July 1954 opened in Vladeck Houses with a wide array of programs: dancing, knitting, discussions, choral groups, bus trips, and more—all, as with Henry Street clubs and classes, about building sense of family. To celebrate its first anniversary, New

FIGURE 2.9. While turn-of-the-century immigrants arrived by steamship, Puerto Ricans arrived in New York City in the first airplane diaspora. Like those before them, they sought opportunity on the Lower East Side. These newcomers had just landed at Newark Airport on April 29, 1947, headed for New York City. Courtesy of the Library of Congress/Telegram & Sun photo by Dick DeMarsico.

York City's new mayor, Robert Wagner, stopped in with Helen Hall and board chair Winslow Carlton (who provided 100 long-stemmed red, white, and pink carnations for the women); member Abraham Schienbloom played his original composition "The Good Companions Waltz" on the piano.[108]

It wasn't only residents who were leaving the Lower East Side. Manufacturers were also leaving, headed for lower operating costs in the American South, taking with them the kinds of jobs that had sustained earlier newcomers. They were departing just as thousands of people of color arrived, including African Americans and West Indians from

Harlem, Black migrants from the American South as part of the second Great Migration, and Puerto Ricans from East Harlem and Puerto Rico (fig. 2.9).[109] A Henry Street study, *Making New Neighbors in an Old Neighborhood*, examined the challenges that newcomers faced—in particular, Puerto Ricans. It observed that not only were they arriving at the time of a declining manufacturing sector, but they had to compete with more established ethnic groups; they had the dual challenges of language and cultural adaptation; and they faced, like Black residents, unrelenting discrimination.[110]

In the face of changing neighborhoods, some settlements, having lost their initial base of European immigrants and unable or unwilling to adapt, moved out of the neighborhoods where they had begun their lives or closed. Some, like Henry Street, stayed. As its clubs, classes, and camps embraced the new neighbors with open arms, Henry Street was also trying to help residents, old and new, with the consequences of massive changes.[111]

## BATTLING JUVENILE DELINQUENCY IN AN UNSETTLED NEIGHBORHOOD

In the 1940s and 1950s, social work was again moving away from the idea that individual problems were produced by social conditions. It focused instead upon the individual, particularly individual maladjustment and juvenile delinquency. And, on the ground as it always had been, Henry Street was seeing a rise in juvenile delinquency. "Families were rootless in their new communities," said Helen Hall. "Many teenage gangs were formed to keep intruders out, giving an impetus to gang warfare which was often further stimulated by the ethnic and racial differences of those moving in."[112] War's end in 1945, she wrote, "began ten years when the disruption of neighborhoods and its concomitant of gang warfare was of top concern." Then, she said, "from 1955 to approximately 1965, drug addiction and individual violence became most disturbing to neighborhood life."[113] Seven gangs are said to have operated on the Lower East

Side in the 1950s and early 1960s. Gang violence reached record highs in the late 1950s, and the rise in juvenile delinquency between 1951 and 1960 among Lower East Side youth was the highest of any neighborhood in New York City.[114]

In 1946, Henry Street created the Mental Hygiene Clinic (later renamed the Community Consultation Center, or CCC), one of the first clinics of its kind in the United States,[115] in response to seeing a rising number of disturbed children in its groups. The case of an eight-year-old girl named Janet helped trigger it. While in a Henry Street club program, Janet became violent and unmanageable. Counselors quickly sought help for her—only to find that the earliest appointment they could get for her at a psychiatric clinic, and one far uptown at that, was in six months. At that point, the Settlement took the issue into its own hands: it raised the funds to support a psychiatric caseworker and a part-time psychiatrist, and continued to expand its mental health work.[116]

Two years later, a conversation that Helen Hall had with longtime supporter Edith Lehman about the neighborhood's troubles led to the opening of a new Henry Street arts and recreation center for local youth. At a foreign-policy dinner, Hall had been seated next to Lehman, who asked her what was happening in the Settlement's neighborhood. "As gang warfare was going on under my windows at the time," said Hall, "I described it pretty vividly and I guess with considerable feeling."[117] After Lehman shared the conversation with her husband, former New York governor and soon-to-be US senator Herbert Lehman, the two decided to donate funds to support a center in the name of their son, Lieutenant Peter Lehman (fig. 2.10). A former volunteer youth leader at Henry Street, the 27-year-old had been killed in England during a training flight crash.[118]

The four-story building at 301 Henry Street replaced two older structures, and its Colonial Revival façade was intended to reflect the Settlement's historic original home, just yards away. Some 1,500 people attended its November 28, 1948, dedication, where local children pressed up against police barriers to better see the speakers. When Herbert

FIGURE 2.10. US Army Air Force Lieutenant Peter Lehman, killed during World War II, had been a Henry Street volunteer; so had his father, Herbert. As with many other families, their commitment continued through the generations: C. J. Wise, Herbert Lehman's great-granddaughter, joined the Settlement's board of directors in 2003. Henry Street Settlement Collection.

Lehman addressed the crowd, he talked of Peter's work at the Settlement, and evoked the ideals that Henry Street had long stood for when he said he knew his son would, "in his kindly heart, wish that 'Pete's House' may be a center where many of our young people of all faiths and races and national origins can meet in friendship and good-will."[119] Board chair Newbold Morris spoke about how the building was an inspiration to all who shared the Settlement's belief in the power of providing opportunity. Also speaking that day was Frank Boyden, who headed Deerfield Academy in rural western Massachusetts, where Pete Lehman had attended boarding school. Afterward, Boyden wrote Helen Hall to tell her how much he and his wife appreciated the warm reception they had received, how impressed they were by Henry Street's work, and how he had witnessed something beautiful and unexpected. "Coming from a small country town where of necessity there is a community spirit and a feeling of unity," he wrote, "I had not supposed that the same spirit could be developed in a great city with a changing population."[120]

Fifteen years later, in 1963, the ability of Henry Street to serve young people expanded when the four-story Charles and Stella Guttman Building opened next to Pete's House. By joining the two structures with interior halls, the Settlement created a sizable complex to house its youth services. In another full-circle moment that suggested the Settlement's impact and abiding place in its neighbors' hearts, it was a gift from a former Henry Streeter, Charles Guttman, who had been born in 1892 to an immigrant family, grew up on the Lower East Side, and took part in Settlement programs. When Henry Street sent him to its summer sleepaway camp, it was his first experience in a rural environment— and a transformative moment. "Henry Street Settlement took me and a lot of Irish and Italian kids and sent us off to the country," he said. "You can't explain what a thrill it was. I'll never forget it—and there's no way I can really pay them back." After accumulating substantial wealth as a businessman, in 1959 Guttman and his wife Stella created a charitable foundation dedicated to the "improvement and benefit of mankind, and the alleviation of suffering." Through the foundation, Guttman decided to repay the debt he felt to the Settlement by helping children who faced the kinds of challenges and difficulties he had. He donated three-quarters of a million dollars toward the construction of his namesake building on Henry Street. His contribution, he professed at the building's dedication, "doesn't even the score, but at least it serves to mark an experience that helped open a poor boy's eyes to the possibilities of life in America."[121]

The October 5, 1963, *Henry Street Settlement News* provided a preview for curious readers: "You oldtimers, who went to the old 301 Kindergar-

ten Room, or you Mothers, who took your children to Play School—
WAIT UNTIL YOU SEE THE NEW PLAY ROOM!" There
would be more space, it said, for club projects, drama, dance, and music,
and "finally," beamed the *News*, "the gym is air conditioned!" Pete's
House Productions, a division of the Settlement's Arts for Living Program, with Joe Balfior directing, would mount performances. And there
was a new instrument group and folksinging groups that would, it noted
with relief, "meet in this club room instead of a locker room as they did
this past year." On the façade, mosaics artistically arranged into color-
ful, floating designs and fantastical flora and fauna with the theme of a
"friendly jungle" greeted all who crossed the center's threshold. Fittingly,
noted the Settlement, the 70-foot-long, 6-foot-high, glazed-ceramic-
tile mural, created by the community under the supervision of Lilli Ann
Killen, director of Henry Street's art department, "incorporated the
names of the four adults and 40 children who had created it."[122]

All of these new initiatives were part of a Settlement strategy to help
young people thrive and, in particular, to avoid the dangers of juvenile
delinquency and gang warfare. But a new menace was just around the
corner: teenage narcotic use. In the years after World War II, New York
City became the nation's heroin capital; in the early 1950s, a stretch of
Henry Street became a hangout for drug pushers and users, earning it
the nickname "Junkie Alley."[123] The Settlement had seen drug addiction
in the neighborhood before, in the 1920s, but then it was minimal, and
most addicts were adults. This new situation—which came to Henry
Street's attention in 1951 when social workers at the Mental Hygiene
Clinic were approached by the younger brothers of teenaged experi-
menters, fearful of following in their siblings' paths—was alarming.

Henry Street social worker Ralph Tefferteller, who had long worked
with young people and on the issue of juvenile delinquency, spearheaded
a study to put a human face on the scourge.[124] Tefferteller interviewed addicts to learn about them and the impact of their addiction on their loved
ones and on community life. He talked with people like Dom Abruzzi,
who recalled being 16 when he first snorted heroin; "I got in on that," he

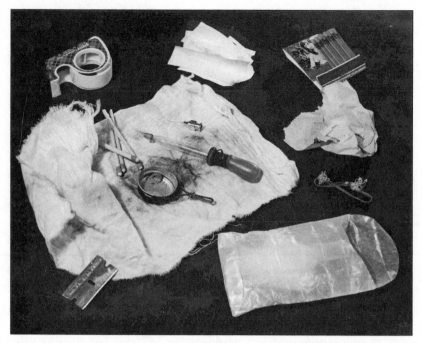

FIGURE 2.11. Drug paraphernalia: one of the photographs that illustrated *The Addict in the Street* (1971), the product of a multiyear Henry Street study of drug addiction on the Lower East Side. Courtesy of the Social Welfare History Archives, University of Minnesota Libraries.

said, "because it was so cheap—a dollar and a half apiece to split a three-dollar bag—and everybody was getting so high and seemed so happy." But what followed was a vicious, continuous cycle of prison, rehab, addiction, and pain. Tefferteller also spoke with family members, like Mrs. Greenberg, who blamed herself for her son's addiction and wondered what went wrong: "I used to go someplace, I took him with me . . . I bought him ice cream. I bought him toys. I don't know why I failed. I don't know where I failed. I don't know what happened to him." With stories like these, and with the help of journalist Jeremy Larner, Tefferteller wrote *The Addict in the Street* (fig. 2.11). The two do not excuse addicts; in short, they call addiction "a copout."[125] But they also—as Henry Street always had—looked at the issue as environmental. Larner writes,

To begin with, these addicts—like most addicts who are not doctors, nurses or druggists, grew up in a crowded, lower-class neighborhood where they were introduced to heroin as teenagers. Bored and delinquent at school, they couldn't face the prospect of starting at the bottom of the social ladder. College was unthinkable, and once school was left behind, there was little to do but hang around the neighborhood, and no group with which to identify but one's comrades on the corner: in brief, no place to aspire to. Small wonder that, when asked why they started on heroin, almost every one of them included in his answer the phrase, *to kill time.*[126]

## Mobilization for Youth

As juvenile delinquency continued to rise, Henry Street, in collaboration with a number of Lower East Side groups, forged an innovative response, one that would become a model for future antipoverty programs.[127] It was called Mobilization for Youth (MFY).

Henry Street was well positioned to understand and respond to juvenile delinquency, given it had long fostered close personal relationships with local youth and had purposefully drawn their parents into its work, making them partners in the effort. In addition, as Hall and Settlement Program Director Ruth Tefferteller wrote in a joint report on pre-delinquent gangs, as "a neighborhood agency we know many children, often from babyhood on, and we are in the position to measure and evaluate success or failure in family and neighborhood relationships, our own included."[128]

The experimental program was developed to saturate a selected area of the Lower East Side with a broad swath of skills and resources to fight juvenile delinquency, combining the community's own leadership and organization with professional social services on the massive scale needed to systematically and effectively deal with the rising problem (fig. 2.12).[129] The project was conceived at a May 1957 Henry Street board meeting. "It is the Board's custom," said Hall, "after a business meet-

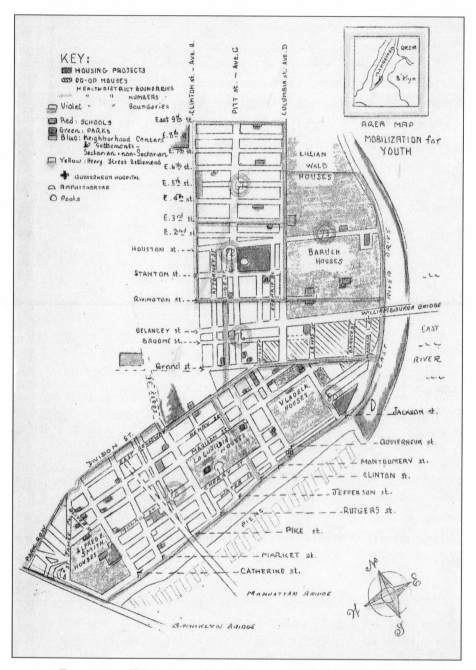

KEY:
▨ HOUSING PROJECTS
▨ CO-OP HOUSES
⸺ HEALTH DISTRICT BOUNDARIES
⸺ " " NUMBERS
▢ Violet " " Boundaries
▣ Red: SCHOOLS
▣ Green: PARKS
▣ Blue: Neighborhood Centers
⚶ Settlements-
Sectarian + non-Sectarian
▢ Yellow: Henry Street Settlement
✚ GOUVERNEUR HOSPITAL
△ AMPHITHEATRE
○ Pools

CLINTON st. ~ AVE. B
PITT st. ~ AVE. C
COLUMBIA st. ~ AVE. D

East 9th st.
E. 8th st.
E. 7th st.
E. 6th st.
E. 5th st.
E. 4th st.
E. 3rd st.
E. 2nd st.
HOUSTON st.
STANTON st.
RIVINGTON st.
DELANCEY st.
BROOME st.
Grand st.

LILLIAN WALD HOUSES

BARUCH HOUSES

WILLIAMSBURGH BRIDGE

EAST
RIVER

VLADECK HOUSES

JACKSON st.
GOUVERNEUR st.
MONTGOMERY st.
CLINTON st.
JEFFERSON st.
RUTGERS st.
PIKE st.
MARKET st.
CATHERINE st.

DIVISION ST.
EAST BROADWAY
HENRY st.
MADISON st.
LA GUARDIA HOUSES
CHERRY st.
WATER st.
MONROE st.

PIERS

ALFRED E. SMITH HOUSES

MANHATTAN BRIDGE

BROOKLYN BRIDGE

MANHATTAN
QUEENS
B'klyn

AREA MAP
MOBILIZATION for YOUTH

N E S W

FIGURE 2.12. This 1959 map shows the area covered by Mobilization for Youth, with Henry Street roughly at center. The antipoverty program joined community and social-service programs to help address juvenile delinquency on the Lower East Side. Courtesy of the Social Welfare History Archives, University of Minnesota Libraries.

ing and dinner, to assemble again to discuss informally one or another phase of the Settlement's many-faceted program. Juvenile delinquency was the subject of the evening's discussion." That evening, Hall had invited guests to join the discussion, among them wealthy businessman Jacob M. Kaplan, who provided seed money from his foundation.[130]

Conflicts over who would manage the project soon emerged. According to Henry Street's initial grant proposal to the National Institute of Mental Health (NIMH), it would administer the program; the head of Mobilization for Youth would report to Helen Hall, and there would be a council to represent participating area agencies. Other area settlements and service agencies, though, pushed to have it run by the Lower East Side Neighborhood Association (LENA), which had grown out of a 1954 meeting at Henry Street.[131] LENA was composed of churches, settlements, and civic groups, and had been created to deal with rising ethnic tensions on the Lower East Side.[132]

Ultimately, the two sides compromised. Henry Street would have fiscal management, with an MFY board made up of representatives from LENA, the local settlement houses, and participating agencies.[133] When Henry Street went to NIMH to fund the project, Hall recalled, they learned that the institute would support only a trial of aspects that engaged preadolescents in educational and recreational activity.[134] But, she argued, what made Mobilization for Youth unique and innovative was its broad, encompassing approach of saturating the neighborhood. Ultimately NIMH, together with the city of New York, the federal government, and the Ford Foundation, funded a revised plan.[135]

Although pioneered by Henry Street, within several years Mobilization for Youth was taken over by Columbia University under the direction of sociologists Richard Clowin and Lloyd Ohlin, and then launched nationally by President John F. Kennedy in 1962. Invigorated by the rising civil-rights movement, MFY staff and community members (who were largely low-income Black and Puerto Rican mothers) focused on direct-action organizing. Often confrontational—MFY leaders felt it was the best approach for obtaining ever-elusive social justice—the organization's radical approach made it a target for unfounded charges of communism. Nevertheless, MFY helped to lay the groundwork for the national War on Poverty Community Action Program and, along with other strategies, helped bring about a decline in gangs.[136]

## A CITY IN CRISIS, THE WAR ON POVERTY, AND HELEN HALL'S PARTING WORDS: "I TOLD YOU SO"

In 1965, the *New York Herald Tribune* ran a series titled "New York City in Crisis." It painted a bleak picture of poverty in the Big Apple. "Nearly one-fifth of the city's people live in poverty conditions," it wrote, "many in cramped, inadequately heated, unsanitary, rat-infested apartments," with more than 70,000 young people "out-of-work and out of school."

When Lyndon Johnson defeated Barry Goldwater in the presidential election of 1964, he sought to expand government's role in addressing issues around poverty and to increase then-meager benefits to the poor. During his campaign, Johnson had described his vision of a "Great Society" "where no child will go unfed and no youngster will go unschooled; where every child has a good teacher and every teacher has good pay, and both have good classrooms; where every human being has dignity and every worker has a job."[137] Now, as president, he hoped to make real his notion of a more beneficent and inclusive nation.

In his first State of the Union address, Johnson—building on proposals initiated by President Kennedy—proposed a "Nationwide War on the Sources of Poverty" to "strike away the barriers to full participation" faced by the poor in American society. He developed the Economic Opportunity Act of 1964, which would encompass several different initiatives, including Head Start, Job Corps, Volunteers in Service to America (VISTA), the Neighborhood Youth Corps, a university work-study program, education and training for adults, and what would be the most controversial: Community Action Programs (CAPs).

At the heart of the massive initiative was the idea that the residents of the communities affected would have a voice, and be closely involved in authentic, meaningful ways. Using as models two programs that had mobilized communities to act—the Henry Street–pioneered Mobilization for Youth and a program developed by community organizer Saul Alinsky in the impoverished "Back of the Yards" area of Chicago— the federal government sought to give over control to the local level through CAPs, so that programs would better target local needs. Those needs would be determined in concert with the poor, who would have "maximum feasible participation." For the federal government, it was a radical idea, one that broke sharply with past government social-reform programs.[138]

Funding through War on Poverty programs exponentially expanded the amount of federal money spent on social-welfare programs. Support for social services and community-based nonprofit programs increased, and settlement houses thrived. For Henry Street, as for many other settlements, though, it would change how it funded its work. For most of its existence, it had relied almost completely on private funding from benefactors, identifying pressing issues and then seeking support. Now, substantial government funding for social problems—something settlement houses had long fought for—was available, and, in fact, essential, given that need dramatically outweighed private funding. There was a flipside, though. Henry Street needed to be more reactive, and less proactive. It needed to tap available federal funds for specific issues identified not by Henry Street, but by others. Like other social service organizations at the time, Henry Street would grow to rely on this increased government funding (and be susceptible to its vagaries).

The difference between old and new ways of funding becomes clear when comparing the years 1933 (when Hall arrived at Henry Street) and 1965 (two years before she left). In 1933, Hall and the board were responsible for raising funds. Their sources were, as they had been for Lillian Wald, small and local; most donors were individuals. By 1965, 75 percent of the Settlement funding came from national foundations and federal programs. Settlement programs would be increasingly driven by the funding that was available.[139]

The 1960s were a time of tremendous change, in society and at Henry Street. Helen Hall was in her 70s and nearing retirement. Through her three decades at the Settlement, she had nurtured the seed that Lillian Wald had planted, and planted her own. In the foreword to a report titled "Impact Beyond the Neighborhood: Visitors to the Henry Street Settlement 1964–1965–1966," she sums up the Settlement's importance, its uniqueness, and its reputation:

> Visitors come from all over the United States and from all over the world; from universities near and far, and from nurses' training schools. They come in groups, in pairs and singly. We are a part of many courses in sociology, in youth leadership, in clinical psychology; in health administration; in music, ceramics, painting and the performing arts. Visitors are sent by the Department of Health, Education and Welfare; the Department of Labor; the Department of State; the United Nations. . . . They come for an afternoon, an evening, for dinner, for lunch, for a whole day, and even for a few days or weeks, to study the work more intensively. . . .
>
> We are by no means the only social agency inundated with foreign visitors these days; the desire to see American social work has spread around the world. But I suspect that our name, the visibility of settlement work, and the multiplicity of our programs play a part in our number of visitors. Not many agencies have in simultaneous operation a club program for all ages, recreation and athletics, a Mental Health Clinic, a Music School, a Pottery and Art Department, Home Planning Workshops, a Playhouse School of Dance and Drama, a large old-age program, and large tile murals both inside and out, produced by our various art classes.[140]

As Helen Hall neared retirement, she also looked about at the sea changes in how settlements functioned financially and at the War on Poverty's clarion call for community participation. Writing a draft of an article to appear in the United Neighborhood Houses' *UNH News*, she reflected on the trends she saw. "I have lived through many panaceas in social work," she wrote.

> At the present moment, the inclined-to-be-domineering community organizer is pretty prevalent as a new solution, yet they can make it hard to tell whether the group organized is expressing the leader's feelings or their own.
>
> Now comes "maximum feasible participation," bringing with it a renewed and broader emphasis on neighborhood participation all along the line, which is very much to the good. But again, this is not a panacea. We know there is no easy road to better housing, no easy road to decent health care or to adequate education, no easy road to self-respecting relief methods. However, this is the road we are on and the more of our neighbors we can get to travel on it, the faster we can go. This has always been the settlements' belief.[141]

In response to the charge some raised that settlements had become elite, old-fashioned, and distanced from their communities, Hall replied:

> I have . . . lived through the period of centralization in social work, have listened to continuous comment about how old-fashioned the settlements are, have lived through the time when sociologists told us there were no such things as neighborhoods in cities; and now today I find that settlements have become the "Establishment," whatever that means.
>
> So it might be pertinent at this point to point out that at last, from the settlements' standpoint, the world has caught up with our basic assumptions, held throughout the years, that there are such places as neighborhoods in cities, although they are now called ghettos; and that services, to be most effective, must be given where people live; that planning those services must be shared with our neighbors, now known as the "poor." The settlements might well put a sign out over their buildings reading 'I told you so.' This wouldn't be modest but it would certainly be true.[142]

The somewhat critical undertone of Hall's words—about the "inclined-to-be-domineering community organizer" who made it difficult to tell if they were "expressing the leader's feelings or their own"; about settlements being the "'Establishment,' whatever that means"; that "our neighbors" were "now known as 'the poor'"—takes on clearer meaning when examined through the lens of her final years at Henry Street and the changes in social work and society. She likely felt battered by the younger, more militant community organizers who had taken over Mobilization for Youth. As historian Janice Andrews writes, Hall had been "caught up in a trend that was far larger than herself—a trend that was both ageist and sexist—the movement in the settlement houses from older female-dominated leadership to younger male-dominated leadership."[143] She had spent 30 arduous if rewarding years at Henry Street. She had always privileged the Settlement's relationship with its neighbors; she now watched as settlements were accused of being elitist organizations that prioritized working with individuals who were upwardly mobile and sought out their services over those who might most need their help. And, like Lillian Wald, Hall had always favored collaboration over confrontation; she now watched as Mobilization for Youth pushed for a social shift that went beyond empowerment to advocating for confrontation, believing it the only way to change the status quo.

She was probably also exhausted after a fractious strike by Settlement staff members who wanted to create a union. The strike had become increasingly personal; an open letter accused Hall of being a proponent of "the same philosophies as are voiced by the American Association of Manufacturers and the reactionaries who have tried to strangle labor," declaring that "Miss Hall, YOU are not Henry Street Settlement! Your EMPLOYEES are Henry Street Settlement!" While the 10-week strike eventually went into binding arbitration that favored the Henry Street board, for Hall, it had been a difficult ending to a decades-long career in social services and reform, one served with distinction.[144]

In 1967, Hall retired. Friends and colleagues honored her in June at a dinner held at Manhattan's upscale Plaza Hotel Ballroom. Entertainment included performances by the Henry Street Settlement Music School, Pete's House Playhouse, and the Alwin Nikolais Dance Company. In the speech that she wrote for the occasion, Hall touched again on the implications of current trends. She shared her fears that "in big new programs, such as are being initiated by the war against poverty, mistakes will continue to be made. Many inexperienced people are involved in working from allocation to allocation, from termination date to termination date, through government red tape, enough at times to strangle all movement."[145]

Hall also extolled the importance of collaboration, of being a "neighbor" in the community and on the ground—and of partnerships. While there were many that made the Settlement run, she was very clear that one was paramount:

> The most important partnership of course is with neighbors, which sets the pace and pattern for everything that goes on inside and outside our doors. It is this partnership which helps most in making us effective at City Hall, Washington, and all the points in between. It is the misery we see at first-hand which sent us to Washington and sparked the long fight for Social Security. It was gangs on our street corners and in our buildings, gangs fighting under my windows that set us planning Mobilization for Youth. It was the drug addicts themselves who gave Ralph Tefferteller the material for his book. This quality of first-handedness is the salient quality of the settlement.[146]

The party was a fitting close to a brilliant career for Hall, who was one of the last of the second generation of settlement house heads. Along the course of her three-decade journey at Henry Street, she had worked tirelessly with the board, staff, volunteers, supporters, funders, office holders, and community members to make an impact on the neighborhood and nation. She had brought the Settlement through the depths of the Depression (and confronted charges of communism along the way); had advocated for issues that were important to people in need on the Lower East Side and beyond, from consumer pricing to affordable housing; had helped make Social Security a reality; and had fought indefatigably for universal health care—although, to her lasting regret, it never came to pass. She had welcomed newcomers from the American South, Puerto Rico, and the West Indies with open arms; had helped neighbors make it through the uncertainties of a world war and a changing economy; and had met the postwar challenges of juvenile delinquency, gang warfare, and drug addiction with new programs and a bold new plan—Mobilization for Youth (and faced charges of elitism). And she had supported the Settlement's everyday work, from checking in on neighbors in need to sitting in on music classes. She had also seen her influence decline in a new era, called forth by the 1960s, that would call for a new kind of leader.

# 3

## LASTING NEIGHBOR AND STEADY INFLUENCE

### The Power of Relationship, Late 1960s to Today

FOR TWO HOT DAYS IN AUGUST 1968, A STREET FESTIVAL marked the Settlement's 75th birthday. Rock and roll, Latin rhythms, and the strains of African, Jewish, Spanish, and American folk music filled the air on Henry Street. Neighbors mingled, munched on soul food, and enjoyed performances by Settlement children and adults. The event recalled the 20th anniversary in 1913, when Henry Street mounted a pageant on the same stretch of thoroughfare. Then, it had called upon its neighbors—largely Jewish immigrants from Eastern Europe—to celebrate their cultures. "This time," noted the Settlement's bilingual newsletter, "the accent is Spanish, instead of Yiddish," proudly noting that the block party was "another proof that Negroes, Hispanics, Jews, Chinese, Italians—all nationalities, colors, and races—can live and play together in harmony, and that peace is the rule, rather than the exception."[1]

The newsletter captured the transformation of the neighborhood. Internal migration and external immigration—spurred by the 1965 Hart-Celler Act, which eased long-standing restrictions to open up immigration from Asia, the Caribbean, Africa, and the Middle East— had converted a place once known as the Jewish Lower East Side into the most ethnically and racially diverse neighborhood in a diverse New York City. But more importantly, it captured Lillian Wald's enduring vision of brotherhood.

By now, the federal system of public welfare that Lillian Wald, Helen Hall, and the settlement movement had fought for was a reality. Increasingly, settlements were reliant on government funding, which typically supported programs but not all-important overhead and capital expenses. And, with the constant seesawing of American attitudes toward poverty—about who was worthy, about whether poverty was a social problem or an individual weakness—their funding was especially susceptible to conservative swings. Operating in an environment far removed from the reform fervor of the Progressive Era, and heavily reliant on federal and foundation funding priorities (instead of individual donors who had supported *their* priorities), settlements that had been strongly activist—like Henry Street—now focused more on social-service work. That's not to say that they weren't guided by their early principles, or that they were unimportant. On the ground, in their communities, and in the lives of their neighbors, they were uniquely situated to see, as Helen Hall posited in 1971, "the so-called 'closed' cases after they are closed, to see the child on his way to trouble, the family on its way to breaking up."[2]

## SETTLING AT THE HOUSE ON HENRY STREET—AND SHAKING THINGS UP

Just months before the August 1968 street festival, 51-year-old social worker Bertram Beck, hired in 1967 to succeed Helen Hall, had moved to 265 Henry Street along with his wife, Deborah, and their four-month-old daughter, Rachel. Beck and his family now occupied the second-floor rooms that Hall, and before her Lillian Wald, had. Deborah Beck described the full-circle moment when they called on a pediatrician to examine their daughter, who fell sick shortly after they moved in. When the doctor arrived, he confided that he had been a violin student at the Henry Street Music School many years earlier, and believed that because of it, he had gained admission to Harvard University.

Hall's former bedroom now became a playroom for Rachel and her sister, Melissa, born in 1969.[3] One of the rooms in their new quarters served as Bertram Beck's office, often doubling as a reception room for

pre-dinner cocktails at Henry Street board meetings. After drinks, the
board would move to the Settlement's spacious dining room. There, in
the same place where Jacob Schiff had once swapped Hebrew phrases
with a neighborhood tailor, and Florence Kelley and Lillian Wald had
sat over steaming cups of coffee brainstorming what would become the
United States Children's Bureau, they shared a meal. Family photographs show the intermingling of public and private life, of Beck hold-
ing hands with Rachel and Melissa on the townhouse steps or gleefully
dancing with staff members in their living quarters. The girls took guitar
lessons and made pottery in Henry Street classes; their mother took
sewing lessons with Ruth Taube at the Settlement's Home Planning
Workshop. And the family now found itself following some of the long-
standing rhythms of the life of the house, like the daily lunch, where
around the dining table staff chatted about who was getting married or
the latest Yankees game. "That was part of the spirit: everyone was there
as a whole, not just as workers," reminisces Deborah Beck.[4]

When Bertram Beck arrived, he was heading Mobilization for Youth,
the project that Henry Street had pioneered but no longer managed.
(The organization had hired Beck as it tried to reconcile forces advocating political activism and funders worried about overt radicalism; Beck
continue to run it until 1969, while also overseeing the Settlement.)
Charismatic, energetic, and hardworking, Beck (fig. 3.1) was intent
on more fully incorporating the neighborhood's diverse voices in the
Settlement's life. That the Henry Street board had selected him as the
Settlement's third leader was telling. Outgoing director Helen Hall had
vigorously lobbied for longtime Settlement social worker Ralph Tefferteller to be her successor,[5] but the board decided otherwise. Beck
represented a new breed of social worker and was part of a new chapter
in urban reform and liberalism.

As was the case for Lillian Wald and Helen Hall before him, a specific moment—a spark—had steered Beck toward his life's work. While
a student at Antioch College, he had a job covering the courts for a local
progressive newspaper. It was the end of the Great Depression, and he

FIGURE 3.1. Bertram Beck with New York Senator Robert Kennedy (left), who came to the Lower East Side in 1965 seeking models for antipoverty programs—like Mobilization for Youth. Beck was then heading the job training and work program pioneered by Henry Street. Courtesy of the Beck Family Archive.

was so struck by the human struggles he witnessed that he decided to become a social worker. He headed to the University of Chicago School of Social (today Service) Administration.[6]

Beck graduated in 1942 with a master's degree in social work and took a job as a psychiatric social worker for the United States Air Force. After World War II ended, he joined the Community Service Society of New York as a family caseworker. Later, he assumed a leadership role at the Bureau of Public Affairs, where he concentrated on issues surrounding urban youth. From there, he went on to direct the Special Juvenile Delinquency Project of the United States Children's Bureau in Washington, DC (first envisioned over coffee at Henry Street Settlement decades before) in the 1950s and, in 1965, became executive director of Mobilization for Youth.[7]

Beck's arrival at Henry Street coincided with several significant new shifts in social work—not just in how it was funded, but in levels of professionalization, in gender roles, and in cultural diversity.

In the 1940s, almost no one held a master's degree in social work; by the late 1950s, most professional positions were held by MSWs. Beck, who had been elected to the initial board of the National Association of Social Workers (NASW) in 1955, actively supported professionalization. While it was by now an anomaly for social workers to live where they worked—professionals felt that their degrees gave them the legitimacy they had once earned by their residence in impoverished neighborhoods and their relationships with neighbors—Beck bucked the trend at the request of Helen Hall, who considered residency an essential aspect of settlement life.[8]

The gender makeup of settlement workers was also changing. Ever since the settlement house movement expanded to the United States from England in the late 1800s, staff and leadership were largely female, making settlements among the few institutions in American public life where women had significant power. With the rise of male social workers, women lost a crucial institutional base. Historian Judith Trolander notes that in 1910, two-thirds of settlement workers were female; in 1960,

40 percent; in 1967, 33 percent; in 1973, 29 percent.[9] Those who led settlements, now more frequently male, were also more likely to be people of color (half by 1975), whereas they had once been a tiny minority.[10]

Fueled by the 1960s' rising voices for societal change, civil rights activism, and the mandates of the War on Poverty, Beck, who was white, was an unwavering advocate for inclusion. Any attack on poverty, he believed, must incorporate in meaningful ways the voices of those living in poverty (especially in New York City, which was divided by race and ethnicity: in 1969, 8.4 percent of whites lived below the poverty line, compared to 23.7 percent of Black people and 27.9 percent of Latinos[11]). Beck said that the voices that most needed to be elevated were the voices of those who most commonly faced systemic discrimination, and whose voices America had often sought to silence: people of color. He encouraged social workers to look past class and status to fully embrace those who lacked professional training or formal education, and to bring them into real positions of power. "This," he argued, "is precisely what the antipoverty program asks of all establishments." Moreover, he asked, "These are the changes we ask of others. Can we ask less of ourselves?"[12]

Beck took a multipronged approach to diversifying the Settlement and incorporating the voices of its community. For one, he formed a neighborhood board. That in itself wasn't new—Helen Hall had also created one—but unlike hers, his would be a feeder group for the board of trustees, giving community members real seats at the table. At the October 14, 1970, Henry Street board meeting, he said he envisioned an advisory committee for each of the Settlement's program areas, whose members, together, would elect two people to the neighborhood board, one of whom would serve on the Henry Street board. Then, he said, together with staff, they "would develop a permanent proposal for neighborhood participation in shaping Henry Street policy."[13]

Beck also diversified his personnel. He hired to the mostly white staff people whose cultures and ethnicities reflected the neighborhood's makeup—African American, Asian, and Latino (and often bilingual)—and made Atkins Preston, a Black Southerner, his associate director.[14]

Astutely aware of the power of words and perceptions, in 1970 Beck rebranded the Settlement to better reflect the relationship of the Settlement staff to those who used its services. While it retained "Henry Street Settlement" as its legal name, it was now called the "Urban Life Center." The goal, noted the June 22, 1970, board minutes, was to convey "the notion of interaction between the staff and people who live in the neighborhood."[15]

In addition, Beck initiated new programs and reworked existing ones to prioritize community leadership building, seeing in the future a new corps of neighborhood leaders. Rafael Jaquez, who today works at the Settlement, was a participant—and, in a common refrain for Henry Streeters, that participation changed his life. Jaquez moved to the Lower East Side from the Dominican Republic in 1963, when he was nine years old. He had imagined that in America, everything would be "shiny and made of glass and chrome," but that wasn't the case. He remembers seeing an article on the front page of the New York *Daily News* in 1970 that called the stretch of Madison Street between Rutgers and Jefferson—a stone's throw from the Settlement—the most dangerous block in the United States. That was his block.

Jaquez went to Henry Street's sleepaway camp in the summer; during the school year, he joined in its recreational activities and received help with his homework. When he was 14, he went to a meeting he thought was going to be about summer jobs but turned out to be about a new Henry Street initiative: the Pioneer Counselor-in-Training Program ("Pioneers"). The program was conceived by the Settlement's Youth Services head, James H. Robinson Jr., a warm bear of a man dedicated to helping others. Robinson had attended the historically Black St. Augustine's College in a segregated Raleigh, North Carolina, and obtained his master's at Columbia University's School of Social Work; he came to Henry Street in 1967. In the spring of 1968, Robinson designed the Pioneers program, which had a dual purpose: to train Lower East Side young men for (paying) jobs as Camp Henry counselors and to teach leadership skills. The Pioneers' motto was "Enter to learn, go forth to serve," and training included sessions in child psychology, counseling, and heritage (in 1974, the program expanded to include young women).[16] When Jaquez, who had grown up without his biological father and had an alcoholic stepfather, joined the Pioneers, he found in Robinson a role model, mentor, and second father, as so many others would. As the July 13, 1970, Settlement board meeting notes reflected, Robinson "viewed activities of interest to young people as a means of engaging them in programs. Once engaged, they were exposed not only to the activity per se but to a total environment designed to build their own sense of self-esteem and community concern . . . providing a 'reverse culture' wherein young people of the neighborhood find an alternative to drugs and violence."[17]

Robinson also enlisted Jaquez for Operation Athlete, a program Henry Street had created to help young people enter college through academic preparation and access to athletic scholarships. Jaquez took up fencing, which, as Robinson admitted, wasn't exactly an "inner-city sport." Jaquez recalls going to an event where he and his Henry Street teammates wore sweatsuits, didn't have all the "right" equipment, and "were the only kids of color there." But they belonged right where they were, and their success spoke for itself: Jaquez received numerous college offers and a scholarship to St. John's College because of his fencing prowess. Increasingly Jaquez exercised his voice. He honed his leadership skills. He became a youth council member. Encouraged by staff who talked to him and his fellow club members on equal terms—as if they were adults, he said—he became a Henry Street board representative. At his first meeting, he found himself sitting between two prominent board members, Judge Jacob Markowitz and longtime funder Herbert Abrons. Jaquez was nervous. Abrons noticed, and asked him if he was the new board member. When he replied in the affirmative, Abrons, said Jaquez, "gave me a nudge and said, 'Don't worry kid, I'll teach you the ropes.'" The newbie quickly learned how things worked. Understanding that the board distributed money, he asked that the subject of a broken water well at Camp Henry be added to the next meeting's agenda for discussion. It was—and the board allocated monies to fix it. "We were not," said Jaquez, "to be overlooked."[18]

Jaquez's leadership training helped him become who he is today: program director of the UPS Community Internship Program (CIP), a collaborative project forged by Bertram Beck in concert with the United Parcel Service (UPS) in 1968. It was, in many ways, a collaboration born out of Beck's focus on developing community. UPS came, says Jaquez, "as a response from corporate America looking at what was going on in the country at the time—the civil rights movement—because at that time they only had white men running the company." The novel program, more than 50 years old, still brings UPS managers to Henry Street to intern in programs throughout the agency, from senior services to shelter for the homeless, working directly with clients and staff. Its goal remains the same: to create greater sensitivity to the social conditions affecting both UPS employees and customers as well as to build job opportunities at UPS for low-income people.[19] By sharing with managers from around the world all that he has learned about the needs and struggles of the Lower East Side—managers who then share with their companies and their communities—Jaquez creates a ripple effect that gives life to the Pioneers' motto he had learned so long ago: "Enter to learn, go forth to serve."[20]

### Making Inclusivity Visible

Like Lillian Wald and Helen Hall before him, Beck saw the arts as a critical and mandatory aspect of the Settlement's work. The changes he now implemented in the arts provide the most visible example of how he was trying to diversify the Settlement's offerings and more fully include its neighbors' voices. At the Playhouse, Betty Young—who had grown up as a Henry Street club member and codirected the Playhouse with dancer and choreographer Alwin Nikolais[21]—convened a group of neighborhood members to plan an advisory committee that would weigh in on better ways to incorporate community representation. At an

April 27, 1969, meeting, Young told the gathered group that "because the enrollment at the Playhouse mirrors the diverse racial, cultural and economic elements which characterize this community, it is possible and desirable to create, from among the participants, an advisory committee which will represent all points of view."[22] Beck also began to forge new relationships to feature new programming (fig. 3.2). For example, in 1969 he brought in the Puerto Rican theater troupe Nuevo Teatro Pobre de América (America's New Poor Theater) for a series of performances. The group, founded in 1963, presented work rooted in political and social issues of both New York's and Puerto Rico's lower and middle classes. In the 1970s, the Settlement instituted the Latino Playwrights Lab, directed by Puerto Rican actress Carla Pinza, to prepare and mount new work. Lorca Peress, who became part of the workshop's acting company, recalled telling her father, Maurice Peress—a well-known conductor—that she was going to be performing at the workshop; he delightedly regaled her with stories of his childhood violin lessons at the Settlement. Peress loved the work. For her, "part of the magic of theater and the magic of the Henry Street Settlement [was that it] allowed us to be creative." Peress also loved learning more about herself and who she was: "I am half Puerto Rican and half Jewish (a true New Yorker)," she said, and the "merging of Latino and Jewish cultures in and around Henry Street was extremely stimulating for me . . . Henry Street gave me a place in which I could explore, grow and learn to understand the New York culture of both my heritages."[23]

The departure of Alwin Nikolais from Henry Street's dance and drama program in 1970, and Beck's response, is a lens into the new executive director's vision for the arts and the organization. Nikolais had brought international attention to the Settlement; as one Henry Street board member noted, the "Alwin Nikolais Dance Theatre, in addition to its own intrinsic worth, is important as a showcase for the Settlement for it illustrates again that Henry Street's tradition nurtures first-rate performance in the arts as well as in community services." And word of mouth about his pathbreaking performances was one of the main ways

Henry Street Settlement
**NEW FEDERAL THEATRE**
466 GRAND STREET, NYC

ANNOUNCES
THE STAGE READING SCHEDULE OF THE

# LATINO PLAYWRIGHTS
# READING SERIES, Inc.

## Carla Pinza PRODUCER

ALL READINGS IN ENGLISH

### "ONE LOUSY SUNDAY"

MONDAY, APRIL 3, 1978 at 7:00PM

BY OSVALDO DRAGUN
DIRECTED BY ANITA VELEZ

### "DESECRATION"

MONDAY, APRIL 24, 1978 at 7:00PM

BY RAY FLORES
DIRECTED BY PAT GOLDEN

### "LOOKING FOR TOMORROW"

MONDAY, MAY 22, 1978 at 7:00PM

BY RINGO REYES
DIRECTED BY MARVIN CAMILLO

### PUERTO RICAN & OTHER HISPANIC WOMEN

Poetry Reading

MONDAY, JUNE 19, 1978 at 7:00PM

## ADMISSION FREE

THIS SERIES IS OPEN TO LATINO AND NON-LATINO PLAYWRIGHTS WHO HAVE PLAYS
THAT DEAL WITH HISPANIC THEMES.
STUDENTS INTERESTED IN THE ACTING TRAINING UNIT OF THE WORKSHOP SHOULD
CALL 711-9334 or 766-9295.

THIS SERIES IS BEING DEDICATED TO THE MEMORY OF FINI MORENO, MARINA BROOKS,
AND ALFIDA FERNANDEZ FOR THEIR CONTRIBUTION TO THE ARTS AND HISPANIC COMM-
UNITY OF THE CITY OF NEW YORK.
This program is sponsored in part by the Department of Cultural Affairs
for the City of New York.

FIGURE 3.2. Program for the Latino Playwrights Reading Series, 1978. This legacy of Bertram Beck's push for diversity brought emerging and acclaimed artists to the Settlement, including, for example, actress Anita Velez (later Velez-Mitchelle), listed here as the director for *One Lousy Sunday*. Courtesy of the Social Welfare History Archives, University of Minnesota Libraries.

that people found out about the Henry Street School of Dance and Drama. But with his renown came new demands on his dance company's time, and performance commitments created long absences from Henry Street. In early June of 1970, Nikolais submitted his resignation to Bertram Beck; immediately after, Betty Young, the Playhouse's co-director, resigned to join Nikolais and his staff. The Murray Louis Dance Company, which, like Nikolais, was facing the demands of extended touring, also left.[24]

In his letter of resignation, Nikolais told the board that the "combination of administrative latitude and perspective of Miss Helen Hall and the members of the board together with the idealism of those of us at the Playhouse was a remarkable one." He was proud of their accomplishments, but the time commitment was too great and he wanted to focus on his own work. While Bertram Beck recognized what Nikolais brought to the Settlement, he took his departure in stride. He understood, he said, that Nikolais was "at a stage in his life where his major energies must go into the development of his own art."[25]

Now, Beck took a hard look at the Settlement's arts programming and began to envision an approach that he felt would better reflect, and be more relevant to, its diverse Lower East Side community, especially its newer Black, Puerto Rican, and Chinese populations; he also wanted to remove any sense that the arts at Henry Street were taking place in an ivory tower. In memos and funding proposals, he laid out his plans. The School of Dance and Drama would transition to a series of workshops on drama, dance, music, photography, and motion pictures. They would have an in-house dance company, with workshops in "modern dance, Afro dance, Puerto Rican dance, ballet and children's dance." In theater, they would offer workshops in Puerto Rican and Black theater, in community drama, and in children's theater. Arts workshops, he said, would feature crafts that today sound quintessentially 1960s—tie-dye, batik—alongside earlier mainstays like pottery. Beck also envisioned film workshops, a movie club, still photography classes, and an eclectic menu of groups for steel-drum, opera, jazz, rock, and electronic music.

Beck quickly followed through with plans, even as he continued to reexamine the arts program to make stronger connections with the world beyond the Settlement and to consider ways of moving away from what he called "the formal music school concept." His choice of words to describe the plan captures the user-driven format he envisioned and its somewhat counterculture, communal approach. Beck says his new model would be a "cooperative," in which "cooperators" would be "actively involved in all phases of planning, funding, and operation," to pool talent and money in order to "share in a self-help program to present their own concerts and original works." He wanted workshops to emphasize the interrelationship of the arts to society in three areas: a study program for learning technical skills; a performance program, whose main goal would be "to illuminate and project the musics of a multi-racial, multi-ethnic community through the study and public presentation of such musics, and by so doing, bridge the gap between the cultures, establishing lines of communication"; and a music therapy program that would focus on the elderly and those with special needs.[26]

In 1970, a new chapter in Henry Street's arts programming—and in the flowering Black Arts Movement—began when Bertram Beck invited Woodie King Jr. to oversee the Settlement's arts programs. King spent his teenage years in Detroit, where he passed many of his after-school hours at Franklin Settlement, making Henry Street a familiar setting. He arrived in New York City in 1964 after graduating from the Will-O-Way School of Theatre in Bloomfield Hills. Bertram Beck, who had taken over as head of Mobilization for Youth in early 1965, was attracted to the 27-year-old's fresh ideas and hired him to oversee MFY's arts programming. At MFY, with its ample War on Poverty funding, King had a generous budget to pay for music, dance, theater, and visual art. He set about recruiting neighborhood young people for the various programs at a time, he said, when "the Lower East Side was infested with gangs and drugs, so this was a social-work move."

Later, when Beck moved to Henry Street, he invited King to head up the Settlement's Arts for Living Program. King now oversaw Henry

Street's Asian, Latino, and Jewish theater programs—and the New Federal Theatre, which he created as an outgrowth of his work at MFY. Initially funded by Henry Street and a small grant from the Ghetto Arts Program at the New York State Council on the Arts,[27] the New Federal Theatre (its name inspired by the Great Depression's Federal Theatre program) had its inaugural season in 1970–71.[28]

It was a groundbreaking moment. The New Federal Theatre pushed to integrate people of color and women into mainstream theater at a time when entrenched racism and sexism had largely shut them out.[29] It tied Henry Street into the Black Arts Movement, which had emerged in the mid-1960s. A sister of the Black Power Movement, it was ignited by poet, writer, and activist Amiri Baraka, whose work exposed structural racism and elevated black pride and identity (and would spawn rhythm and poetry, or rap). The Black Arts Movement was dedicated to creating art for Black audiences by Black artists affirming their autonomy.[30]

Beck, whose goal was to diversify and make more inclusive Henry Street's arts, was extremely supportive of King, whose desire to give voice to people of color and their work meshed with his vision for Henry Street. King was African American, and most of the plays he mounted at the theater were by Black playwrights, bringing to Henry Street some of the most innovative work of the time. As he later recalled, "Many white-controlled theatres produce only European plays that are directed to their own need to glorify the past," while "African Americans are not integral to their past in any kind of positive way. That [left] me with a large canvas of untold stories."[31]

With King leading it, the theater quickly garnered attention for its provocative programming and artistic excellence. Starting in 1970, recalls King, "we had a hit show each year for 10 years," with such acclaimed actors as Ruby Dee, Morgan Freeman, Laurence Fishburne, Debbie Allen, Phylicia Rashad, and Denzel Washington bringing words to life. The December 1977 issue of *Black Enterprise* touted King's "emergence as one of black theater's shrewdest and most resourceful producers," writing that he "has transformed the small New Federal Theater on New York's lower eastside from a center for Yiddish productions to New York City's major generator of contemporary black plays. And he puts his shows on with the kind of money commercial producers spend on just a week's advertising."[32]

A program statement for the New Federal Theatre described the project's success. In "only seven years of operation, the New Federal Theatre has carved an enviable and special niche for itself in the theatrical world," it noted. Not only had it moved past a shoestring budget to one of roughly $300,000, but it

> has brought minority theatre to the audience for which it was originally designed—that of the Lower East Side, at the same time bringing to national attention minority playwrights and actors and sponsoring various ethnic theatres. In achieving its current status, it has moved . . . from an essentially ethnocentric effort, Black, to a multi-ethnic endeavor; from showcase to Off-Broadway productions.[33]

Over time, King mounted dozens of plays. Some, in arrangement with Joseph Papp's New York Shakespeare Festival, were moved uptown after opening at Henry Street.[34] The first partnership with Papp was for Ed Bullins's *Taking of Miss Janie,* which won a Drama Critics' Circle Award as best play of the year and three Obie Awards in 1975 (fig. 3.3). "Papp would come to see our plays," said King; "we'd put up the money to do it, if it received favorable audiences, he'd give us the money we used back, and move it uptown. At that time, African American theater was not done off Broadway or on Broadway. If it was done, it was more of an exploitation."

In what was by now an established way of working at Henry Street, the theater blended activism with art and with teaching and mentoring young people. King calls it "a professional theater involving community," where young people in and around Henry Street—Black, Latino, Asian—would work on the productions. For Ed Bullins's *Black Girl,* he recalls, "we had young people working, building sets, as assistant

FIGURE 3.3. Standing in front of the Henry Street Settlement Playhouse are Settlement head Bertram Beck (second from left); Woodie King Jr., founder and head of the Settlement's New Federal Theatre (far right); playwright Ed Bullins (far left); and producer and director Joseph Papp, who often took King's productions uptown. Henry Street Settlement Collection.

stage managers, working on the lighting crew, costumes." These young people were exposed to brilliant, creative minds and social currents. In Bullins—the avant-garde playwright and activist (and former Minister of Culture for the Black Panthers) who engaged audiences with critical issues around race—they had a front-row view of the power of art and social activism.

Looking back years later, King recalled that his proudest moments were the ones in which he had created positive action out of rejection, the "times when traditional theatre producers denied me access and we prevailed."[35] Two of them were acclaimed productions that brought widespread attention to his work and the Settlement. In 1974, King produced *for colored girls who have considered suicide / when the rainbow is enuf*, a landmark choreopoem written by Black feminist playwright and poet Ntozake Shange. Shange recalled that the first "theater" space for the groundbreaking production was a small Henry Street lecture hall, transformed on opening night into "a divine space, supplicants flocking from everywhere"—and a space so crowded that she had to elbow her way in. From there, King mounted *for colored girls* with the Settlement's New Federal Theatre; it then went to Joseph Papp's Public Theatre, and, finally, to Broadway's Booth Theatre, where it had a breakthrough run. King later staged playwright Laurence Holder's *When the Chickens Came Home to Roost*, with a 26-year-old Denzel Washington playing the role of civil rights activist Malcolm X in a blistering, highly acclaimed performance. Washington recalls his amazement watching "500, 600, 700 people lining up to get in—every night there were famous people, Diana Ross coming . . . it took on a life of its own."[36] Until financial problems at Henry Street prompted it to find new quarters uptown, the New Federal Theatre brought together audiences, Settlement youth—and, seamlessly, uptown and downtown crowds. Today, the company continues to break new ground from its home on West 42nd Street, with Woodie King Jr. its producing director.

## A BOLD STATEMENT

Since Henry Street Settlement's earliest days, the arts had been seen as an integral part of wellbeing and a means for individual and community self-expression. Often, they had an activist component, bringing the issues of the day—rising milk prices, anti-immigrant fervor, the desire for peace in a world at war—to a broad audience, inviting to the stage and the classroom some of the most forward-thinking artists of the time. Aimed at the neighborhood but also at an uptown audience, the arts had helped the Settlement make its case for its work, its values, and its orientation in ways that took advantage of a medium that reached new and larger audiences. The project that Beck now launched—a new arts center—would physically and programmatically make his push for inclusion visible. He wanted a bold statement and he got it, by taking advantage of a federal grant program to bring music, performance, and art under one brand-new roof.

The Henry Street board had been raising money for a modern arts facility ever since the Music School, located behind the Playhouse, was torn down in 1963 as part of the city's 14-block Seward Park Urban Renewal Project.[37] The demolition pushed classes into temporary quarters in ground-floor apartments in Hillman Houses (affordable cooperative housing built by the Amalgamated Clothing Workers Union) or wherever space was available, including the dining room of 265 Henry Street, Pete's House, and nearby St. Augustine's Church.[38] By 1969, the board had hired architects, who were working on plans for a new building. But when construction estimates came in too high, the board began to rethink its strategy.[39] Just as it paused to consider its next move, Beck happened to have lunch with local congressman Emmanuel Celler (a namesake of the 1965 Hart-Celler Act). As they ate, Celler told Beck about a promising opportunity. President Richard Nixon had put aside money in the Economic Development Agency for communities that had 100 percent working drawings for projects and were ready to move to construction. It seemed like a perfect fit for Henry Street. But there was a hitch: the application deadline was the next day.[40]

Beck returned to the office and, working feverishly with his wife and staff members, managed to get the drawings and an application in by the deadline. Henry Street was successful. The project went out for public bid, and construction for the new Arts for Living Center proceeded with the design by architect Lo Yi Chan of the firm Prentice & Chan, Ohlhausen. In October 1975, it opened to fanfare as the first arts center to be designed and built specifically for a predominantly low-income neighborhood (fig. 3.4).[41] First Lady Betty Ford was on hand for the dedication, joined by New York City Mayor Abraham Beame, former

FIGURE 3.4. The Abrons Arts Center, which opened in 1975 as the Arts for Living Center. With its open, welcoming architecture and varied offerings, it gave the arts a showcase for aspirations of community and diversity building. Henry Street Settlement Collection.

mayor Robert F. Wagner, National Endowment for the Arts Chair Nancy Hanks, former Henry Street Settlement head Helen Hall, and many others.

The center's architecture spoke clearly to Beck's aspirations for the arts. It blended seamlessly with the adjacent 1915 Henry Street Playhouse (now a designated national landmark). But it did more, as critic Ada Louise Huxtable expressed in her favorable *New York Times* review, titled "Henry Street's New Building—An Urban Triumph." She praised the way the wide, expansive steps of its courtyard amphitheater served as an open invitation to the street and its steady stream of city life. And its name, she said—the Arts for Living Center—summed up "everything that urban architecture should be. It is a building meant to serve and expand the life of a community, and no better definition of architecture exists than that."[42] The building had done what it was supposed to. Its look, its break with the earlier architecture surrounding it, its purpose: all were clear expressions of what Beck, with the board's support, backing, and help, was trying to do.

## PROBLEMS—BOTH INTERNAL AND EXTERNAL—ARISE

Financial problems, though, quickly followed the opening. Not only were the building and its expanded programs proving expensive to operate, but the city was in crisis, threatening funding and the neighborhood's wellbeing. Facing bankruptcy, New York asked the federal government to bail the city out. The front-page headline of the October 29, 1975, New York *Daily News* captured the response and the political climate: "Ford to City: Drop Dead."[43] Further troubled by rising inflation and a stagnant national economy drained by the continuing war in Vietnam, the city fell into a decline. Crime and poverty rates rose. As services failed, uncollected garbage piled high on streets. Residents and landlords fled. By 1975, in a 40-block area on the Lower East Side, the number of abandoned houses had risen from 4 to 100 in just four years (fig. 3.5).[44]

The financial crisis aggravated long-standing issues. Among the most serious was homelessness, which had begun to grow in the early 1960s as job opportunities for the poorest New Yorkers shrank in tandem with economic changes and a growing dearth of low-income housing. By the early 1970s, the city was suffering through the worst homeless crisis since the Great Depression of the 1930s. Whereas in the past people who were homeless had mostly been single, white, and often older men, they were now increasingly younger people, people of color, and women and children who lacked shelter.[45]

To house its rising homeless population, New York City paid exorbitant prices to privately held "welfare hotels," many of them rundown and riddled with drugs and crime. Whole families were crowded into single, decrepit rooms.[46] After conditions at the worst welfare hotels

FIGURE 3.5. A child stands in a burned-out lot on the Lower East Side. In the 1970s and 1980s, residents faced new problems as swaths of old buildings fell prey to abandonment and arson. Henry Street Settlement Collection.

were publicized, New York City Mayor John Lindsay demanded a solution from his agencies. The Housing Authority turned to Henry Street for help, and its response helped to pioneer a new way to address homelessness and its related issues.[47] Daniel ("Danny") Kronenfeld, then an instructor at the Columbia University School of Social Work, had recently co-authored a groundbreaking paper on the "temporary family residence," an alternative to welfare hotels.[48] Bertram Beck recruited Kronenfeld (who had once been a community organizer at Mobilization for Youth) to create a model program that would draw on his pioneering ideas to address the neighborhood's, and the city's, urgent problem.

Kronenfeld responded to the challenge. His vision took physical form in 1972 as Henry Street Settlement's Urban Family Center (UFC), the country's first apartment-style, temporary shelter with on-site social services for homeless families with children, and Kronenfeld was its director (fig. 3.6). At the UFC, a six-story walkup building on the Lower East Side, each family had its own furnished apartment, complete with a kitchen. When they arrived, they were assigned a social worker, and together they laid out the goals for what typically was a six-month stay before moving into permanent housing. Then, the staff met collectively to determine the best way to help holistically. While Kronenfeld held that homelessness was primarily a housing problem, not a social one, the program helped clients to focus on the issues that had made them homeless and to find ways to improve their economic future. Staff members facilitated finding permanent housing; counseled clients in how to defend themselves from unscrupulous landlords; offered guidance in searching for stable employment; focused on the kinds of personal issues that had typically been ignored, such as managing personal finances or shepherding children into and through school; and offered all-important follow-up.[49]

It was a supportive environment, Kronenfeld recalls, and an interesting place to live because of the various people who resided there and the skills, temperaments, and personalities they brought. In general, people were happy to be there, considering that they typically came from a bad

FIGURE 3.6. Children living at the Urban Family Center, opened in 1972 as the nation's first shelter of its kind, for homeless families. Henry Street Settlement Collection.

situation or bad housing. "Just having heat in the winter," said Kronenfeld, "was a blessing." For the next 13 years, until he was tapped to run the Settlement, Kronenfeld lived at the UFC. He dedicated himself to its work—sometimes to an extreme. Affable and unpretentious, he tells a story that reveals his dedication. "One of my weaknesses as a social worker," he recalled in a 2018 interview, "is I tended to do too much for people I was working with." That quality led to what Kronenfeld calls "an interesting episode" in his life at Henry Street.

> When we opened the facility, we made the decision that if a person had to get to a health facility we would drive them, rather than call an ambulance. And when a person came down after hours and had to get to a medical facility, there was always a social worker on call, who would get the van and take them there.

Well, I soon had a bunch of worn-out social workers, who were being awakened every night to take somebody to the clinic, often for trivial things. . . . It became clear that I would have to do something with how this was handled. So I then instituted a policy whereby if anybody came to the office after 12, having to go to the clinic or medical facility, I would be the person who took them. And there was a period of time when it seemed almost every night, I had to get up and take somebody to the clinic in the neighborhood.

This went on for a couple of weeks, when I would show up with a different woman, almost every night. And then take them back [to the UFC] after they were finished at the clinic. And then it became clear to me I better tell the nurses who I was. So I went on to tell them about the Urban Family Center, and my being director there, and they were over-joyed, because they said, the last couple of nights, they noticed I was coming in with different women, and wondered, "Who was this guy? Who comes here every night with a different woman, brings her here, and then disappears?" Well, when they huddled together they came up with the conclusion that I must be a pimp, and these were the women in my stable. I had a good laugh because I'd been called worse things as a social worker than a pimp.[50]

The program blossomed, soon becoming a model for transitional housing, one studied nationwide by others attempting to combat pov-erty and homelessness in American cities. As UFC social worker Ve-rona Middleton-Jeter (who would eventually succeed Kronenfeld as the shelter's director) observed, it had an immeasurable impact: it "played a major role" she said, "in bringing respect to the way homeless peo-ple were and are treated." Five years after the Urban Family Center opened, the Shelter for Domestic Violence Survivors, one of the first publicly funded shelters of its type, opened under the UFC's auspices. Middleton-Jeter recalled that the UFC became involved with the issue of domestic violence "because a woman could go to a . . . welfare center and say, 'My husband just beat me. I need a place to live,' and they'd just say, 'tough.' So then, if that same woman went back the next day and said, 'I'm homeless. I need a place to stay,' they'd say 'oh, we've got a place to send you.'" As a result, the UFC was seeing rising numbers of battered women. At the time, says Middleton-Jeter, the women's movement had brought the issue of domestic violence onto a national stage, and while the momentum was important, she feared that the voices of low-income women of color would be lost among the movement's largely white, middle-class makeup. By creating a shelter for domestic survivors, Middleton-Jeter avowed, she could ensure that "what was decided about poor women would not be based on some theoretical middle-class white woman's way of thinking."[51]

## A Perfect Storm

In 1977, Bertram Beck left Henry Street to become general director of the Community Service Society of New York City.[52] It had been a decade since he and his family had come to Henry Street, and, as his wife recalled, he felt that he had given it his best. To send him off in style, the staff staged a play affectionately titled *The Wizard of Henry Street*—and gave Beck a crown and scepter "in a display of love and affection."[53] Beck had overseen many changes that had made the Settlement increasingly diverse and inclusive and enhanced Henry Street's stature (among them obtaining national historic landmark status for the headquarters—the now connected buildings at 263, 265, and 267 Henry Street, in 1976—just before he left). He had done so despite the crippling effects of the city's fiscal social crisis and a poor economy. But more difficult years now lay ahead, as these challenges were compounded by a perfect storm of funding and leadership issues that threatened to close Henry Street's doors as it neared 100 years in operation.

Finding Beck's successor would prove fractious. The board received 125 resumes; interviewed 16 applicants; narrowed them down to 5; and from that, winnowed it to 3. Among the three top candidates was Atkins Preston, known as "Kin," Henry Street's associate director. Many community members favored his candidacy; he was talented, he had an excellent track record at Henry Street, and he was African American. But the board chose another candidate: Frank Seever, director of the historic Chicago Commons, a person with extensive experience heading a multimillion-dollar settlement—but also an outsider, and white.

The community was outraged. "The night of the Board meeting at which Seever was to be first proposed," recalled Richard Abrons, a longtime board member, "there were pickets outside and community leaders presented a petition for Kin with five thousand signatures." The board minutes for the months surrounding the hire suggest the extent to which the board was grappling with the issue. At the November 28, 1977, board meeting, amid continuing tensions, board member Herbert Abrons asked Preston to speak to the group. Preston began by saying that he was trying to minimize disruptions amid ongoing protests; the "Arts for Living Center was under siege," he said—and many in the community, he noted, were "disenchanted with the Settlement." Preston said he felt that he had "not functioned at Henry Street as a black associate executive but as an associate executive director who was black," but that "recent events had caused him to consider whether he was a victim of prejudice"—especially in light of the fact that the board had only recently passed an affirmative action policy. On the side of hiring Seever were those who felt that Atkins could have made a good director, but that Seever was the best person for the job: he had a proven track record running a large organization similar to Henry Street and was extremely successful at raising private funds—in fact, more so than Henry Street had been. On the side of hiring Preston, transition committee member Lorraine Albritton said that "the system had kept black people out of the mainstream," and that she was unconcerned if Preston had not "actually functioned as executive director"; he was well qualified and "had every capacity to develop."[54]

Given all the talk of inclusion and diversity at Henry Street, and the hard work to include neighbors on all levels during Bertram Beck's tenure, the board's choice of Seever must have felt like a slap in the face to Preston and the community. But in the end, the board stayed with its decision, and Frank Seever soon arrived at Henry Street to get to work.

In his book *An Agent of Change*, Seever describes coming to Henry Street and feeling a sense of hostility from the community members serving on the board who had favored hiring Preston. He also recalls that some staff members, unhappy about his selection, resigned in protest. His biggest challenge, he felt, would be to "bridge the gap between the board factions and neutralize the political maneuvering of the staff."[55] But staff and board divisions weren't the only challenges Seever faced. The board minutes reflect a growing concern over a swelling deficit. On November 20, 1978, they note that the market was bad; capital funds were forecast to be depleted in four years; and cutting expenses was not necessarily an option, since many programs were funded through public sources. That meant any cuts would have to be in programs that were funded by unrestricted private funds. Seever warned the board that it was facing a two-punch problem: one, they were in a conservative funding climate, and two, public funding, on which Henry Street was so reliant, paid for programs but not for permanent staff positions or utilities—and the utilities costs for the new, grand arts center alone were $250,000 per year. Things only got worse, and one year later, Seever left to return to Chicago Commons full time. This time, the board promoted internally, hiring Niathan Allen, who had been working at Henry Street as deputy administrator.[56] He was the Settlement's first Black executive director, and he was inheriting a dire, potentially ruinous fiscal situation.

Given the dimensions of Henry Street's financial problems, Allen faced what must have felt like an insurmountable challenge, even though to the public, the Settlement would have looked as if it were prospering. In October 1981, Woodie King Jr.'s New Federal Theatre opened with a production of *Boy and Tarzan Appear in a Clearing* by poet, writer, and activist Amiri Baraka. More than 100 fall classes and workshops were in full swing. The number of dance students was three times what it had been less than 10 years before; the music department had increased to 800 students from 130. New Yorkers could come to Henry Street to attend a symphony orchestra concert or workshops in opera, jazz, or Latin music.[57]

In 1981, consultant Joseph Wesley Zeiler, who had been hired by the board to examine the new arts programs and find solutions for the challenges they were facing, submitted his report—*A Reconsideration of the Arts for Living Center at the Henry Street Settlement*—to executive director Allen. Written from the findings of eight months of interviews, questionnaires, and group meetings, he laid out his findings, the issues, and his conclusions. He observed that the Arts for Living Center was healthier than it had been for some years, which he attributed to Allen's care and to the work of its former director, Barbara Tate, to connect more closely with the community. And it was true, he said, that the arts center was a "major setting in the cultural life of New York City"; that it was the vehicle through which many people knew of Henry Street; and that it was a "primary part of the Settlement's overall place in the city, even the nation." But here was the crux of the problem: the arts center had opened in a time of expansion, fueled by unprecedented government funding. That expansion was over, warned Zeiler, "and the rules," he said, "are changing drastically." Now, all types of community programs were threatened by new federal policies and a new recession. It was unlikely, he believed, that the private sector would replace government funding. [58]

Zeiler's advice to the board echoed what other settlements were also seeing: that while the 1960s War on Poverty had launched a vast array of social welfare programs run by government social workers, federal welfare spending, which supplied settlements, was waning. That decline was part of a broader picture, of a growing ideology in America that railed against the welfare state and sought to reduce federal aid to people who were poor.

In 1981, Ronald Reagan, a conservative Republican, came into office on the heels of President Jimmy Carter. The American public was worried about a poor economy, fewer jobs, and inflation. Reagan masterminded a changed course. Glorifying a romanticized view of the 19th century as a golden age when individualism reigned, and enamored of the notion of self-sufficiency, Reagan was disinclined to see poverty as a social or environmental problem, and revived the question of who among the poor were deserving.[59] He aimed to shrink government spending on social programs (while boosting military spending); to reduce government regulations; and to cut taxes, mostly for affluent Americans. All this was happening while factory closings, layoffs, and other uncontrollable factors were swelling the ranks of those in poverty, and a stagnant minimum wage meant that having a job no longer translated into a way out. To some, the underclass had become America's enemy.[60] As National Rainbow Coalition head Jesse Jackson succinctly put it, "The policies of the present administration have effectively unleashed a war on the poor."[61]

By fall of 1982, things had spiraled even further downward at Henry Street. At its September 13 meeting, the board discussed renting out or closing its landmark buildings because they were now looking at themselves "in a liquidation posture." Then, facing a budget deficit of $800,000 after having already run a deficit for the four years prior, Henry Street did what seemed unimaginable: it closed the arts center. The Settlement's music, visual arts, and dance programs, all of which involved some 1,200 people each year, were now suspended; the New Federal Theatre operated on a reduced basis. In addition, a host of social-service programs were scheduled to operate on a reduced basis, and 32 employees throughout the Settlement were slated to lose their jobs.[62] Eventually, a coalition rallied to save the arts center from closing permanently. Financial support came from a benefit concert at Lincoln Center's Avery Fisher Hall, with luminary bandleader Count Basie joined by singers Carmen McRae and Tony Bennett.[63] Funds also came in the form of grants from the New York State Council on the Arts and the National Endowment for the Arts. But issues remained—as they did for the city around them.

## Tackling AIDS, Resurging Homelessness, and the Impact of Rising Crime

In the 1980s, New York City was paying the price of the 1970s fiscal crisis and feeling the pain of the decline of its once massive industrial economy. As historian Robert W. Snyder writes, "Bankers, Republicans, and fiscal conservatives seized on the opportunity to discipline New York, restructure its political economy, and set an example for other municipalities that embraced anything that smacked of socialism in the city. Eventually bankers, unions, and elected officials crafted a solution, but it came at a price. New York's social services would be drastically reduced and so money would be saved. The savings were clear but so, too, was the cost."[64] City government axed jobs; teachers lost one-fourth of their numbers; subway riders noticed far fewer trains; and garbage was piling up on the streets.

And there was more. In the 1980s—and in the decade to come—the city faced rising crime, drug use, and homelessness; it grappled with poor housing, inadequate health care, and a new scourge, AIDS; and, after decades of neglect, an aging, decaying urban infrastructure. In a January 23, 1987, *Wall Street Journal* article, James H. Robinson Jr., Henry Street's director of youth services, described the city he saw around him. "Before, I just fought heroin, but crack is twice as dangerous," he said. "Institutional racism is worse now. Cops are younger and more frightened. The kids coming in are worse off. There's more neglect at home and child abuse. The schools are worse. Illiteracy is up. Kids are dropping out in junior-high. The church has less effect." Within the context of these enormous challenges, Henry Street remained an anchor in the community, responding to the AIDS and homelessness crises and, as crack increasingly made streets unsafe, helping to keep teens off the streets with innovative leadership programs.

The challenge of AIDS (acquired immune deficiency syndrome) emerged in the public eye on June 5, 1981, when the Centers for Disease Control (CDC) issued a report on a rare disease attacking previously healthy gay men in Los Angeles. Within days of seeing the press reports, doctors from around the United States were reporting similar cases to the CDC. The numbers of AIDS cases mounted steadily. With no cure on the horizon and, as the disease began to ravage communities, with no medical understanding of how to combat it, panic rose. So too did prejudice, homophobia, and racism directed not just at those who had the disease but at those believed to be infected—the high-risk groups identified by the CDC as gay men, intravenous drug users, Haitians, and hemophiliacs.[65]

Henry Street was one of the earliest responders to the crisis. It first picked up on the problem in 1979 through its mental health center, the Community Consultation Center (CCC), when a Henry Street employee died from what was believed to be tuberculosis, but was later recognized as AIDS-related causes. In the years to come, the CCC found that several of its clients were infected with the virus, and that some had lost, or were about to lose, family members to the disease. Drawn into the emerging crisis, it became one of the first mental health clinics in the nation to provide services specifically for those dealing with HIV and AIDS, prompting New York City's Department of Mental Health to name Henry Street the official provider of AIDS Mental Health Services for the Lower East Side in 1988. The work, led by the CCC leadership team of Larraine Ahto and Florence Sampieri along with Director of AIDS Services Lela Charney, was especially challenging in the early days. Many people who contracted HIV/AIDS kept silent, fearing ostracism and discrimination, and most people saw the disease as a physical issue, not a mental health one. But through its work, the CCC was able to see the interconnected webs of impact and obstacles that HIV/AIDS bred, and to meaningfully respond. It offered family treatment to mothers who, facing death, had to plan for their children's care; to grandparents unexpectedly transformed into caregivers; to youngsters traumatized by a relative's illness.

In 1988, a call from a guidance counselor at nearby PS 20 prompted the CCC to pioneer the first in-school bereavement groups for young children. The counselor was concerned that a number of well-performing students were now coming to school unkempt and unprepared. All had one major life event in common: they'd recently lost a parent. Given how unusual it was for so many young parents to be dying, the CCC staff suspected the deaths were from AIDS (although would not know for sure until later). In response to the counselor's concerns, the CCC organized a clinical team to go into the school and offer bereavement counseling. Their group sessions quickly expanded, as children brought in friends and cousins who were also suffering. While new funding guidelines eventually forced the end of the sessions, the CCC's collaboration with schools became an important means of identifying children—and through them, their parents—in need. Because of their pathbreaking work on intergenerational care, in 1992 the federal government awarded the CCC a multiyear grant, part of its Special Projects of National Significance, to fund its work. The CCC went on to establish supportive housing for HIV/AIDS-affected families, meeting the needs of low-income families at risk of being plunged into homelessness (or having to place children in foster care) when a parent had a long hospital stay. Created in collaboration with the New York City Housing Authority and the New York City Human Resources Administration, the housing was a unique experiment that came to fruition, after numerous bureaucratic hurdles, in 2003.[66]

As homelessness saw a resurgence nationally in the 1980s—increasingly attracting attention from social policymakers—New York City felt the impact. "Whenever I pick up a newspaper, or listen to the news," declared New York City Mayor Ed Koch, "I find stories about one of our most pressing problems—that of the homeless."[67] Exactly who was homeless, though, had changed from 1972, when the Settlement first opened the Urban Family Center. In July 1983, Verona Middleton-Jeter, the UFC's associate director, testified about the shift. Speaking before the US House of Representatives' Select Committee on Children, Youth, and Families, she explained that during the UFC's first five years, most clients were Black and Puerto Rican families headed by single-parent females. Now, they were seeing more families that were white; that were headed by two parents; and that had children in foster-care placement. They were also seeing more victims of fire and of domestic abuse.

As an eyewitness to the unfolding crisis, Middleton-Jeter described the wider problems that were pushing New Yorkers into homelessness: "unemployment, the high cost of energy, the lack of affordable low-income housing, gentrification of working class and low-income communities, racial and sexual discrimination, social security benefits terminated for children at an earlier age, and increased violence in the family." And, just as Lillian Wald and Helen Hall had so effectively done, she put a human face on the dilemma by sharing real stories about real people she had encountered. She told the story of a 25-year-old mother of two who had been supporting her family with the income from a steady job as a department-store cashier—until her landlord spiked her rent, and, unable to pay it, she was evicted. While the Department of Social Services found the family temporary housing in a midtown hotel, the conditions there were deplorable. A gauntlet of drug addicts in and in front of the hotel made the young mother so fearful for her children's safety that she escorted them to and from their school. The lengthy and time-consuming trip, coupled with her desperate search for an apartment, frequently made her late to work—and she was fired. And now a woman who had always prided herself on her work ethic found herself on welfare, one of thousands pushed into poverty by a spiraling set of circumstances. And, with a wrenching story about a mother of three, Middleton-Jeter illustrated the impact of homelessness on mental health. The young mother had come to the UFC depressed and anxious. Crying as her six-year-old son did his best to comfort her, the woman shared her anguish with Middleton-Jeter: "You don't know what it is to be without a home, with not even a shack to call your own. Losing your home must be as bad as losing your mind, and not having a home is driving me out of my mind."[68]

As it had always done in times of need, Henry Street responded, adapting its services to new trends; in the process, the Urban Family

Center was adopted as a model for the New York City shelter system. In 1986, the Shelter Management Training program (now the Center for Training) opened to bring the UFC's experience with current and formerly homeless families to other workers in shelters. Later, the program expanded to serve managers of public housing facilities, further expanding its impact.

In one of many full-circle moments that characterize Henry Street and its impact, one of the people Henry Street's shelter system served was Theather Huggins (fig. 3.7). In 1985 Huggins was 30 years old, a mother, and homeless. Fleeing violence at home, she found refuge at Henry Street—as well as a path forward. Shortly after arriving, her fellow residents elected her to serve as a neighborhood scout. Charged with identifying the neighborhood institutions and services they would need once they left for permanent housing—schools, hospitals, and

FIGURE 3.7. Theather Huggins, today an on-call crisis worker at the Settlement, stands by the entrance to the townhouse that Lillian Wald made home in 1895. Henry Street Settlement Collection.

FIGURE 3.8. In 1991, Mayor David Dinkins was on hand to dedicate Helen's House at its opening ceremony; the building boosted Henry Street's capacity to provide much-needed homeless services. Among those listening as he spoke were (to the right of the mayor, left to right) Settlement board chair Audrey Rosenman, Manhattan Borough President Ruth Messinger, and Henry Street Executive Director Danny Kronenfeld. Henry Street Settlement Collection/George Hirose.

laundromats—she did the job so well that she was hired, after training and certification, as a full-time shelter employee. Seeking more, she obtained a degree in sociology. Today Huggins is a residential specialist and crisis worker at the Urban Family Center, leading support groups and helping residents with a host of issues, including adapting to life at the UFC, securing permanent housing, navigating the court system, and finding child care. "I don't have to imagine how someone is feeling," says Huggins. "I know how overwhelming, humiliating, and embarrassing arriving at a shelter can be."[69]

Henry Street expanded its homeless services when it created Helen's House (fig. 3.8), named in honor of Helen Hall. Opened in 1991, it was funded by the New York City Department of Homeless Services. The transitional housing program provided temporary accommodations with on-site social services for single mothers and their preschool children, and included efficiency apartments, day care space, and a community room. Ruth Messinger, who was then Manhattan borough president, attended its dedication. Looking back, she reflected on the hope in the moment, and the reality that time would reveal: "there were probably more people thinking then that we would figure out how to end homelessness with programs like Helen's House, with improvements in city shelter spaces," she said; "each exposé was met with some powerful new initiatives to expand services. Now more people seem to see it as a problem they just have to live with."[70]

As parents watched New York City crime rates and drug use rise in the last decades of the 20th century, they wondered how they could protect their children from the dangers of the streets. Henry Street was there with robust youth leadership programs. Debbie Cox, now an administrator in Henry Street's Workforce Development Center, credits both the Pioneers and the Cadet Corps (fig. 3.9) with developing her leadership skills and keeping her busy during her teens and twenties. James H. Robinson Jr., head of Henry Street's youth services, pushed a 17-year-old Debbie to join the Pioneers in 1981. She fondly recalls learning poetry, traditional African and Puerto Rican dances, drawing, and karate, and discussing Black history and where the members' families came from. Jim Robinson invited in speakers—lawyers, doctors, and others who had been through the Pioneers program—and the "big brothers and sisters" mentored those who now followed in their footsteps. "We learned you have to be your own person," Cox says. "If you took the training seriously, you became a leader. We followed the 'each one teach one' model, so we were then involved in teaching the next group." She adds, "We were very close knit; it was like one big family, and we were responsible for each other."

"Henry Street was big in the '80s and '90s," Cox says. "It had a huge influence on young people in the neighborhood. We were really lucky to have someone in a position—Jim Robinson—to see a need and bring in all these programs." Cox credits Robinson's guidance with helping her

FIGURE 3.9. James Robinson presents an award to Michelle Charley at a graduation ceremony for the Cadet Corps at nearby St. Augustine's Church (around 1987). Through programs like the Cadets, Robinson fostered a sense of family and helped young people grow their own leadership skills. Henry Street Settlement Collection.

thrive in school and beyond. It was about being able to see your future, she says. "If I didn't have Jim Robinson, where would I be today? That's why I carry that torch of leadership in his honor." At 18, Cox applied the leadership skills she'd gained from the Pioneers program to the Cadet Corps, where she stayed for 12 years, mentoring a new generation as a commanding officer. The program, which was a branch of the New York City Mission Society's Harlem Unit (James Robinson had become a member of the organization in 1951, and brought Henry Street into its fold), followed a military-style regimen that was intended to foster discipline, responsibility, and respect. Cadets were divided by age and gender and taught to do marching and rifle drills. Most participants learned about it by word of mouth. "When we first started it, there was a small group, but then when you saw your friends doing drills, then you wanted to do it," Cox says. The squads vied against other organizations in drills and even went to Madison Square Garden and West Point to compete. "To this day, people send me photos and say they were in the Cadets," Cox says. "They had great leaders they looked up to. Even though it was military, it was fun. And we had a huge parent organization that raised money if a young person couldn't get a uniform. Ruth Taube, Henry Street's sewing teacher, made the skirts for the girls."[71]

In 1997, Henry Street expanded its youth programs and possibilities for leadership training when it took over the Boys Brotherhood Republic (BBR) on East Sixth Street. Started in New York City in 1932, it was modeled on Chicago's BBR, founded in 1914 when a salesman named Jack Robbins sought to help a gang of seven teenaged boys by creating a club-like, miniature municipality governed solely by young people. Henry Street renamed it Boys & Girls Republic (BGR) and opened it up to girls. It has a unique approach: to this day, young people who participate become "citizens" of the "Republic." They run for office and elect their own officials to run their community, including a mayor, city clerk, judge, and city council members. Citizens who break the rules face court trials by their peers.[72]

Roy Givens describes what BGR meant to him as a parent. "When I first learned of BGR," he says, "I was in a bad place: single father, two preteen kids, I do long hours at my job, I work for the city, with mandatory overtime. Babysitters were too expensive . . . I was in trouble." He visited other programs, but it was with BGR that he found what he was looking for. "A few of the other centers didn't look quite attentive to the kids," he recalls, "but here I saw they had programs and they were organized, and it just felt right."[73]

Boys & Girls Republic fosters independence and accountability. For kids, it's about friendships, about having a voice, about making their own choices—and about building confidence. In 1998, 11-year-old Luis Checa participated in BGR; his fellow citizens elected him mayor. "When I was first elected mayor," he recalls, "I was a shy kid. I had to run meetings; I couldn't be shy anymore. It helped me grow so much." Checa went on to obtain a degree in public administration at John Jay College of Criminal Justice and today is still involved with BGR—but now as an employee, as the sports and recreation coordinator. "This place is just like home," he says. "A lot of us grew up here. I know what the kids want because I wanted the same things when I was their age."[74]

## SAVING THE SETTLEMENT

At Henry Street in the early 1980s (as well as at other settlements facing the impact of reduced social-welfare funding), a constant, troubling board-meeting topic was adequate funding—or more precisely, lack of it. Executive Director Niathan Allen came under increasing pressure to fix the longstanding problem, and in November 1982, he left the Settlement. Michael L. Frey, who had been recently hired as Henry Street's chief operating officer, was named as his successor. Board minutes suggest that internally, it was a difficult time to lead. At a 1983 board meeting, chair John Morning called out his fellow members for their poor attendance. Moreover, he raised concern about the tenor of their recent meetings which, he said, had become "angry, embroiled and ineffective," a reality that prompted trustee Nancy Aronson to take on the role of conciliator.

At the May 21, 1984, board meeting, Frey did his best to rally the group. He reminded everyone of Henry Street's value to the community, as a place that "belongs to everyone and means many different things to many people." And, he said, "we are, in fact, the only Settlement House with an active neighborhood association. Henry Street should be taking full advantage of its potential." Those were the positives. Frey then addressed the negatives. He reminded the board that Henry Street had been skirting financial ruin for the past several years, and, he felt, had become more distanced from the community since Bertram Beck's departure. To jumpstart funding, he instituted a capital campaign because, he said, "We must recognize that institutional costs can no longer be covered by government funds. In this regard, we need to build a larger and more permanent financial base." But while the campaign got off to a good start, the Settlement's deficit was rising at an alarming rate. At the February 25, 1985, board meeting, trustee Richard Abrons reported that for fiscal year 1984, the deficit was approximately $516,000—an increase of more than $300,000 over the year before. A month later, lacking board support, Michael Frey resigned. After long tenures by Lillian Wald and Helen Hall, followed by Bertram Beck's 10-year stint, Henry Street had now had three directors in just seven years. Not surprisingly, with Frey's departure, the Settlement felt rudderless—and, it was still running a financial deficit. The board found its stabilizing force in the spring of 1985.[75]

For its April 1, 1985, meeting, Henry Street's board met at the law offices of one of its members. In the conference room at Rosenman, Colin, Freund, Lewis & Cohen, Board Chair John Morning called the meeting to order. The mood was serious but optimistic. After the third of three short-lived executive directors had resigned, a beloved in-house staff member of 13 years—the slightly rumpled but eminently qualified social worker Danny Kronenfeld, head of the Urban Family Center—would take the helm (fig. 3.10). His hiring was a prayer in dire times, because Henry Street was on the brink of closing. Kronenfeld had the right set of skills to bring the Settlement out of the red. Born in the Bronx in 1932 to immigrant parents, Kronenfeld had gone through the New York City public school system, and his exposure to diverse students had helped inform his consciousness on race relations and social justice. He graduated cum laude from the City College of New York, pursued graduate studies at the University of Wisconsin-Madison, and earned a master of social work degree from Columbia University. Before coming to the Settlement, he'd worked as a community organizer for Mobilization for Youth, the Ittleson Center for Child Research and Day Treatment, and the Bronx YMHA. And, as many staff members would attest, he was a mensch.

Kronenfeld became executive director on the heels of a conservative backlash that had ushered in huge social cuts and efforts to reduce government's role in the lives of its citizens. As President Ronald

Figure 3.10. Danny Kronenfeld poses with Verona Middleton-Jeter, who would succeed him as executive director. Henry Street Settlement Collection.

Reagan would famously summarize his position, "I've always felt the nine most terrifying words in the English language are: 'I'm from the government and I'm here to help.'"[76] Undaunted, Kronenfeld swung into action, assuring the board that they should expect to see "a new burst of energy" from the staff as morale lifted. Along with his daughters, Leah and Jenny, who had lived with him at the UFC, he moved to 265 Henry Street, the place where Lillian Wald had first settled almost 100 years before. Deeply committed to the Settlement's long track record of finding solutions to the neighborhood's pressing problems, Kronenfeld vowed that "if there was a problem to be solved, Henry Street Settlement should determine how to solve it."[77]

The board rallied around Kronenfeld; "Danny," board member Richard Abrons would later say, "saved the Settlement. He built its programs and ensured its future."[78] Abrons attributed Kronenfeld's success to a number of factors. One, he was an excellent fundraiser (when he took over, said Abrons, the Settlement's budget was $6 million; 16 years later, when he left, it was $30 million). He was also "the soul of integrity, a fine person with a good sense of humor" and was "so nice and competent," said Abrons, "that the board, which had been dormant during the previous three executive directors, rallied around him." And it probably didn't hurt that after his promotion, Kronenfeld played in a weekly poker game at the apartment of longtime board member Fred Papert, partner in Papert Koenig Lois, a leading American advertising agency. "At this game were a lot of big-time city officials," notes Abrons, "so he got to know people at that level."[79]

While Kronenfeld faced a difficult climb toward solvency, not all was dire, as a December 9, 1985, memo from a fundraising consultant noted. In some areas, money was coming in. "The affection of much of the outside world for Henry Street continued on," she wrote, "possibly because of the Settlement's great name, possibly because of hard work by board members, possibly because most programs kept going of their own accord—including, notably, the Arts for Living Center which simply wouldn't stay closed."[80] In fact, by the February 24, 1986, board meeting, the Settlement was close to a breakeven point, and had already taken in more private monies than it had in all of the previous year. In September, Kronenfeld reported that things were continuing to go well, enough so that they could start to focus more on programming again.[81]

The mood was increasingly positive, and a visit from someone who was arguably the world's most famous woman helped, bringing the Settlement international headlines and increased recognition of its work. On February 2, 1989, a limousine pulled up to Henry Street, and out stepped Diana, the Princess of Wales. It was her first solo visit to New York City and, knowing that the press followed her wherever she went, she used her celebrity to draw attention to causes that mattered to her. While the British Embassy in Washington, DC, had proposed several sites for her to visit on her brief trip, one of the few she personally chose to visit was the Settlement, because it had a reputation for being one of the best-managed social programs in the country.[82]

Princess Diana visited with children at Henry Street's day care center (fig. 3.11), then met with eight former shelter residents, who shared their stories with her. Henry Street board chair Richard Abrons remembered the day, the pride in the air, and the excitement as a star-struck crowd gathered outside the Settlement in hopes of getting a glimpse of the much-loved royal: "One woman was so overcome by the idea she was talking to the princess," Abrons recalled, "that she just couldn't get the words out." For director Danny Kronenfeld, it was an ideal opportunity to draw attention to—and hopefully increase funding for—the Settlement's work. It also helped that in 1993, the Settlement was again in the international news when Kronenfeld was selected as one of 53 Americans invited to attend President Bill Clinton's inaugural luncheon as a "Face of Hope," where he was seated next to the new president.

In Henry Street's 1992–94 report, Kronenfeld acknowledged the good work his team had accomplished, but also the problems they still faced. While they were providing a broad array of services to more than 25,000 low-income and at-risk New Yorkers each year, many of their neighbors were still facing a multitude of problems, problems that were especially acute on the Lower East Side—which, he pointed out, was among the "most ethnically diverse and economically disadvantaged areas in the city." And once again, the Settlement would have to meet the swings in social funding, as President Clinton assumed office in 1993 and made welfare reform a major goal of his administration. When he signed into law the Personal Responsibility and Work Opportunity Act of 1996, which he promised would "end welfare as we have come to know it," it marked a major shift in how people who were poor received federal assistance. At the same time, poverty was on the rise. In 1990, roughly 1.38 million New Yorkers—about 19.3 percent of the city's population—lived below the poverty line; 10 years later, 1.67 million people (21.2 percent) did.[83]

FIGURE 3.11. Princess Diana stops to chat with children in Henry Street's day care center while on her 1989 visit to see the renowned Urban Family Center. Henry Street Settlement Collection.

Kronenfeld and Henry Street would meet these challenges on many levels, whether focusing on homelessness, the elderly, new immigrants, or the unexpected—like the devastating terrorist attacks of 9/11 and their aftermath. But benefitting from Kronenfeld's skills as a fundraiser and his ability to obtain government grants, the Settlement's staff doubled and its budget increased dramatically, enabling it to grow or adapt existing programs. In addition to opening Helen's House—which had expanded the Settlement's work with homelessness—Kronenfeld instituted the Senior Companions Program, which paired older volunteers with frail or infirm elderly clients. Also for elderly neighbors, Henry Street created the Vladeck Cares Supportive Service Program, the first naturally occurring retirement community program in public housing, across the street from its headquarters, in the Vladeck apartment complex.

Henry Street also adapted its programs to meet the needs of the changing neighborhood, as, in the last decades of the 20th century, a growing number of Chinese immigrants, pushed by economic restructuring in their home country, settled on the Lower East Side. The newcomers expanded—and rejuvenated—the existing Chinatown community that until the 1970s had been the first home for most Chinese immigrants coming to New York City. While Chinatown originally was home to Cantonese residents, these newcomers were now Fuzhounese. Many of them arrived as undocumented immigrants and were relegated by language issues and low education levels to poor-paying jobs.[84]

Just as it always had, Henry Street responded to the shift in demographics. As Danny Kronenfeld noted in the Settlement's 1998 *Biennial Report*, the organization had intensified its outreach and engagement with its newest neighbors in comprehensive ways. For example, Henry Street's mental health day program was now 68 percent Asian. In the fall of 1997, the Settlement had hired the Senior Center's first Chinese-speaking caseworker; programming at the arts center included Chinese folk arts and a Chinese music ensemble; and Henry Street's mental health clinic had launched an Asian bicultural unit to address the specific counseling needs of Chinese families.

## HENRY STREET IN THE 21ST CENTURY

On September 11, 2001, an unforeseen crisis affirmed the value of the Settlement as an on-the-ground neighborhood responder. That morning, Henry Street staff members heard a loud boom, felt their offices shake, and looked outside to see a plume of smoke rising from the World Trade Center. As the city was plunged into unspeakable tragedy, the Settlement jumped to action. "Within the hour, a long line of bleeding, dust-covered evacuees began to walk down the street, passing our agency's door," recalled former Henry Street social worker Vita Iacovone. The CCC distributed food and water, supplied telephones to evacuees to call family members, and provided free counseling services.[85] On September 11 and in the days following, Henry Street continued to respond to neighbors' needs. One poignant thank-you came from a housebound senior who depended on the Settlement's Meals on Wheels program. "Despite black smoke, closed streets and silent phones, I received every meal, even on September 11th," the grateful recipient wrote in a letter about Henry Street to the *Daily News*. The meal deliverers must, she said, "be added to the list of magnificent heroes."[86]

In 2002, after rescuing Henry Street from the precipice of financial ruin—and shepherding it through the dark days of 9/11—Danny Kronenfeld retired. Verona Middleton-Jeter, who had succeeded him as the head of the Urban Family Center, now succeeded him as the head of the Settlement, becoming its first Black female director. She had grown up in rural South Carolina, and got her introduction to social work when she was recruited to work at a residential treatment center in Westchester. Wanting to make a difference in the lives of people who were poor, she obtained her master's degree in social work from Smith College in Northampton, Massachusetts.

One of Middleton-Jeter's first official functions was to celebrate the opening of Henry Street's Workforce Development Center (WDC) in 2003, an event spawned, in part, by the longtime observations of Urban Family Center workers. Located on the third floor of 99 Essex Street, just blocks from the Williamsburg Bridge, the WDC's mission spoke to the entrenched problems of a changing city. Ever since the postwar exodus of industry from New York City, the jobs that once sustained immigrants without high levels of technical skills had largely vanished—or were so underpaid and under-unionized that they made it impossible to earn a living wage. At the Urban Family Center, Danny Kronenfeld and the staff had seen how it played out in real people's lives from working with second generations of families with the same problems that their parents had experienced. Believing that employment was key to self-sufficiency, Kronenfeld had persuasively made his case to benefactor Rita Abrons Aranow for a program devoted to developing job skills. Aranow contributed $4 million to kick it off, and in 2003 the WDC had come to fruition as a one-stop location for comprehensive employment services and adult basic education, a place where one could learn English, get an internship, or get help transitioning out of homelessness.

Within two years, according to then–chief administrator David Garza, 48 clients had achieved the equivalent of a high-school diploma with a GED, and 427 clients had been placed in good jobs. One of those who benefited from this longtime, thriving program is Wei Zhan (fig. 3.12). A chef in his native China, he moved to New York in 1991, following in the footsteps of other family members and seeking opportunity. His grueling 14-hour shifts at a Chinatown restaurant left him little time for anything but work. Thanks to the Workforce Development Center, he was able to keep feeding hungry New Yorkers—but also to spend time with his wife and two children. After completing an intensive training program, Henry Street hired him for its Meals on Wheels program, and in 2019, he delivered 95 meals, five days a week, to homebound seniors on the Lower East Side. The WDC, one of the Settlement's defining and largest programs, in 2019 moved to 178 Broome Street, part of the new Essex Crossing mega-development on the Lower East Side. [87]

And in 2004, a year after the WDC opened, Henry Street opened the Neighborhood Resource Center, which it had spearheaded in response to 9/11. Backed by government funds earmarked to help address the

FIGURE 3.12. Wei Zhan, who delivers meals and good cheer to Henry Street neighbors, found a welcome hand and a door of opportunity at Henry Street's Workforce Development Center. Henry Street Settlement Collection/David Grossman.

aftermath of the terrorist attacks, the walk-in center, located at the CCC, served clients affected by 9/11 by providing financial, legal, housing, and crisis counseling, as well as advocacy services.[88] Today it serves as a hub for community members who need help applying for food stamps, health insurance, and other public benefits.

Throughout the early 2000s, the Settlement continued to focus on issues of homelessness, health care, employment—and, as always, the arts. The Abrons Arts Center continued its longtime emphasis on the innovative and the experimental in theater, music, dance, and visual art, gaining a reputation, as a *New York Times* article observed, as "one of the last standing locations for avant garde performance downtown." And the Settlement was planning for the future, with its first-ever strategic plan.

Unveiled in 2006, the five-year road map was designed to strengthen and improve the agency's infrastructure, increase investment in staff, and consolidate and streamline services. Much as nurse Jane Hitchcock had categorized Henry Street's work in 1907 as four "branches of usefulness," the Settlement, almost 100 years later, defined its services in four distinct clusters, which it identified as Health and Wellness, Youth and Workforce Development, Transitional and Supportive Housing, and Visual and Supporting Arts (the Abrons Arts Center).[89]

As was clear by now, as a nonprofit, Henry Street, like other settlements, had always been especially susceptible to political and economic swings, and once again its financial viability was threatened when the Great Recession hit in late 2007. The global phenomenon, sparked by the US subprime mortgage crisis, ushered in rising unemployment and debt. In New York City, the first few years of the recession plunged 200,000 more city residents into poverty; out of an overall population of 8.1 million people, 1.7 million were now poor. Henry Street was hit hard, as rising demand for services met with diminished resources.[90] After cutting almost 30 positions—mostly administrative and maintenance— there was nothing else to cut, and no place to go. "It's not like you could run down to the basement," said Middleton-Jeter, "because the basement is leaking and the storm is raging there."[91] In light of the financial hardship, in 1982 the Settlement sold Camp Henry, which had fallen into disrepair—although its name is preserved in the organization's Lower East Side summer day camp. (Echo Hill, the beloved girls' camp, had earlier converted to a day camp for adults and children, and closed in 1980; it too was sold in 1982.)[92] In 2010, after having served Henry Street for 38 years, Middleton-Jeter retired. Among other accomplishments, she had helped grow the UFC and pioneered key programs for survivors of domestic abuse. Perhaps one of her greatest legacies is how she helped change public attitudes about homeless people. "We were there to help them help themselves—we weren't there to do it for them," she said; "we knew they were coming to us with skills and knowledge about life, and treated them like it." [93] In other words, respect.

FIGURE 3.13. President and CEO David Garza, shown here in 2012 as he helped deliver critical supplies to neighbors in the aftermath of Hurricane Sandy. Henry Street Settlement Collection/Rob Bennett.

In its search for Middleton-Jeter's successor, the board spread a wide net. From a field of 75 candidates that included heads of nonprofits and city programs, David Garza—the Workforce Development Center's chief administrator—rose to the top of the list. The board chose Garza, citing, among other attributes, his track record at the WDC, where he'd forged productive partnerships with corporations, agencies, and local private-sector entities; his high regard in the community; his deep commitment to Henry Street; and his passion for his work. In 2010, Garza (fig. 3.13) became the Settlement's new Executive Director (a title later changed to President and CEO), dedicated to championing the Settlement's longstanding values and to opening doors to all. "The reason I work in this field," he says, "is really about hope—it's about giving people hope for a better future."[94]

## Looking Back, and Moving Forward

David Garza leans back in his office chair at 265 Henry Street, the townhouse that Lillian Wald moved into in 1895 to help impoverished neighbors on the Lower East Side, and reflects on his path to the Settlement, and what it meant to celebrate 125 years in 2018. As a $41 million organization with well over 100 discrete funding sources and a staff of 700, Henry Street today serves more than 50,000 people through offerings that span all stages in life. These include preschool, afterschool, and college success programs; partnerships with dozens of Lower East Side schools that provide social workers' expertise and arts-in-education programming; programs for its homeless shelters and retirement community; and, through the Abrons Arts Center, classes, programs, and events.

Garza is a born-and-bred New Yorker. One of three children of a single mother, he grew up in a largely blue-collar Brooklyn neighborhood in modest circumstances. He watched his mother work nights as a nurse, returning in the morning to help her children get ready for school. As he put it in a 2019 interview, "I can't say I knew the full struggle of poverty, although I do know what a ketchup sandwich tastes like. But my mother? She knew the struggle."[95] Accepted into Harvard University, he left for college with a suitcase and $300 in his pocket. Upon graduating, he felt that he had to translate his degree into financial success so he could help his mother. Garza returned to New York City, where he pursued a career in retail management and television production. He was successful, but unfulfilled.

In 2000, Garza was volunteering in the restoration of the Church of St. Teresa on Henry Street when he happened to meet Danny Kronenfeld, then Henry Street's executive director. That's when the fuse was lit. Garza was intrigued by the Settlement's work, in part because he had a background in psychology and had considered going into social work. When a job opened up at Henry Street—helping low-income jobseekers transition from public assistance to work—he applied. Hired on a Friday, Garza started on Monday. Thrust into a new job, he was immediately confronted by the myriad challenges the Settlement's clients faced on a daily basis—as well as the challenges Henry Street faced in the wake of the Great Recession. But "our ability to create change," he said, was "beyond my wildest expectations." It was early on, when he helped a client obtain employment, that he truly realized the value of the work and knew that he was exactly where he was meant to be. The client came back to show his pay stub to Garza, not necessarily because he'd gotten the job, but because he had no one else to show it to. To Garza, that represented the DNA at the core of Henry Street—what he calls "the transformational power of relationship and support." As Garza sees it, if you "open doors to new opportunities and help individuals take the critical steps forward, that can make the difference between merely surviving and living a full life. Multiply that by the 50,000 people we serve each year, and you cannot lose sight of the exponential power and importance of this work."

When Garza became executive director, the city and nation were still feeling the impact of the recent financial downturn. Garza now found himself, he said, "staring down the mouth at the same social conditions that described the core reasons upon which we were founded. Same issues; different characteristics, different characters."[96] Poverty still existed. Jobs that didn't require special skills were difficult to find and often paid too little to subsist on. Low-income housing was increasingly difficult to secure, especially with rising gentrification. Issues of race played into higher poverty rates among people of color.[97]

Garza felt that the Settlement's service areas—education and employment, health and wellness, transitional and supportive housing, and performing and visual arts—were the right mix for the challenges at hand. But he was bothered by his sense that Henry Street's ability to listen to community members and respond to the needs they expressed— the essence of a settlement house—was hampered by the constraints of government contracts and the bureaucracy that comes with them.

That's when he decided, as he describes it, to "put the street back in Henry Street." Once, public health nurses had traveled the cobblestone streets of New York City as the Settlement's eyes and ears on the ground; now, through conversations—lots of them—the Settlement would reengage with the people who knew the neighborhood's problems best. They would listen, reflect on what they had heard, and act.

The first step is listening. Listening deeply and without judgment is crucial for Garza, who believes that communities are strengthened by authentic human connections. In a time characterized by bitter divisiveness—and one in which our technological devices have shortened our attention spans and pulled us into cycles of rapid-fire call-and-response—he has thought long and hard about how to connect people in meaningful ways. His advice is useful to anyone who has ever wanted to connect with another human being. "You need to be as viscerally present and in the moment as possible, because that lays the very necessary fertile ground for human connection," he argues. "I think that people sometimes go into conversations over-intellectualizing their own objectives. Or sometimes they're looking for specific answers to specific questions. That can accelerate right past the human connection. Stop; be present; and do whatever you can, at the most fundamentally respectful level, to be human together."[98]

To listen, Garza and Settlement staff members began by talking with key stakeholders—participants in every Henry Street service area; New York City Housing Authority resident association leaders; local residents; partner organizations. They went to their own homeless shelters and asked residents to share their views and ideas. When that still didn't feel like quite enough, they kept going. Garza created a community advisory board, one that built on the work of earlier executive directors but took it to a new level, one that Garza feels is more authentically representative than it has ever been. "The Community Advisory Board provides governance and oversight from a unique vantage point," he says. "We have our fiduciary governing board of 40 people and the Community Advisory Board is close to 40 people. Their work is a reflection of our identity as a settlement house—that it's critically important to listen to the community we serve in order to respond with services that meet this generation's issues—with economic development, gentrification, and volatile financial shifts in the city's landscape." And, in keeping with his leadership tenet that if you don't resource a function, you don't get it, he hired several staff members to oversee community engagement.

Listening to what was happening on Henry Street's doorstep and in its neighborhood was just the first step in what became an entrenched practice. As the cycle unfolds, information gathered on the ground is studied and reflected on. Then, it's distilled to the most salient actionable points. From there, Garza and his team decide whether the response should be a program change, a new program, a budget adjustment, or government policy advocacy. Always—and this is key, says Garza—their thinking is filtered through the unique historical perspective of the settlement approach, and in particular, Henry Street's set of values and the blueprint set out by Lillian Wald. This approach has been enhanced by a deeper understanding of the Settlement's place in the city and nation, gleaned through the history project that Garza championed and that came to fruition in 2018: onsite and web-based exhibitions, a walking tour, a school curriculum, and the hiring of a public historian to open up discussions with staff, neighbors, schoolchildren, scholars, elected officials, policy makers, and others about the issues that have long motivated Henry Street.

Then it's time to act. Launching a new initiative usually means that funding has to be identified. Today, Henry Street relies on a blend of government and private funding. Garza describes it as an important mix of bricks and mortar, one that fluctuates with the times. Government funding is critically important for the Settlement's viability, he says, largely supporting such services as those for homeless people, children, and seniors. But Garza also sees it as representative of changing political winds, acting "as a kind of moral barometer of where the country is and where New York City is." Private funding, he notes, provides more of an opportunity to be innovative or experimental, or to address a service need that might not fall into the structural buckets of public funding. Both are essential.

Listen, reflect, act—and do it through the lens of the Settlement's history and core values. This is the formula that Garza is using to reenergize the Settlement for the 21st century. The formula has spawned and informed new initiatives that address homelessness, gentrification, and income disparity; tackle the needs of out-of-school and out-of-work young people; infuse the arts into everyday life; and more. For example, having listened to shelter residents describe the need for better aftercare once they left Henry Street, the Settlement partnered with CAMBA (a Brooklyn-based social service agency) and Win (the largest provider of family shelter and supportive housing in New York City) to approach the City Council for support, because, as David Garza says, "it wasn't just a Lower East Side issue or a Henry Street Settlement issue; it was a citywide-system issue."

In 2006, Henry Street took the lead in an innovative collaboration in partnership with Community Board 3 and other workforce-orientated local nonprofits, including four other settlement houses, called the Lower East Side Employment Network (LESEN). The collaboration was a response to major real estate development projects that would dramatically change the face of the neighborhood—and bring about significant hiring. By serving as a central employment clearinghouse, LESEN mitigates competition for jobs among the partner organizations and serves as a single point of access for employers seeking talent, ensuring that the employment prospects that come with most major projects are available to the neighborhood residents who need them most. Because LESEN was in place by the time the sprawling Essex Crossing development took shape, the community board and a city zoning task force were able to negotiate local-hiring commitments from that developer. In 2019, LESEN placed its 900th employee in new economic developments on the Lower East Side and elsewhere throughout the city. [99]

Henry Street is also one of five organizations to successfully compete for funding from the Manhattan District Attorney's Office's Criminal Justice Investment Initiative to create its Youth Opportunity Hub. The initiative, which redistributes criminal forfeiture funds obtained through legal settlements with major banks, aims to make services more accessible to at-risk children, teens, and young adults. It does so by linking neighborhood service providers to offer one-stop, comprehensive support—with the goal of preventing vulnerable young people from becoming involved in the criminal justice system. From its base in Henry Street's youth services building, the Settlement and five other local settlements have hired nine social workers, who engage young people in a range of educational and employment programs.[100]

As part of Henry Street's long-standing devotion to the arts and belief in their importance to individual wellbeing and society at large, under current artistic director Craig T. Peterson the Settlement continues to forge the kinds of social and cultural intersections that had always defined Henry Street, from the anti-war play staged at the Neighborhood Playhouse in World War I to the exhibition of artists' responses to AIDS in 1989. Arts programs, performances, residencies, and classes are frequently inspired by the issues people are talking about on the street— such as unjust power structures, racial inequality, mass incarceration, and LGBTQ rights—sparking activism and imagination and giving voice to voices that are not always heard.[101] A new Social Practice Residency enables the Abrons Arts Center to support four artists who are undertaking a variety of creative endeavors; the inaugural cohort explored issues including domestic violence, indigenous knowledge, gentrification, and gun violence. Moreover, Henry Street's intergenerational chorus, made up of singers from age four to senior citizens, rehearses weekly and has sung in the *Mile-Long Opera* on Manhattan's High Line in 2018, and in Theater of War's *Antigone in Ferguson* in 2019, a groundbreaking performance that explored community reactions to police violence.

And, guided by Lillian Wald's belief that the arts are essential, Henry Street has woven them into its programs through PATHS (Promoting the Arts Throughout Henry Street), an initiative that joins the arts with each of the Settlement's service areas in innovative ways. On any given day, you can see the synergy in action: in a mental health recovery program, a ceramics teacher guides participants in the mindfulness and flexibility of making pottery; at a work-training program session, improv artists help participants learn how to think on their feet in job interviews; at an afterschool program, a dance instructor leads fourth graders through the muscle-flexing moves of a street dance—popping—to burn off energy (and absorb the collateral benefits that music, it's been shown, can provide to math and study skills).[102]

The most recent concrete example of President and CEO David Garza's desire to reenergize the Settlement for the 21st century is the relocation of its neighborhood center from East Broadway into a remodeled former firehouse at 269 Henry Street. The newly adapted firehouse, built in 1883, had been vacant ever since Engine Company No. 15 relocated to 19 Pitt Street after 9/11. Henry Street worked for more than a decade to purchase the decommissioned building from New York City, buying it for one dollar in 2017. The funds for its renovation and design were among the fruits of the Settlement's $20 million capital campaign, completed in 2018. The center is named for Henry Street board member Dale Jones Burch, the lead campaign donor, whose family has been involved with and supported the Settlement for generations. The new center provides a wide array of free services to neighborhood residents, including screenings for benefits and income supports (such as Supplemental Security Income, Access-A-Ride, affordable housing, and eviction protection); SNAP (food stamps program); employment services; health insurance enrollment; and legal and financial services. The onsite Parent Center offers supportive and educational group sessions for parents-to-be, parents, and guardians to help them address the challenges and celebrate the joys of raising children.

On a brilliantly sunny October 23, 2019, friends, neighbors, Settlement board and staff, funders, and elected officials gathered for the center's formal opening. Red-and-white balloons danced in the air as four-year-olds from the Settlement's Early Education Center, sporting red fire hats, welcomed the crowd with a heartfelt rendition of Randy Cohen's "You've Got a Friend in Me." As emcee David Garza invited the project's supporters—and two of the Settlement's current clients—to the podium to speak, attendees heard sentiments with a similar theme: of the power of love and of human beings choosing to help other human beings. In closing, Garza homed in on the heart of the story: that "now, more than ever, in a world where 'progress' is defined or aligned with corporate profit and personal gain, it's comforting that today we make 'progress' for the sake of real human progress with a core of compassion, dignity, and service." After closing with a rap he had written in honor of the day, Garza led the group in the ceremonial opening. Scissors sliced through the red ribbon stretched across the building's ornate cast-iron façade and it fluttered to the ground. With that, the former firehouse, given new life by Henry Street so that it could serve its community, returned to its role as a first responder.

The moment of rebirth captured the essence of Henry Street. Like the firehouse, the Settlement was a 19th-century first responder that had to change to meet the changing needs of its neighbors and neighborhood. Its ability to move with the times had been especially important from the late 1960s to the late 2010s, a 50-year period characterized by the end of postwar prosperity; rising deindustrialization (and the disappearance of jobs that once sustained newcomers); stagnant or falling wages for low-income workers; sustained conservatism; and changing funding sources.

Over the course of the half century, Henry Street had built an arts center; responded to calls for greater community inclusion; weathered the urban crisis, a strike, and a sit-in; faced political swings; offered robust youth leadership programs at a time of rising crime and drug use; teetered on the brink of collapse; tackled the challenges of homelessness and HIV/AIDS; ridden out the Great Recession; expanded its programs; and recharged for the 21st century. In the face of persistent poverty, it had managed to be a strong, resilient anchor and a vital and caring neighbor in a vibrant and always changing neighborhood. It was no small feat.

# CONCLUSION

## The Enduring Lessons of the House on Henry Street

"I think I know who Lillian Wald is; I don't need to live in her time. I've read enough about her, and through Henry Street's programs, I can see that her vision, her dream, lives."
—Rafael Jaquez, former Henry Street youth participant and program director of Henry Street UPS Community Internship Program, 2019

THE HOUSE ON HENRY STREET STANDS IN THE HEART OF THE Lower East Side, a place that has long been a first stop for immigrants coming to the United States. The neighborhood is still ethnically diverse—with almost 40 percent of its population foreign born—but, as Settlement head David Garza puts it, "it's also a neighborhood that's synonymous with struggle and with overcoming obstacles to make it in the city." This vibrant community is the repository of some of the country's most intractable problems. Poverty still persists, and with it the kinds of issues that, as Lillian Wald well knew, impact residents' wellbeing. Out of all of New York City's neighborhoods, the Lower East Side is one of the highest in income disparity. On one side of the neighborhood, the median household income is $124,000 per year; on the other, it's $15,000, which is among the most dramatic disparities in the city. Over half of Henry Street's neighbors are income insecure; 36.1 percent of low-income households are severely rent burdened (meaning they spend more than 50 percent of their income on rent) and at risk of homelessness; 31 percent of adults over 65 are living below the poverty line; and 60 percent of students are economically disadvantaged.[1]

In this community, Henry Street is part of what the United Neighborhood Houses (UNH)—founded in 1919 to unify settlements' collective efforts—today calls "the settlement house advantage." It is about caring and belonging, about being a place where you are greeted as a neighbor with "skills and abilities," not as a client "with deficits and problems." Alive and well in a neighborhood whose intense poverty inspired Lillian Wald to found it in 1893, Henry Street is a reminder of how the settlement house movement has enriched, and continues to enrich, the country's social welfare and cultural landscape.

It does bear saying, though, that settlements today are not the same start-up organizations they were in the late 1800s, when they were buoyed by Progressive Era reform fervor. Most historians, in fact, see settlements' zenith in the years around World War I, and note that despite marked surges in social activism in the 1930s and 1960s, their overall influence waned over the course of the 20th century. However, that's not to say that their best days are behind them, as Henry Street demonstrates. It's true that settlement houses no longer have the direct influence in the corridors of power they once did, and that activism today is more likely to be on a local level than a national one. But judging settlements' contemporary effectiveness against their Progressive Era selves—when the world around them has changed so profoundly— feels unfair. Perhaps it is not so much surprising that settlements have changed, but impressive that they have managed to endure through changing times.

Henry Street Settlement has been a leader in the same neighborhood for more than 125 years. To thrive, it has had to adapt to shifting demographics, changing ways of funding, a fluctuating political environment, and the extensive demolition and rebuilding of surrounding housing. Henry Street's capacity to change with the times—and even inform them—has made it an enduring institution that could evolve and make life better for successive generations of New Yorkers.

To understand the impact that the Settlement has made and continues to make, one need only listen to the voices of those who have crossed the threshold of the House on Henry Street. Listen to Richard Abrons's story: his parents, Louis Abrons and Anne Schroeder, met at a Henry Street dance in 1905. Eight years earlier, Lillian Wald had helped Anne's destitute, widowed mother by hiring her to sew nurses' uniforms so she could support her five children. Louis was also involved in Henry Street as a member of a club whose leader, Herbert H. Lehman—the banker turned public servant—helped fund his college education. The family never forgot how Henry Street alleviated their poverty and their concerns. For 52 years until his death in 2019 at the age of 92, Richard Abrons—businessman, philanthropist, and author—served on the Settlement's board of directors, advocating for the place that gave his family a chance. Anne Abrons, another family member who serves on the board, now carries the story forward.

Listen to the words of settlement-worker-turned-novelist Ernest Poole, who wrote in Henry Street's guest book in 1927, "Here when I was still a youngster, thank God, I came into a personal intimate home with windows looking all over the world. And I come here again and again and again."[2] Listen to the words of the Henry Street Oldtimers, who in 1940 avowed that "the Settlement of today is probably a more integral part of the community than ever before," and that "those of us for whom life took on an added zest, because of our association with Henry Street, more than a generation ago, acknowledge our obligation for helping to bring the privileges of the Settlement to the young people of this generation."[3]

Listen to the words of Sue Ann Santos-Hoahng. Today an attorney, judge, and Settlement board member, she grew up on the Lower East Side in the 1960s along with her brother and four sisters. Her father worked six days a week, 14 hours a day. It put food on the table, but there were no extras. She recalls the Henry Street summer trips to Echo Hill Farm that allowed her family to "do things together—where given our income it just wouldn't have happened," and the clubs and activities she enjoyed at the Settlement. "The ethnic mixture . . . was so diverse, yet we all got along," recalls Santos-Hoahng, who is of Chinese and Puerto Rican heritage. "Henry Street Settlement taught us to re-spect each other's culture and to learn from the differences."[4] Listen to Marina Gutierrez, who as a struggling artist in the 1980s was given studio space at the Abrons Arts Center and found in the crossroads of culture and community the "comradeship of people who were serious about their work" which allowed her to pursue a life as an artist.

Or talk to one of Henry Street's current family members. Javier Egipciaco, a former youth-services client, will tell you that "Henry Street wasn't just a street name; it was a foundation of the Lower East Side." Ask Shaquasia Williams, a transitional-housing client, who was homeless before she came to Henry Street. The Settlement, she says, has helped her become more independent, to have confidence in herself. "I see my life now," she says, "because of what I've done at Henry Street."[5]

In 1893, a 26-year-old nurse answered a child's plea for help and cre-ated a place guided by the power of association and a blueprint dedi-cated to the belief that, by crossing class divides and bridging differences, we could make a better world. As Lillian Wald's corps of public health nurses traveled out and through the city, crossing tenement rooftops and climbing over houseboats at the river's edge, they came to know their neighbors and their issues in ways that few other settlements did. Wald, the nurses who traveled throughout the city, neighbors, visitors, Henry Streeters, and the board members, philanthropists, and govern-ment officials who supported the Settlement's initiatives, past and pres-ent, express the power of taking action, and the ability of individuals to effect change by working together—even in the most dire, trying circumstances.

Henry Street Settlement is living testimony to the power of people coming together. In her 1934 book *Windows on Henry Street*, which she wrote as she was retiring, Lillian Wald shares that the lesson she learned in her years on Henry Street was that "people rise and fall together, that no one group or nation dare be an economic or a social law unto itself."[6] These words bookend the closing to her 1915 memoir, *The House on Henry Street*, where she wrote, "All of us who have worked together have worked not only for each other but for the cause of human progress; that is the beginning and should be the end of the House on Henry Street."[7]

That end is not in sight; poverty persists. And so the House on Henry Street continues to be the heart of the Settlement and a community anchor, a stable and steady influence, drawing on the core strengths established long ago by Lillian Wald and, always, moving with the times. Its history is a usable one, and its enduring lessons are as meaningful now as they were then:

Each of us is whole and worthy.
Poverty is a social issue.
There is power in bridging differences.
Neighbors matter.
In times of need, act.

# ACKNOWLEDGMENTS

WHEN NURSE LILLIAN WALD RUSHED THROUGH THE CROWDED streets of the Lower East Side in 1893, headed to the bedside of a young mother in need, she set in motion a series of events that led to the creation of Henry Street Settlement. This book takes its name from the memoir she wrote in 1915 to share the work of the Settlement and her vision for a more just society, a book aptly named *The House on Henry Street*. Today, the world is a better place because of the house, her vision, and their enduring power. I am eternally grateful for the privilege of telling the Settlement's incredible story, which belongs, of course, to the people who created it and lived it.

I had known about the storied Henry Street Settlement for years, but my first visit to its headquarters at number 265 was in 2013, when I met with Susan LaRosa, then Henry Street's vice president for marketing and communication, to discuss a potential project connected to the Settlement's upcoming 125th anniversary. LaRosa, a historian and tireless proponent of Lillian Wald and her legacy, had been fielding requests for visits from nursing and social work programs, Lower East Side buffs, historians, and others, who wanted to see where history had been made. While LaRosa always obliged, she wanted to do more. Determined to better meet the demand, she had been brainstorming with a consultant, cultural anthropologist Sally Yerkovich, about how the Settlement could tell the story in a more permanent and public way. Their conversations blossomed into a funding application to the National Endowment for the Humanities (NEH) to plan and execute a suite of visitor experiences that focused largely on the Settlement's founding years: an onsite exhibition, a web-based exhibit, a walking tour, a school curriculum, and a series of public programs. With successful planning and implementation grants, both under NEH's Division of Public Programs, the project launched.

Hired through the NEH grants to curate the onsite and online exhibitions and write the resource document that would inform and support the work of the exhibition team, I quickly became enveloped in Henry Street's rich history and inspired by the Settlement's work today. And so when the research document was complete, I was driven to continue; 20,000 words became 70,000 words and a book (although in doing so it quickly became clear that the Settlement's rich history could actually fill many volumes). My thinking and writing have been informed and enriched by my work on the exhibition and by the energizing exchange of ideas with the team of designers, evaluators, and scholars who were assembled to create it. President and CEO David Garza was the project's champion from the beginning and has been a constant source of inspiration. Susan LaRosa, as the project's instigator, director, and muse, was indescribable—the perfect combination of expertise, knowledge, imagination, and good humor. Sally Yerkovich as project manager was the humanities and logistical mastermind who conceived of the project with LaRosa, wrote the successful NEH grants, assembled and guided the process and the team, and imbued the project with her deep talent. Keith Ragone, our brilliant exhibition designer, brought to the table not just a designer's eye but an interpreter's perspective and an artist's sense of disruption. Bluecadet did a poetic job in creating the media elements and website, and evaluator Ellen Leerburger helped us all understand, importantly, what visitors wanted to know. Katie Vogel, hired through the NEH grant to be a public historian overseeing programs for clients and the public, also did yeoman's work obtaining images and permissions, developing web elements, and acting as an important sounding board. When Sally Yerkovich left to take on a position at the American Scandinavian Foundation, strategic planning consultant Janet Rassweiler took over as project manager, and I am indebted to her for her smart, perceptive, invaluable input on all elements. When LaRosa retired at the close of the exhibition project, she graciously continued to provide information and moral support. Barbara Kancelbaum, who took on LaRosa's position, has been a wonderful ally and a crack editor.

Part of this talented team was an esteemed group of consulting scholars, whose work was funded by the NEH grants. Along with our programming partners, the Tenement Museum and the Museum at Eldridge Street (represented, respectively, by Annie Polland and Hannah Griff-Sleven), they provided invaluable guidance during the project's planning and implementation, all of which shaped my thinking for this book. I cannot thank them enough: Marjorie N. Feld, Robert Fisher, John P. Harrington, Kathryn Kish Sklar, Judith Trolander, Morris Vogel, Joshua Freeman, Joshua Brown (and the American Social History Project), Alan M. Kraut, and Jack (John Kuo Wei) Tchen.

Rich archives were an important source of research for Henry Street's story. The most extensive collection of Settlement-related materials is housed at the University of Minnesota Social Welfare History Archives (where Linnea Anderson provided invaluable assistance). Copious materials can also be found at Columbia University's Health Sciences Library and Butler Library, and at the New York Public Library's main and performing arts branches; material on the Neighborhood Playhouse can be found in the library of the Neighborhood Playhouse School of the Theatre. Photographic collections were important sources, too, among them those at the Museum of the City of New York, the Library of Congress, and the USC School of Cinematic Arts Hugh M. Hefner Moving Image Archive. Also key was the existing body of scholarship on Henry Street and settlements in general, especially the work of Marjorie Feld, Judith Trolander, Robert Fisher, Michael Fabricant, Blanche Wiesen Cook, and John Harrington. Urban historian Robert W. Snyder provided expert, invaluable advice and insightful edits on the manuscript for which I am eternally grateful. In addition, Henry Street Settlement's archival collection and ongoing work to document client, staff, and board stories in its many online and print publications have been essential.

Throughout the process, Henry Street Settlement has been an incomparable, no-strings-attached partner. I extend gratitude for the support of its Board of Trustees, its team members and clients, elected officials, and the many foundations and individuals who make its work possible.

Heartfelt thanks go to Farley Chase of Chase Literary Agency for all his help making this book a reality. Having NYU Press take it on as publisher is an honor and something I imagine would have pleased Lillian Wald immensely. I am indebted to the press's terrific staff, especially editor Clara Platter; sales and marketing director Mary Beth Jarrad and her team; editing, design, and production director Martin Coleman; copyeditor James Harbeck; and designer Charles B. Hames. And finally, I want to thank my husband Gerry and daughters Zoë and Isabelle for their unwavering support, encouragement, and wonderfulness.

In writing this book, I could not help but think of the stories my father, Max Snyder, told me about his Russian immigrant parents, Benjamin and Rose, who, fleeing pogroms, arrived in New York City in the early 1900s. I honor their courage and resilience and that of all newcomers, past and present, as well as all those who have reached out to welcome them—like the people of Henry Street and all those who, like them, are creating a more just world.

# NOTES

Archives frequently cited in these notes have been identified by the following abbreviations:

HHP  Helen Hall Papers, Social Welfare History Archives, University of Minnesota Libraries, Minneapolis

HSC  Henry Street Settlement Collection, Henry Street Settlement, New York City

HSM  Henry Street Settlement Music School Records, Social Welfare History Archives, University of Minnesota Libraries, Minneapolis

HSR  Henry Street Settlement Records, Social Welfare History Archives, University of Minnesota Libraries, Minneapolis

LWC: Lillian D. Wald Papers, Rare Book and Manuscript Library, Columbia University Library, New York City

LWN  Lillian D. Wald Papers, Manuscripts and Archives, The New York Public Library Humanities and Social Sciences Library, New York City

VNS:  Visiting Nurse Service of New York Records, Archives & Special Collections, Columbia University Health Sciences Library, New York City

## PART 1: A BAPTISM OF FIRE

1 Mary Adelaide Nutting and Lavinia L. Dock, *A History of Nursing: The Evolution of Nursing Systems from the Earliest Times to the Foundation of the First English and American Training Schools for Nurses*, vol. 3 (New York: G. P. Putnam's Sons, 1912), 216; Lillian D. Wald, "The House on Henry Street," *Atlantic Monthly*, March 1915, 289.

2 Lillian D. Wald, *The House on Henry Street* (1915; repr., London: Forgotten Books, 2012), 6.

3 Marjorie N. Feld, *Lillian Wald: A Biography* (Chapel Hill: The University of North Carolina Press, 2008), 35.

4 Carol Groneman and David M. Reimers, "Immigration," in Kenneth T. Jackson, ed., *The Encyclopedia of New York City* (New Haven: Yale University Press, 1995), 583.

5 Isaac Metzker, ed., *A Bintel Brief: Sixty Years of Letters from the Lower East Side to the Jewish Daily Forward* (New York: Schocken Books, 1971), 132, 76.

6 Max Weren, "I Love America," in *Good News* 1, no. 4, July 1955, HSC. *Good News* was the newsletter of the Good Companions, a Henry Street group for seniors founded in 1954 and still active today. It included news as well as short pieces of prose and poetry by members. This reminiscence is from one of the newsletter's editors, Max Weren.

7 Martha Dolinko interview in Jeff Kisseloff, *You Must Remember This: An Oral History of Manhattan from the 1890s to World War II* (New York: Harcourt Brace Jovanovich, 1989), 17.

8 Thomas J. Schlereth, *Victorian America: Transformations in Everyday Life 1876–1915* (New York: HarperPerennial, 1991), 104.

9 Jacob Riis, *How the Other Half Lives,* Hasia R. Diner, ed. (New York: W. W. Norton, 2010), 63.

10 Irving Howe, *World of Our Fathers: The Journey of the East European Jews to America and the Life They Found and Made* (New York: Harcourt Brace Jovanovich, 1976), 80–83.

11 Quoted in Minnie D. Louis, "A Retrospect: Recollections of the Beginning of a Great Work," *New Era Illustrated Magazine* 6, no. 1 (December 1904): 64.

12 Morris Rosenfeld, *Songs from the Ghetto* (Boston: Small, Manyard and Company, 1900), 3.

13 Michael McGerr, *A Fierce Discontent: The Rise and Fall of the Progressive Movement in America 1870–1920* (New York: Free Press, 2003), 17–18; National Child Labor Committee, *Children Who Work in the Tenements: Little Laborers Unprotected by Child Labor Law* (New York: National Child Labor Committee, 1908), Harvard Library, https://iiif.lib.harvard.edu.

14 Howe, *World of Our Fathers*, 149–52.

15 Ernest Poole is quoted in "The March of Events," The World's Work 7, no. 1 (November 1903): 4056; Ralph da Costa Nunez and Ethan G. Sribnick, *The Poor*

*Among Us: A History of Family Poverty and Homelessness in New York City* (New York: White Tiger Press, 2013), 115.

**16** "Lillian Wald," *VCU Libraries Social Welfare History Project*, accessed July 28, 2019, http://socialwelfare.library.vcu.edu; Feld, *Lillian Wald*, 20.

**17** See Doris Groshen Daniels, *Always a Sister: The Feminism of Lillian D. Wald* (New York: The Feminist Press at The City University of New York, 1989), 6–17, for more on this account of her early life.

**18** B. A. Backer, "Lillian Wald: Connecting Caring with Activism," *Nursing & Health Care* 14, no. 3 (March 1993): 122–9; Daniels, *Always a Sister*, 18; Marjorie N. Feld, "Lillian D. Wald," *Jewish Women: A Comprehensive Historical Encyclopedia*, March 20, 2009, the Jewish Women's Archive, accessed August 25, 2014, https://jwa.org.

**19** "Cornell University—New York Hospital School of Nursing," *Weill Cornell Medicine Samuel J. Wood Library*, notes that this was later the New York Hospital School of Nursing, and then the Cornell University-New York Hospital School of Nursing. See https://library.weill.cornell.edu.

**20** Lillian D. Wald to George Ludlum, May 27, 1889, from "Copy of letter sent by Lillian D. Wald to the New York Hospital in Applying for admission to the School of Nursing . . . from files of the Cornell University-New York Hospital School of Nursing" ("Excerpts from this letter," reads a note on the copy, "were read by Miss Dunbar at the Tea on March 10, 1952, the anniversary of Miss Wald's birthday"), LWN, MssCol 3201, Reel 1, Box 2.

**21** Feld, *Lillian Wald*, 33; "Minnie Louis," *Jewish Foundation for Education of Women*, accessed September 23, 2018, www.jfew.org; Anne M. Filiaci, "Medical School and Epiphany," *Lillian Wald—Public Health Progressive*, accessed September 2, 2018, www.lillianwald.com. For a more complete history of the school, see Louis, "A Retrospect: Recollections of the Beginning of a Great Work." The school's stated mission was to elevate "the character and condition of the Jewish poor of the city of New York by imparting to them ethical, religious and secular instruction, and by relieving their physical wants."

**22** Wald, *The House on Henry Street*, 7.

**23** See Lavinia L. Dock and Isabel Matiland Stewart, *A Short History of Nursing from the Earliest Times to the Present* (New York: G. P. Putnam's Sons, The Knickerbocker Press, 1920), 195–7. William Rathbone, a Liverpool merchant and philanthropist, is credited with conceiving the idea of a visiting nurse service to provide medical care to poor individuals in 1859. Rathbone had engaged a private nurse to tend his ailing wife; when she died, it occurred to him, he later wrote, to pay the nurse to "go into one of the poorest districts of Liverpool and try, in nursing the poor, to relieve suffering and to teach them the rules of health and comfort." See "William Rathbone and the Beginning of District Nursing," *Qni Heritage*, accessed September 18, 2018, www.districtnursing150.org.uk; Yssabella Waters, *Visiting Nursing in the United States* (Philadelphia: Fell, 1909).

**24** Elizabeth Fee and Liping Bu, "The Origins of Public Health Nursing: The Henry Street Visiting Nurse Service," *American Journal of Public Health* 100, no. 7 (July 2010): 1206–7; Paul Berman, "Looking Back: Mary Maud Brewster: A Closer Look at a Long-neglected Public Health Pioneer," *American Journal of Nursing* 110, no. 8 (August 2010), 62. Berman writes that Brewster was born in Pennsylvania on October 4, 1864.

**25** Wald, *The House on Henry Street*, 8–9.

**26** Lillian Wald, "We Called Our Enterprise Public Health Nursing," foreword to Marguerite Wales, *The Public Health Nurse in Action* (New York: Macmillan, 1941), xi.

**27** Nightingale makes the argument in her introduction to William Rathbone, *Sketch of The History and Progress of District Nursing* (London: Macmillan, 1890), 11–14; Louise Selanders, "Florence Nightingale in Absentia: Nursing and the 1893 Columbian Exposition," *Journal of Holistic Nursing* 28, no. 4 (December 2010), 308. As Selanders writes, "Environmental alteration became the critical factor in health promotion."

**28** Henry Street Settlement, *Report of the Henry Street Settlement 1893–1913, Published by the Henry Street Settlement on Its Twentieth Anniversary* (New York: Henry Street Settlement, 1913), accessed November 1, 2019, https://collections.nlm.nih.gov, 13–14.

**29** Ibid.; Wald would later say, "Perhaps it was an advantage that we were so early exposed to the extraordinary sufferings and the variety of pain and poverty in that winter of 1893–94, memorable because of extreme economic depression." Wald, *The House on Henry Street*, 17.

**30** Wald, *The House on Henry Street*, 10.

**31** Nunez and Sribnick, *The Poor Among Us*, 122. For an easily accessed, extensive resource on early settlement houses, see the Virginia Commonwealth University Libraries' *Social Welfare History Project* website at http://socialwelfare.library.vcu.edu.

**32** "Our History," *Toynbee Hall*, accessed September 19, 2019, www.toynbeehall.org.uk.

**33** Allen F. Davis, *Spearheads for Reform: The Social Settlement and the Progressive Movement, 1890–1914* (New York: Oxford University Press, 1967), 12, 266n24.

**34** Alice Boardman Smuts, *Science in the Service of Children, 1893–1935* (New Haven: Yale University Press, 2006), 27.

**35** See Floris Barnett Cash, "Radicals or Realists: African American Women and the Settlement House Spirit in New York City," *Afro-Americans in New York Life and History: New York* 15, no. 1 (January 31, 1991): 7–17; Lina D. Miller, *The New York Charities Directory: A Reference Book of Social Service,* 28th ed. (New York: Charity Organization Society, 1919), 168.

**36** See Smuts, *Science in the Service of Children*, 27–8; Nunez and Sribnick, *The Poor Among Us*, 134; and Wald, *The House on Henry Street*, v.

**37** Nunez and Sribnick, *The Poor Among Us*, 137.

38 Olivia Howard Dunbar, "A Great Profession for Women—Social Service," *New York Times*, July 31, 1910.

39 *Hebrew Standard*, January 21, 1910, cited in Feld, *Lillian Wald*, 41.

40 Wald, *The House on Henry Street*, 69–70.

41 Louise W. Knight, *Jane Addams, Spirit in Action* (New York: W. W. Norton, 2010), 67.

42 Stephen Birmingham, *The Jews in America Trilogy* (Open Media: 2016).

43 Seth Korelitz, "Minnie Dessau Louis 1841–1922," *Jewish Women: A Comprehensive Historical Encyclopedia*, Jewish Women's Archive, accessed September 19, 2018, http://jwa.org.

44 M. Fromenson, "Because of His 'Confounded' Good Nature: An Exclusive Interview with Felix M. Warburg," *American Hebrew* 110, no. 13 (February 10, 1922): 355, 364; Feld, *Lillian Wald*, 36–41.

45 Birmingham, *The Jews in America Trilogy*.

46 See Backer, "Lillian Wald: Connecting Caring with Activism," 124. The story was told by Nina Warburg about her mother, Betty Loeb, on a radio talk given by Rita Morgenthau on October 15, 1953, LWN, Microfilm Reel 1, Box 1, Letters by Lillian D. Wald, 1893–1917.

47 See Naomi W. Cohen, *Jacob H. Schiff: A Study in American Jewish Leadership* (Hanover: Brandeis University Press/University Press of New England, 1999), 70–71.

48 Jacob H. Schiff, inscription to Lillian Wald, 1909, Henry Street Settlement Guest Book, HSC.

49 Lillian D. Wald to Jacob H. Schiff, August 29, 1893, LWN, Microfilm Reel 1, Box 1.

50 Wald to Schiff, February 2, 1894, LWN, Microfilm Reel 1, Box 1.

51 Wald to Schiff, August 29, 1893, LWN, Microfilm Reel 1, Box 2.

52 Henry Street Settlement, *Report of the Henry Street Settlement 1893–1913*, 13.

53 Wald, *The House on Henry Street*, 281.

54 Ibid., 13.

55 R. L. Duffus, *Lillian Wald: Neighbor and Crusader* (New York: Macmillan, 1939), 39.

56 Nutting and Dock, *A History of Nursing*, 220.

57 Wald, *The House on Henry Street*, 24.

58 The street was named after New York City–born Henry Rutgers, a Revolutionary War hero, elected official, and later philanthropist; New Jersey's Rutgers University is also named for him.

59 Wald, *The House on Henry Street*, 24.

60 Joyce Mendelsohn, *The Lower East Side Remembered and Revisited: A History and Guide to a Legendary New York Neighborhood* (New York: Columbia University Press, 2009), 52; "The Whole City Seethed," from *Di arbiter tsaytung*, 1892, in Tony Michels, ed., *Jewish Radicals: A Documentary History* (New York: New York University Press, 2012), 91.

**61**  Lisa Buckley, *Settlement Houses on the Lower East Side*, unpublished manuscript, 2007, 9. Buckley draws on building files in the New York City Municipal Archives; Karen Buhler-Wilkerson, *No Place Like Home: A History of Nursing and Home Care in the United States* (Baltimore: Johns Hopkins University Press, 2003), 107.

**62**  Wald, *The House on Henry Street*, 171–2.

**63**  "President's Message" in *Sixteenth Annual Founder's Day Dinner-Dance of the Henry Oldtimers, Inc. Commemorating the Birthday of Lillian D. Wald. Guest of Honor Harold A. Spears. Saturday, March Twelfth, 1955, The Waldorf-Astoria*, 1955, Box 147, Folder NN—Related Organizations—History Old Timers, University of Minnesota Libraries, Minneapolis, Minnesota.

**64**  Wald, *The House on Henry Street*, 82–4.

**65**  Smuts, *Science in the Service of Children*, 27; Estelle Freedman, "Separatism as Strategy: Female Institution Building and American Feminism, 1870–1930," *Feminist Studies*, 5 (1979): 518–19.

**66**  Alice Lewisohn Crowley, *The Neighborhood Playhouse: Leaves from a Theatre Scrapbook* (New York: Theatre Arts Books, 1959), 8.

**67**  Duffus, *Lillian Wald*, 69, v–vii. Duffus's book is especially interesting because of his relationship with Wald while writing it. He not only went through her papers, but had, as he puts it in his foreword, "many interviews, which have been a delight to me over a period of two years."

**68**  "Jane E. Hitchcock, 1863–1969," *American Association for the History of Nursing*, accessed October 15, 2019, www.aahn.org.

**69**  Carole E. Estabrooks, "Lavinia Lloyd Dock: The Henry Street Years," in Ellen D. Baer, Patricia D'Antonio, Sylvia Rinker, and Joan E. Lynaugh, eds., *Enduring Issues in American Nursing* (New York: Springer, 2002); Karen Buhler-Wilkerson, in *No Place Like Home: A History of Nursing and Home Care in the United States* (Baltimore: John Hopkins University Press, 2001), 102, says Dock and Wald met at the Chicago Congress; also see Presbyterian Hospital, *Annual Report of the Presbyterian Hospital in the City of New York, 1904* (repr., London: Forgotten Books, 2013), 185.

**70**  Leo Trachtenberg, "Philanthropy That Worked," *City Journal*, Winter 1998, www.city-journal.org. Trachtenberg notes that little is known about Mary Brewster. She had poor health, left Henry Street, and married. She was with the Settlement at least until September 1897, when she is mentioned in a *New York Times* article as still being there. Paul Berman, in "Looking Back: Mary Maud Brewster," 62–3, notes that when she was married in 1898, she listed Henry Street as her home address, suggesting she was living there at least until then.

**71**  Arlisha R. Norwood, "Florence Kelley," *National Women's History Museum*, accessed September 20, 2018, www.nwhm.org. For more on Kelley, see Kathryn Kish Sklar, *Florence Kelley and the Nation's Work: The Rise of Women's Political Culture, 1830–1900* (New Haven: Yale University Press, 1995).

72  Sarah Leavitt, *From Catharine Beecher to Martha Stewart: A Cultural History of Domestic Advice* (Chapel Hill: University of North Carolina Press, 2002), 78. Kittredge, writes Leavitt, "devoted her life to helping people and concentrated many of her efforts on ensuring better food and homes for the underprivileged." See also Feld, *Lillian Wald*, 35; Clare Coss, ed., *Lillian D. Wald: Progressive Activist* (New York: The Feminist Press at the City University of New York, 1989), 9. The information about Arthur is from Billy J. Harbin, Kim Marra, and Robert A. Schanke, eds., *The Gay & Lesbian Theatrical Legacy: A Biographical Dictionary of Major Figures in American Stage History in the Pre-Stonewall Era* (Ann Arbor: University of Michigan Press, 2005), 30.

73  For more on Wald's relationships with her female network, see Blanche Wiesen Cook, "Female Support Networks and Political Activism: Lillian Wald, Crystal Eastman, Emma Goldman," in Wayne R. Dynes and Stephen Donaldson, eds., *Homosexuality and Government, Politics, and Prison* (New York: Garland Publishing, 1992). Kittredge's poem and letter, dated 1904, are from LWC, Mabel Hyde Kittredge Correspondence Box 6, folder titled "April 28, 1904."

74  "Women of Valor: Lillian Wald," *Jewish Women's Archive*, accessed September 24, 2018, http://jwa.org; Feld, *Lillian Wald*, 98–99; Henry Street Settlement, *Report of the Henry Street Settlement 1893–1913*, 26.

75  Program, 40th anniversary, Henry Street Settlement, 1933, VNS, Box 194, Folder 30; Jane Elizabeth Hitchcock, "Methods of Nursing in the Nurses' Settlement, New York City," *American Journal of Nursing* 7, no. 6 (March 1907): 460.

76  Nurse Zing Ling Tai is identified in a 1927 silent film, *The Henry Street Visiting Nurse*, which is in the collection of the Hugh M. Hefner Moving Image Archive at the USC School of Cinematic Arts and can be viewed at https://uschefnerarchive.com/vnsny-visiting-nurse-service-of-new-york/.

77  Rose Gollup Cohen, *Out of the Shadow: A Russian Jewish Girlhood on the Lower East Side* (New York: Doran, 1918; repr., Ithaca: Cornell University Press, 1995), 230–1.

78  Hitchcock, "Methods of Nursing in the Nurses' Settlement," 460. A 1910 survey listed "The Rest at Grand View-on-the-Hudson, New York; Reed Farm, Valley Cottage, N. Y. (for Italian patients); [and] Echo Hill Farm, Yorktown Heights, N. Y. (where a limited number of delicate children are kept for an indefinite period or are partially adopted)"; J. Hansan, "Henry Street Settlement (1910)," *The Social Welfare History Project*, accessed October 17, 2019, www.socialwelfarehistory.com. Hansan draws on material from Robert Archey Woods and Albert Kennedy, eds., *Handbook of Settlements* (New York: Charities Publication Committee, 1911).

79  Elisabeth Lasch-Quinn, *Black Neighbors: Race and the Limits of Reform in the American Settlement House Movement, 1890–1945* (Chapel Hill: The University of North Carolina Press, 1993), 4.

80  Craig Steven Wilder, *A Covenant with Color: Race and Social Power in Brooklyn* (New York: Columbia University Press, 2000), 119.

81  Jane Addams, "Social Control," *Crisis* 1, no. 3 (January 1911): 22. See also Lasch-Quinn, *Black Neighbors*.

82  James H. Perkins (Henry Street Settlement treasurer), letter to the editor, "Aid for Henry Street Settlement," *New York Times*, December 29, 1926; Marie O. Pitts Mosley, "Satisfied to Carry the Bag: Three Black Community Health Nurses' Contributions to Health Care Reform, 1900–1937," *Nursing History Review* 4, no. 1 (1996): 65–8.

83  Patricia D'Antonio, Ellen D. Baer, Sylvia Rinker, and Joan E. Lynaugh, eds., *Nurses' Work: Issues Across Time and Place* (New York: Springer, 2007), 69–74. On the challenges faced by Black women who pursued nursing as a profession, see Darlene Clark Hine, *Black Women in White: Racial Conflict and Cooperation in the Nursing Profession, 1890–1950* (Bloomington: Indiana University Press, 1989).

84  Lawrence C. Washington, "Preserving the History of Black Nurses," *Minority Nurse*, March 30, 2013, https://minoritynurse.com

85  D'Antonio, Baer, Rinker, and Lynaugh, *Nurses' Work*, 70–3; Marcy S. Sacks, *Before Harlem: The Black Experience in New York City Before World War I* (Philadelphia: University of Pennsylvania Press, 2013), 76–8.

86  "No Color Line Drawn at Stillman House," *New York Age*, January 9, 1913; Lasch-Quinn, *Black Neighbors*, 29; Diner, *In the Almost Promised Land: American Jews and Blacks, 1915–1935* (Baltimore: The Johns Hopkins University Press, 1995), 182–3. The collections at the A. C. Long Health Sciences Library in New York City have a number of papers related to nurse Edith Mae Carter, whose story is worthy of deeper study.

87  D'Antonio, Baer, Rinker, and Lynaugh, *Nurses' Work*, 73, 75–76. They cite Dorothy Cooper, supervisor of the Longacre Office of the Henry Street Settlement Visiting Nurse Service, "Longacre," VNS.

88  Darlene Clark Hine, *Black Women in the Nursing Profession* (New York: Garland, 1985), 36.

89  Henry Street Settlement, *Report of the Henry Street Settlement 1893–1918*, 74; Hasiah Diner, *In the Almost Promised Land*, 179.

90  "Helping and Healing People," *MetLife*, accessed August 22, 2014, www.metlife.com; Elizabeth Fee, "Lee K. Frankel (1867–1931): Public Health Leader and Life Insurance Executive," *American Journal of Public Health* 101, no. 10 (October 2011): 1870; "Metropolitan Life Insurance's Health Campaign," *Historical Collections at the Claude Moore Health Sciences Library, University of Virginia*, accessed August 21, 2019, http://exhibits.hsl.virginia.edu; Wald, *The House on Henry Street*, 62–3.

91  Karen Buhler-Wilkerson, "What Is a Public Health Nurse? Historical Visions of Public Health Nursing," *Docplayer*, accessed November 7, 2019, docplayer.net; "Henry Street Settlement: Fortieth Anniversary Program," *VCU Libraries Social Welfare History Project*, accessed September 23, 2018, www.socialwelfarehistory.com. In 1952, the National Organization of Public Health Nurses dissolved when its holdings were transferred to the newly created National League for Nursing.

92  Arthur C. Holden, *The Settlement Idea: A Vision of Social Justice* (New York: Macmillan, 1922), 64.

93  Elisabeth Israels Perry, *Belle Moskowitz: Feminine Politics and the Exercise of Power in the Age of Alfred E. Smith* (New York: Routledge, 2018), ix; Lillian Wald to Karl Hesley, December 5, 1932, Wald MSS, New York Public Library, New York City, cited in Daniels, *Always a Sister*, 45; *Settlement Journal* 11, no. 1 (November 1912), 18–32.

94  Jacob R. Patent, interview with John H. Petito, October 30, 1991, HSC; Abraham Davis spoke at the memorial service for Lillian Wald at Carnegie Hall, 1940, LWN, Microfilm, Reel 1.

95  See W. Barksdale Maynard, "'An Ideal Life in the Woods for Boys': Architecture and Culture in the Earliest Summer Camps," *Winterthur Portfolio* 34, no. 1 (Spring 1999): 3–29.

96  Miriam Hirsch, "Remembrance of Things Past—Miss Wald," *Good News* 1, no. 4, July 1955, 7, HSC; Alice Hartsuyker, *My Mother's Daughter* (San Diego: Hartworks Graphic Arts, 2005), 150–4.

97  "Henry Street Settlement," *VCU Libraries Social Welfare History Project*, accessed August 1, 2019, https://socialwelfare.library.vcu.edu.

98  Estabrooks, "Lavinia Lloyd Dock: The Henry Street Years," 291, citing Lavinia L. Dock, *Short Papers on Nursing Subjects* (New York: M. Louise Longeway, 1900).

99  Wald, *The House on Henry Street*, 310.

100  Crowley, *The Neighborhood Playhouse*, 5–6.

101  John Louis Recchiuti, *Civic Engagement: Social Science and Progressive-Era Reform in New York City* (Philadelphia: University of Pennsylvania Press, 2006), 74–83, citing Frances Perkins, *The Reminiscences of Frances Perkins (1951–1955)* 1, Columbia University Oral History Research Collection, 326–7. Perkins mentions Raymond Fosdick. Fosdick was a lawyer and social reformer; he became active in the Wilson administration and went on to serve as president of the Rockefeller Foundation from 1936 to 1948. On Fosdick, see the publisher's note for "Public Service, International Affairs and Rockefeller Philanthropy, The Papers of Raymond Blaine Fosdick (1883–1972) from the Seeley G. Mudd Manuscript Library, Princeton University," accessed November 7, 2019, ampltd.co.uk.

102  For more on Wald and the exchange of ideas she fostered, see Feld, *Lillian Wald*, 53, 92; Daniel T. Rodgers, *Atlantic Crossings: Social Politics in a Progressive Age* (Cambridge: Harvard College, 1998), 4, 75. The quote by Morgenthau is from "Tribute to Miss Wald," which she delivered at Wald's memorial service in 1940, and is in the collections of the Neighborhood Playhouse School of Theatre's library.

103  Helena Dudley, inscription to Lillian Wald, 1909, Henry Street Settlement Guest Book, HSC. Amelia Earhart signed the same guest book on July 8, 1928.

104  Lillian Wald, "Theodore Roosevelt—the 'Social Worker,'" undated, Box 16, folder 5, LWC, Reel 14.

105  Jacob A. Riis, inscription to Lillian Wald, April 29, 1912, Henry Street Settlement Guest Book, HSC.

**106** Wald, *The House on Henry Street*, 65.

**107** Roy Lubove, "From the Progressives and the Slums: Tenement House Reform in New York City, 1890–1917," 1962, reprinted by permission of the University of Pittsburgh Press, 379–99, in Riis, *How the Other Half Lives*, 380–1.

**108** Wald, *The House on Henry Street*, 306.

**109** Feld, *Lillian Wald*, 19–21.

**110** *The Utilization of the Immigrant* (New York: Free Synagogue, 1907), 2, 11, LWN, Reel 24.

**111** "Samovars at Nurses' Settlement," *New-York Tribune*, June 8, 1902.

**112** Wald, *The House on Henry Street*, 293–4.

**113** Lillian Wald to President Taft, Senator Elihu Root, and Senator James O'Gorman, January 7, 1913, Lillian D. Wald Papers, Rare Book and Manuscript Library, Butler Library, Columbia University, New York City New York, cited in Feld, *Lillian Wald*, 224.

**114** Daniels, *Always a Sister*, 93–5.

**115** Wald, *Windows on Henry Street*, 25. Merriam-Webster defines a walking delegate as "a labor union representative appointed to visit members and their places of employment, to secure enforcement of union rules and agreements, and at times to represent the union in dealing with employers" (accessed October 1, 2019, www.merriam-webster.com).

**116** Wald, *The House on Henry Street*, 282.

**117** Cyrus Adler, *Jacob H. Schiff: His Life and Letters*, vol. 1 (New York: Doubleday, Doran, 1928), 389.

**118** S. J. Kleinberg, *Women in the United States 1830–1945* (New Brunswick: Rutgers University Press, 1999), 105.

**119** Lillian D. Wald, "Organization Amongst Working Women," *Annals of the American Academy of Political and Social Science* 27, no. 3 (May 1, 1906): 638–45.

**120** Jane Bernard Powers, "Leonora O'Reilly," *American National Biography Online*, accessed September 24, 2018, www.anb.org.

**121** For a description of the fire and first-person accounts, see *Remembering The 1911 Triangle Factory Fire,* Cornell University, Kheel Center, accessed October 12, 2018, https://trianglefire.ilr.cornell.edu.

**122** Wald, *The House on Henry Street*, 206.

**123** "Children's Bureau," December 26, 1908, LWN, Microfilm, Reel 24; Michael B. Katz, *In the Shadow of the Poorhouse: A Social History of Welfare in America* (New York: Basic Books, 1986), 117. Katz writes succinctly about how and why children's issues became a magnet that attracted a broad coalition of social reformers.

**124** Wald, *The House on Henry Street*, 96.

**125** "Lillian D. Wald Playground," *NYC Parks.com*, accessed October 17, 2019, www.nycgovparks.org.

**126** "Seward Park Is Opened; Mayor Low Speaks to Vast Crowd Gathered in the Rain," *New York Times*, October 18, 1903.

127 Wald, *The House on Henry Street*, 132–3.

128 Wald, *The House on Henry Street*, 120; E. E. Farrell, "What New York City Does for Its Problem Children," *Ungraded* 11, no. 5 (1925); "Emotional and Intellectual Problems of School Years," S. C. A. A. News 13, no. 8 (May 1925), 7; for more on Farrell, see Cheryl Hanley-Maxwell and Lana Collet-Klingenberg, *Education* (Los Angeles: Sage Publications, 2011) and Kimberly E. Kode, *Elizabeth Farrell and the History of Special Education* (Arlington: Council for Exceptional Children, 2002).

129 Lillian Wald, "The Feeding of School Children," *Charities and the Commons: The Official Organ of the Charity Organization Society of the City of New York*, June 13, 1908, 372.

130 Mary K. Simkhovitch, "Trained Nurses in Public School Service," *The Commons*, July 1934, 13, ACL, Box 190, Folder 18; Lavinia L. Dock, "Training Nurses in Public School Service," ca. 1903, ACL, Box 190, Folder 6; Wald, *The House on Henry Street*, 46–8.

131 Wald, *The House on Henry Street*, 51–2; for more information on Rogers, see Lina L. Rogers, "Some Phases of School Nursing," *American Journal of Nursing* 8, no. 12 (September 1908): 966–74.

132 Catherine A. Paul, "National Child Labor Committee (NCLC): Founded April 25, 1904," *VCU Libraries Social Welfare History Project*, accessed October 17, 2019, https://socialwelfare.library.vcu.edu.

133 Kriste Lindenmeyer, "Children's Bureau," *VCU Libraries Social Welfare History Project*, accessed October 17, 2019, https://socialwelfare.library.vcu.edu; Wald, *The House on Henry Street*, 163–4; Lillian Wald, "Theodore Roosevelt—the 'Social Worker'"; Paul U. Kellogg, speech at the memorial service for Lillian Wald at Carnegie Hall, 1940, LWN, Microfilm, Reel 1. The actual details and the dates differ in various accounts as to exactly how the visit to Roosevelt was arranged and exactly when it was, but, historians agree that Wald and Kelley spearheaded the idea.

134 Kriste Lindenmeyer, *"A Right to Childhood": The U.S. Children's Bureau and Child Welfare, 1912–46* (Champaign: University of Illinois Press, 1997): 1, 9–17; Wald, *The House on Henry Street*, 165; Lillian Wald, "Address to the House Committee Hearing on Establishing a Federal Children's Bureau," 1909, in Coss, *Lillian D. Wald*, 69.

135 National Child Labor Committee Collection, Library of Congress, accessed August 15, 2019, www.loc.gov.

136 See "ACF History," *Administration for Children & Families*, accessed October 22, 2019, www.acf.hhs.gov; *The Children's Bureau Legacy: Ensuring the Right to Childhood* (Washington, DC: The Children's Bureau, US Department of Health & Human Services, 2012).

137 Wald, *The House on Henry Street*, 167.

138 Daniels, *Always a Sister*, 112.

139 Ibid., 3, 113.

140 See Mary E. Garofalo and Elizabeth Fee, "Lavinia Dock (1858–1956): Picketing, Parading, and Protesting," *American Journal of Public Health* 105, no. 2 (February 2015): 276–7.

141 H. H. Russell, "Ten Thousand Women March for the Right to Vote," *HERB: Resources for Teachers*, accessed October 17, 2019, http://herb.ashp.cuny.edu.

142 Wald, *The House on Henry Street*, 266–7.

143 Daniels, *Always a Sister*, 122–3. The quote is from a letter Wald wrote on November 13, 1917.

144 Diner, *In the Almost Promised Land*, 183.

145 Ibid., 118.

146 "Nation's Premier Civil Rights Organization," *NAACP*, accessed October 12, 2018, www.naacp.org; Feld, *Lillian Wald*, 88.

147 Mary White Ovington, "How the National Association for the Advancement of Colored People Began," *The Crisis*, August 1914, 186.

148 Wald, *Windows on Henry Street*, 49.

149 Diner, *In the Almost Promised Land*, 134.

150 "10,000 See Pageant of Henry St. Life," *New York Times*, June 8, 1913.

151 Philip Davis and Grace Kroll, *Street-Land: Its Little People and Big Problems* (Boston: Small, Maynard & Company, 1915), 267–8.

152 *1893–1913 A STREET PAGEANT presented by the members of The Henry Street Settlement to celebrate the twentieth anniversary of the founding of the Settlement On the Evenings of the Sixth and the Seventh of June*, VNS, Folder 20, Box 194; John Collier, "The Stage, a New World," *Survey*, June 1, 1916, 253; Davis and Kroll, *Street-Land*, 267–8; Crowley, *The Neighborhood Playhouse*, 14–15.

153 *Report of the Henry Street Settlement 1893–1913*, 16, 28, 19; Lillian Wald to Charles Evans Hughes, January 7, 1914, LWC, Box 187, Folder 45. He and others were invited to speak at an anniversary event. Notes from a January 9, 1914, special board meeting (LWC, Record Series 8, Henry Street Settlement, Box 131, Folder 4) record their names and illuminate how many worlds intersected at the Settlement: "1. The Nation: Speaker—Miss Lathrop or Miss Addams; 2. The City: Speakers—Mayor Mitchel and a) Department of Education, William Maxwell and Dr. Baker; 3. The Directors: Speaker—Mr. Schiff; 4. The Residents: Speaker—Mrs. Kell[e]y; 5. The Volunteer Workers: Speaker—Mrs. Max Morgenthau; 6. The clubs and the Neighborhood: Speaker—Mr. Lowenkrohn."

154 Henry Street Settlement, *Report of the Henry Street Settlement 1893–1913*, 27.

155 Amy Swerdlow, *Women Strike for Peace: Traditional Motherhood and Radical Politics in the 1960s* (Chicago: University of Chicago Press, 1993), 248.

156 Feld, *Lillian Wald*, 107; Swerdlow, *Women Strike for Peace*, 30, 248; Wald, *Windows on Henry Street*, 286, citing the August 30, 1914, *Herald*.

157  Feld, *Lillian Wald*, 107; Kenneth E. Miller, *From Progressive to New Dealer: Frederic C. Howe and American Liberalism* (University Park: Penn State Press, 2011), 248, citing a form letter signed by Lillian Wald in the Jane Addams Papers, Swarthmore Peace Collection.

158  Feld, *Lillian Wald*, 107–8; on Paul Kellogg, see "The Survey Journal," *Social Welfare History Project*.

159  Kellogg was speaking at Lillian Wald's memorial service at Carnegie Hall in 1940. LWN, Microfilm Reel 1; Benjamin F. Shearer, *Home Front Heroes: A Biographical Dictionary of Americans during Wartime* (Santa Barbara: Greenwood, 2006), 834.

160  Lillian D. Wald to President Woodrow Wilson, November 25, 1915, LWN, Microfilm Reel 1, Box 2.

161  Feld, *Lillian Wald*, 113–4.

162  Wald, *The House on Henry Street*, 79–80; for more on settlements and the arts, see Rebecca A. Sayles, "Cultural Development in an Immigrant Community: Arts Education through the Settlement Movement," *Journal of Arts Management, Law and Society* 23, no. 1 (Spring 1993).

163  Crowley, *The Neighborhood Playhouse*, 4–6; John P. Harrington, *The Life of the Neighborhood Playhouse on Grand Street* (Syracuse: Syracuse University Press, 2007), 8.

164  Linda J. Tomko, *Dancing Class: Gender, Ethnicity, and Social Divides in American Dance, 1890–1920* (Bloomington: Indiana University Press), 111; Sayles, "Cultural Development in an Immigrant Community," 15–24. For more in general on the Lewisohn sisters and their work at Henry Street from their perspective, see Crowley, *The Neighborhood Playhouse*.

165  Robert Francis Egan, "The History of the Music School of the Henry Street Settlement" (PhD diss., New York University, 1967), 147; "The group had no theater," recalled John Collier in a 1916 article in the *Survey*. "It worked in the club rooms and gymnasium of the Henry Street Settlement, building all its own properties and taking them down after the performances given in the gymnasium." Collier, "The Stage, a New World," 253; "The Neighborhood Playhouse," Landmarks Preservation Commission, Designation List LP-2433, March 22, 2011, 4, www.neighborhoodpreservationcenter.org; Henry Street Settlement, *Report of the Henry Street Settlement 1893–1918*, 54–5. The chapter on the Neighborhood Playhouse notes that it "began humbly at the Henry Street Settlement some twelve years ago. On a portable stage with a setting of hemlock boughs, a group of young club members by means of choral chants and rhythmic movement interpreted some of their religious traditions," and that those early festivals "have been the inspiration for much of the subsequent work."

166  Harrington, *The Life of the Neighborhood Playhouse*, 6–8, 47. Since 1976, the official name of the Neighborhood Playhouse has been the Harry De Jur Playhouse.

167 "The Neighborhood Playhouse," *New York World*, as reprinted in Willard Grosvenor Bleyer, *How to Write Special Feature Articles: A Handbook for Reporters, Correspondents and Free-Lance Writers Who Desire to Contribute to Popular Magazines and Magazine Sections of Newspapers* (New York: Houghton Mifflin Company, 1920), 240.

168 "Jephthah's Great, Great, Great Grandchildren," *Survey*, February 20, 1915, 547.

169 Wald, *The House on Henry Street*, 186.

170 Lillian Wald, "Women and War," an address given at the Cooper Union in February of 1915, in Coss, *Lillian D. Wald*, 88.

171 "The Neighborhood Playhouse," *New York World*.

172 Crowley, *The Neighborhood Playhouse*, 41.

173 *The New York Supplement* (St. Paul: West Publishing Company, 1917), 339.

174 Wald, *Windows on Henry Street*, 306.

175 Collier, "The Stage, a New World," 253–4.

176 "The Neighborhood Playhouse," Landmarks Preservation Commission. The Playhouse was built between 1913 and 1915 by the architects Ingalls & Hoffman.

177 "Milestones: 1914–1920/American Entry into World War I, 1917," *US Department of State, Office of the Historian*, accessed August 26, 2014, https://history.state.gov.

178 Wald, *Windows on Henry Street*, 305.

179 "New York Sees 20,000 Parade for Red Cross," *Red Cross Bulletin*, 1, no. 23 (October 9, 1917).

180 Wald, *Windows on Henry Street*, 306.

181 Feld, *Lillian Wald*, 113. See also Judith Rosenbaum, "'The Call to Action': Margaret Sanger, the Brownsville Jewish Women, and Political Activism," in Marion A. Kaplan and Deborah Dash Moore, eds., *Gender and Jewish History* (Bloomington: Indiana University Press, 2011): 261–3.

182 Wald, *Windows on Henry Street*, 305.

183 "Report of Head Worker of Henry Street Directors' Meeting, Oct. 16, 1917," VNS.

184 "Memo for Report of the Head Resident, Henry Street Settlement Directors' Meeting, Dec. 11, 1917," Directors' Minutes, 134, VNS, Box 131, Folder 3.

185 "Victory Day Celebrated by Millions in New York; All Nations Wild With Joy," *Evening World*, November 11, 1918; on the flu's impact, see Gina Kolata, *Flu: The Story of the Great Influenza Pandemic of 1918 and the Search for the Virus that Caused It* (New York: Touchstone, 1999).

186 Permelia Munan Doty, "A Retrospect of the Influenza Epidemic," *Public Health Nurse* 11 (August 1919): 950–1; Lillian Wald to Royal Copeland, October 4, 1918, LWN, Box 3, Reel 2, as cited in Arlene W. Keeling, "Alert to the Necessities of the Emergency': U. S. Nursing During the 1918 Influenza Pandemic," *Public Health Reports*, 125, supp. 3 (2010), 105–12.

187 Lillian Wald, "Influenza: When the City is a Great Field Hospital," *Survey*, February 14, 1920, 1, LWN, Box 3, Reel 2, as cited in Keeling, "Alert to the Necessities of the Emergency."

188 Royal Copeland to Lillian Wald, December 2, 1918, LWN, Box 3, Reel 2, as cited in Keeling, "Alert to the Necessities of the Emergency."

189 Jeffrey S. Gurock, *Jews in Gotham: New York Jews in a Changing City, 1920–2010* (New York: New York University Press, 2012), 26.

190 For the shift in climate, see McGerr, *A Fierce Discontent.*

191 "Lillian Wald," *Women of Valor,* Jewish Women's Archive, accessed October 16, 2018, http://jwa.org.

192 Shearer, *Home Front Heroes,* 834.

193 For Wald and her support of the Russian Revolution, see Feld, *Lillian Wald,* 123–8.

194 New York Legislature, Joint Legislative Committee to Investigate Seditious Activities, *SNAC,* accessed July 1, 2019, https://snaccooperative.org.

195 Shearer, *Home Front Heroes,* 834.

196 Mary Stillman Harkness to Lillian Wald, July 3, 1919, LWC, Box 56, Folder 1, as cited in David Huyssen, *Progressive Inequality: Rich and Poor in New York, 1890–1920* (Cambridge: Harvard College, 2014), 148; Lillian Wald to Lavinia Dock, August 1919, LWN, Box 3, Folder 4, as cited in Beatrice Siegel, *Lillian Wald of Henry Street* (New York: Macmillan, 1983), 152.

197 Directors' Minutes, 1903–18, October 1919, VNS, Box 132, Folder 4.

198 Michael B. Fabricant and Robert Fisher, *Settlement Houses Under Siege: The Struggle to Sustain Community Organizations in New York City* (New York City: Columbia University Press, 2002): 33–5.

199 Meeting notes, October 6, 1925, VNS, Box 132, Folder 36.

200 Meeting notes, November 28, 1927, VNS, Box 132, Folder 47.

201 Clarke A. Chambers, *Seedtime of Reform: American Social Service and Social Action 1918–1933* (Minneapolis: University of Minnesota Press, 1963), 126–8; Paul U. Kellogg, "The Unsettling Settlements," *Survey* 60, no. 4 (May 15, 1928), 218.

202 Harrington, *The Life of the Neighborhood Playhouse,* 145–6.

203 Ibid., 121, 124, 209, 156–7.

204 Ibid., 7–8.

205 "The Neighborhood Playhouse . . . For release Monday, April 11, 1927," VNS, Box 151, Folder 26.

206 Ibid.; Harrington, *The Life of the Neighborhood Playhouse,* 268–9.

207 See Harrington, *The Life of the Neighborhood Playhouse,* 11.

208 Shannon L. Green, "Controversy and Conflict in the Henry Street Settlement Music School, 1927–1935," *Women and Music: A Journal of Gender and Culture,* 8 (2004): 74; Helen Hall, *Unfinished Business in Neighborhood and Nation* (New York: Macmillan, 1971), 120–4.

209 "Music in the Service of Charity," *New York Times,* March 15, 1931.

210 Green, "Controversy and Conflict in the Henry Street Settlement Music School," 75; Lillian Wald to Walter White, May 20, 1935, NAACP Admin. Files, C-362, cited in Diner, *In the Almost Promised Land,* 182, 198.

**211** Green, "Controversy and Conflict in the Henry Street Settlement Music School," 75.

**212** Ibid., 75.

**213** Gary Louis Palmer, "The Hochstein School of Music & Dance: History, Mission, and Vision" (PhD diss., Eastman School of Music, University of Rochester, 2010), 29–30.

**214** Green, "Controversy and Conflict in the Henry Street Settlement Music School," 77.

**215** Marylisa Kinsley, "The More Things Change in Home Care, the More They Stay the Same," *Nurse.com*, November 19, 2007, http://news.nurse.com.

**PART 2: MOVING WITH THE TIMES**

**1** "2,000 Pay Honor to Lillian Wald," *New York Times*, May 24, 1943.

**2** Ibid.

**3** Wald, *Windows on Henry Street*, 227–30.

**4** Ibid., 227.

**5** "Henry Street Settlement and the Depression," unpublished manuscript, HSC; Suzanne Wasserman, "Our Alien Neighbors": Coping with the Depression on the Lower East Side," *American Jewish History* 88, no. 2 (June 2000), 209–32.

**6** Dorothy Day, cited in Studs Terkel, *Hard Times: An Oral History of the Depression* (New York: The New Press, 1970, repr. 1986), 291.

**7** Christina D. Romer and Richard H. Pells, "Great Depression: Economy," *Encyclopaedia Britannica*, accessed September 14, 2018, www.britannica.com; Chambers, *Seedtime of Reform*, 202.

**8** "Report by Mr. Hesley" on the unemployment situation (for Henry Street Settlement board meeting), November 5, 1930, Box 132, Folder 57.

**9** Ibid.

**10** Lillian Wald, "What Keeps the Nurses Going?" *Survey*, November 15, 1932, 590–1.

**11** *American Jewish History*, vol. 8 (Baltimore: John Hopkins University Press for the American Jewish Historical Society, 2000), 227.

**12** Nunez and Sribnick, *The Poor Among Us*, 162.

**13** Susan Quinn, *Furious Improvisation: How the WPA and a Cast of Thousands Made High Art out of Desperate Times* (New York: Walker Publishing, 2008), 5.

**14** "Nursing Service Aids Its Millionth Patient," *New York Times*, July 18, 1932; Judith Ann Trolander, *Settlement Houses and the Great Depression* (Detroit: Wayne State University Press, 1975), 43; Judith Trolander, email to author, September 20, 2013.

**15** "Henry Street Settlement Pioneers: Lillian Wald and Helen Hall," *Social Welfare History Project*, accessed September 14, 2018, www.socialwelfarehistory.com. An editor's note reads: "This entry is an original document prepared and distributed by Henry Street Settlement sometime in the late 1960's when Bertram Beck was the Executive Director (1967–1977)."

**16** Hall, *Unfinished Business*, ix.

**17** "Henry Street Settlement Pioneers: Lillian Wald and Helen Hall," *Social Welfare History Project.*

**18** *Memorial Program in Honor of Helen Hall, Tuesday, April 12, 1983, at the Harry De Jur Henry Street Settlement Playhouse*, HSC. For more on the National Federation of Settlements see John E. Hansan, "National Federation of Settlements," *VCU Libraries Social Welfare History Project*, accessed September 28, 2014, www.socialwelfarehistory.com.

**19** Susan Jenkins Brown, *The Helen Hall Settlement Papers: A Descriptive Bibliography of Community Studies and Other Reports, 1928–1958* (New York; Henry Street Settlement, 1959); Judith Ann Trolander, "Changing Methods of Reform and Advocacy in the Settlement House Movement from the Great Depression to the War on Poverty," unpublished manuscript, 1993, 3, HSC. The paper was delivered at Henry Street Settlement on March 25, 1993, on the occasion of its centennial celebration.

**20** Judith Trolander, email to author, September 20, 2013.

**21** Ruth and Ralph Tefferteller, social workers at Henry Street from 1946 to 1967, also described how Hall "used humor to fight; she used humor to win. . . . These were the secret weapons of her powerful effectiveness in bringing fresh thinking and 'besettedness' for social change in neighborhoods and in the nation as a whole." *Memorial Program*, 1983.

**22** Telegram and notes to Helen Hall, HHP, Box 86, Folder 8.

**23** National Federation of Settlements and Neighborhood Centers, Unemployment Committee, *Case Studies of Unemployment* (Philadelphia: University of Pennsylvania Press, 1931).

**24** National Federation of Settlements and Neighborhood Centers, Unemployment Committee, *Case Studies of Unemployment.*

**25** Helen Hall, "On Family Life in America: Hard Times Lay Heavy Load," *New York Times*, December 3, 1933; Trolander, "Changing Methods of Reform and Activism," 2.

**26** Nunez and Sribnick, *The Poor Among Us*, 166–8; Trolander, "Changing Methods of Reform and Advocacy," 2.

**27** Helen I. Clark, *Social Legislation* (New York: Appleton-Century-Crofts, Inc., 1957), 552; Wald, *Windows on Henry Street*, 326.

**28** Chambers, *Seedtime of Reform*, 255; Marjorie Feld, "Lillian D. Wald: 1867–1940," accessed November 1, 2019, jwa.org.

**29** "Social Security History," *Social Security Administration*, accessed September 14, 2018, www.ssa.gov; Susan Ware, *Notable American Women: A Biographical Dictionary Completing the Twentieth Century*, vol. 5 (Cambridge: Harvard University Press, 2004), 267; Judith Trolander, email to author, September 20, 2013.

**30** Brown, *The Helen Hall Settlement Papers,* 3; for more about Hall's prolific work, see Trolander, *Settlement Houses and the Great Depression.*

**31** Trolander, "Changing Methods of Reform and Advocacy," 10.

**32** Hall, *Unfinished Business*, 277–8.

**33** Douglass W. Orr and Jean Walker Orr, *Health Insurance With Medical Care, The British Experience* (New York: Macmillan, 1938); Henry Street Settlement, "When Sickness Strikes a Family," 1951, reprinted in 1952 in *Building America's Health*, a report to President Truman by the Commission on the Health Needs of the Nation, as part of a five-volume issue; Susan Ware, ed., "Helen Hall," *Notable American Women: A Biographical Dictionary Completing the Twentieth Century* (Cambridge: The Belknap Press of Harvard University, 2004), 267; Hall, *Unfinished Business*, 287.

**34** This quote is from a letter that Mayor Fiorello La Guardia wrote to Helen Hall in July 1944, which is in HHP, Box 12, Folder 5. Several letters in the same box suggest how he drew on Helen Hall's expertise and convey a sense of their friendly relationship. A December 9, 1936, letter from La Guardia to Hall asks her to attend a meeting on December 15, 1936, at the Board of Estimate chamber, City Hall, on housing conditions in New York City; he says he wants her to come because there is a "recent rapid reduction in vacancies in those houses which are subject to the tenement house law," and surveys show a shortage; he wants to "go forward in housing and not backward." In another instance, on March 17, 1937, La Guardia writes to thank Hall for her "painstaking and sympathetic investigation of the matter of the Suffolk Street fire sufferers" and says "I need not tell you how greatly I appreciate it." On June 3, 1937, she replies in affirmative to his request for her to be on the "Local Sponsoring Committee in connection with the Annual Meeting of the American Public Health Associates this fall."

**35** "Robert Wagner: A Featured Biography," *United States Senate*, accessed June 1, 2019, www.senate.gov.

**36** "Life and Legacy of Herbert H. Lehman," *Columbia University Libraries*, accessed June 1, 2019, https://library.columbia.edu; Duane Tananbaum, *Herbert H. Lehman: A Political Biography* (Albany: State University of New York Press, 2016), 1; Trolander, "Changing Methods of Reform and Advocacy," 6–7.

**37** "Helen Hall," *VCU Libraries Social Welfare History Project*, accessed October 16, 2018, https://socialwelfare.library.vcu.edu; Trolander, "Changing Methods of Reform and Advocacy," 5–6.

**38** Hall, *Unfinished Business*, 14.

**39** "January 24th 1934, Station W.I.N.S.," HHP, Box 34, Folder 3.

**40** "Dickstein Says Settlement Aids Reds for CWA," *Jewish Telegraph Agency*, June 29, 1934; Ted Morgan, *McCarthyism in Twentieth-Century America* (New York: Random House Publishing Group, 2004), 146–8. As of 2019, a small stretch of land below Grand Street on the Lower East Side still bears the name it was given in 1963 in honor of the congressman: Dickstein Plaza.

**41** Hall noted that the "arts flourished enormously in WPA days, which brought us many teachers," Hall, *Unfinished Business*, 126; Steven Haifeh and Gregory White

Smith, *Jackson Pollock: An American Saga* (New York: Clarkson N. Potter, Inc., 1989): 264, 271; Henry Adams, *Tom and Jack: The Intertwined Lives of Thomas Hart Benton and Jackson Pollock* (New York: Bloomsbury Press, 2009), 35–7.

42  "Headworker's Report," November 15, 1935, VNS, Box 133, Folder 6; "Memorandum on Workers' Education Center," March 9, 1936, HSR, Box 68, Folder 3; "Dickstein Says Settlement Aids Reds for CWA," *Jewish Telegraph Agency*; "Address by Helen Hall, President/National Federation of Settlements," given in Montreal, June 1935, HHP, Box 34, Folder 4.

43  Lizabeth Cohen, *A Consumer's Republic: The Politics of Mass Consumption in Postwar America* (New York: Vintage, 2003), 36.

44  An obituary for Helen Hall in the January 1983 issue of the journal *The Consumer-Farmer Milk Cooperative* describes her extensive work on behalf of affordable milk for low-income households. It notes that in 1934, she was appointed to the Advisory Committee of the State's Milk Control Board. In 1936, she joined the Milk Consumers Protective Committee and organized a group of settlement mothers who were "representative proof that milk consumption was directly related to income and that low-income households suffered from a lack of it. One famous gathering at Foley Square, in November of 1937, amidst baby carriages, cows, farmers, and city milk consumers, led to the formation of the Consumer-Farmer Milk Cooperative which would quickly become the 'yardstick' for milk prices and the nemesis of the milk trust. In June of 1943, Helen became a member of its Board of Directors, a position she held until her death on August 31, 1982." See "Helen Hall, Consumer-Farmer Board Member, Dies at Age 90," *Consumer-Farmer Cooperator*, no. 48 (January 1983), HSC.

45  Tom Kriger, "The New York Milk Strikes," *The Milk House International Literary Dairy Farming Column*, accessed September 30, 2018, www.themilkhouse.org. For a discussion of the milk strikes and settlements' role, see Thomas J. Kriger, "A Very Unusual Partnership: The Consumer-Farmer Milk Cooperative in New York City, 1938–1971," *New York History* 80, no. 3 (July 1999).

46  In a tribute to Hall, Persia Campbell, "Former Consumer Counsel to the Governor of the State of New York," mentions Hall's march through city streets with a cow and efforts by the Settlement's neighbors to dramatize the milk dilemma. "Helen Hall, Consumer-Farmer Board Member, Dies at Age 90," *Consumer-Farmer Cooperator*.

47  This 1934 study is described in Brown, *The Helen Hall Settlement Papers*, see p. 9, "15. Milk Consumption in Relation to Family Income. Typed report (15 pp.) and 4-page pictorial statistic graphs (offset)."

48  "Statement by Helen Hall to Members of N.Y. State Milk Advisory Committee, May 1934," HHP, Box 88, Folder 1.

49  Robert Justin Goldstein, ed., *Little 'Red Scares': Anti-Communism and Political Repression in the United States, 1921–1946* (London: Routledge, 2016), 221.

50  "Red Charges Denied by Consumer Group," *New York Times*, December 13, 1939.

51 Hall, *Unfinished Business*, 139–40; "This Bank Specializes in 'Bad Risks,'" *Reader's Digest*, February 1954, 135–6; Deborah Beck, interview with the author, April 6, 2015.

52 Helen Hall, "Old-Law Tenements: Henry Street Nurses Find Some Deplorable Conditions" (letter to the editor), *New York Times*, March 24, 1936.

53 Nicholas Dagen Bloom, *Public Housing that Worked: New York in the Twentieth Century* (Philadelphia: University of Pennsylvania Press, 2009), 4.

54 Obituary, Alfred Rheinstein, *New York Times,* May 28, 1974.

55 "Mary Kingsbury Simkhovitch (September 8, 1867–November 15, 1951): Social Worker, Progressive, Social Reformer, Academic and Founder of Greenwich House in New York City," *The Social Welfare History Project*, accessed October 17, 2019, www.socialwelfarehistory.com.

56 Bloom, *Public Housing that Worked*, 46.

57 Ann L. Buttenwieser, "Shelter for What and for Whom? On the Route Toward Vladeck Houses, 1930 to 1940," *Journal of Urban History* 12, no. 4 (August 1, 1986): 391; Bloom, *Public Housing that Worked*, 55–9.

58 Bloom, *Public Housing that Worked*, 59; *Vladeck Houses: A Lesson in Neighborhood History* (New York: New York Housing Authority, 1940), 4, 13.

59 *Vladeck Houses: A Lesson in Neighborhood History*, 3–4.

60 Ibid., 4–6.

61 Buttenwieser, "Shelter for What and For Whom?" 393, 409.

62 "About," *Henry Street Settlement*, accessed September 14, 2014, www.henrystreet.org; *Vladeck Houses: A Lesson in Neighborhood History*, 4, describes how nearby settlements and churches provided various tenant activities.

63 "She's the Treat Keeping the Community Together," *Villager*, January 12, 2019, www.thevillager.com; "President's Awards," *FIT, State University of New York*, accessed November 1, 2019, www.fitnyc.edu.

64 Flier, HSR, Box 43, Folder 1.

65 Sunday Night at Nine Committee to Helen Hall, March 19, 1938, HSR, Box 43, Folder 1; Program, "Sunday Nights at Nine presents A Play on the Progress of Organized Labor," Thursday, May 19, 1938, HSR, Box 44, Folder 6.

66 See Green, "Controversy and Conflict in the Henry Street Settlement Music School," 79–82.

67 See S. Margaret William McCarthy, "Grace Spofford: Educator, Internationalist, and Organization Woman," *Journal of the International Alliance for Women in Music* (February 1996), 17–21; Wald, *Windows on Henry Street*, 14.

68 Elizabeth Bergman Crist, *Music for the Common Man: Aaron Copland During the Depression and War* (New York: Oxford University Press, 2009), 15.

69 H. Howard Taubman, "'Second Hurricane': New 'Play Opera' by Aaron Copland to Have Its Premiere Next Season," *New York Times*, July 26, 1936; Egan, "The History of the Music School of the Henry Street Settlement," 166.

70 McCarthy, "Grace Spofford: Educator, Internationalist, and Organization Woman," 17–21; Robert F. Egan, *Music and the Arts in the Community: The Community Music School in America* (Metuchen: Scarecrow Press, 1989), 181.

71 "The Music School of the Henry Street Settlement, Report of Director, June 1937, for School Year, September 21st, 1936, to June 12th, 1937," HSM, Box 3, Folder 4.

72 See McCarthy, "Grace Spofford: Educator, Internationalist, and Organization Woman." As McCarthy writes of Spofford, "Although many of the students had made names for themselves in the world of music, Spofford's philosophy in educating the underprivileged was that 'we are just as proud of the ones who marry and raise families or follow careers which have nothing to do with music.'"

73 These reminiscences are from the memorial service for Lillian Wald at Carnegie Hall, 1940, LWN, Microfilm, Reel 1, with the exception of the remarks by Samuel Dickstein, which are from "Remarks of Hon. Samuel Dickstein of New York in the House of Representatives, Thursday, September 19, 1940," *Social Welfare History Archives*, accessed October 17, 2019, https://socialwelfare.library.vcu.edu.

74 Hall, *Unfinished Business*, 187.

75 Preface by Helen Hall in Jeremy Larner, ed., *The Addict in the Street. Edited, and with an introduction by Jeremy Larner from tape recordings collected by Ralph Tefferteller* (New York: Grove Press, 1965), 26.

76 This 1941 list included Joseph Willetts of the Rockefeller Foundation; Manhattan Borough President Stanley M. Isaacs; Shelby M. Harrison, general director, Russell Sage Foundation; Samuel Grafton, *New York Post*; Dorothy Bellanca, on the general executive board of the Amalgamated Clothing Workers of America; and Joseph H. Willits, director of the Division of Social Sciences at the Rockefeller Foundation. HHP, Box 98, Folder 8.

77 Hall, *Unfinished Business*, 207; "Luther Halsey Gulick II Papers," Baruch College Archives, www.baruch.cuny.edu; "Luther Gulick Papers," *Harry S. Truman Presidential Library and Museum*, accessed September 18, 2018, www.trumanlibrary.org.

78 Hall, *Unfinished Business,* 207.

79 Ibid., 207–8.

80 A December 2, 1942, report on Settlement activities notes that they are cutting back on day and night home delivery service due to the lack of available nurses as a direct result of the war, LWC, Box 133, Folder 47; Faville's comment is from a January 27, 1943 report, LWC, Box 133, Folder 48.

81 This information is found in LWC, Box 133, Folder 43.

82 A June 10, 1942, report notes that Hall was to be given leave of absence for one year to go abroad with the American Red Cross. She returned in May 1943. LWC, Box 133, Folder 45.

83 *Our Boys*, Henry Street Settlement, July 1944, HSC.

84 Ibid.

**85** Hall, *Unfinished Business*, 187; "Report on the Henry Street Settlement Home Planning Workshops & Craft Rooms in Vladeck Houses," undated, HHP, Box 90, Folder 6.

**86** Hall, *Unfinished Business*, 191.

**87** Ibid.; Robert Hanley, "Jacob Markowitz, 72, 22 Years on Bench," *New York Times*, September 7, 1976.

**88** Judith Karp, "Galamian—A Great Violin Teacher," *New York Times*, April 26, 1981; Egan, "The History of the Music School of the Henry Street Settlement," 312; "Annual Report of Director, Season 1941–42," HSM, "Music School of Henry Street Settlement Annual Report of Director, Season 1942–3," HSM.

**89** Barrie B. Witham, *The Federal Theatre Project: A Case Study* (New York: Cambridge University Press, 2003), 15; Paula Becker, *Federal Theatre Project*, 2002, accessed October 10, 2018, www.historylink.org.

**90** Martin Canin interview, November 3, 1993, Lower East Side Oral History Collection, Tamiment Library, New York University, New York City, accessed April 1, 2019, http://wp.nyu.edu.

**91** Jerry Stiller, *Married to Laughter: A Love Story* (New York: Simon and Schuster, 2000), 52–3.

**92** "Playhouse of Henry Street Settlement 1943–44 Season," HSR, Box 42, Folder 10.

**93** Karen Buhler-Wilkerson, "The Call to the Nurse: Visiting Nurse Service of New York 1893–1943," 15, and Shirley H. Fondiller, "The Promise and the Reality: Visiting Nurse Service of New York 1944–1993," 17, in Ellen Paul Denker, ed., *Healing at Home* (New York: Visiting Nurse Service of New York, 1993); "Henry Street Groups Divide Their Service," *New York Times*, May 25, 1944.

**94** To learn about the work of the Visiting Nurse Service of New York today, visit its website at www.vnsny.org.

**95** Hall, *Unfinished Business*, 84–9.

**96** "Partnership has always seemed to me to be one of the best words in the English language," said Hall; "It connotes so many possibilities in human relationships, and I have thought of it as of necessity applying to the board, staff, and neighbors of a settlement." Hall, *Unfinished Business*, 84.

**97** Hall, *Unfinished Business*, 90.

**98** "Overview of the Post-War Era," Digital History ID 2923, *Digital History*, accessed August 6, 2019, www.digitalhistory.uh.edu.

**99** Jean Ritchie, *Dulcimer People* (New York: Oak Publications, 1975), 9.

**100** An October 1945 letter from the University of the State of New York, State Education Department, Division of Industrial and Technical Education, to the Music School of the Henry Street Settlement, 8 Pitt Street, says that under Section 200, the school is approved for veterans (pertaining to the GI Bill of Rights), HSM, Box 1, Folder 4.

**101** Report to "Helen Hall, The Board of Directors of Henry Street Settlement, and the future Director of the Playhouse" from "Esther Porter Lane, Playhouse

Director, October 1943 to June 1946 and members of the Playhouse Staff for 1945–1946," HSR, Box 42, Folder 11.

**102** Ibid., 43–44.

**103** "Alwin Nikolais Biography," video, the Kennedy Center Honors Medal of the Arts presentation, 1987, uploaded December 4, 2007, www.youtube.com/watch?v=y8-X2SNL1iA.

**104** "Murray Louis," *Nikolais/Louis Foundation for Dance, Inc.*, accessed September 20, 2018, www.nikolaislouis.org; "Alwin Nikolais Biography," video. Louis, notes the website, "became a driving force in the evolution of the aesthetic and pedagogic theory, which today is known as the Nikolais/Louis technique."

**105** "Murray Louis," *Nikolais/Louis Foundation for Dance, Inc.*; "Alwin Nikolais Biography," video.

**106** "Phyllis Lamhut," video, *80 Faces. Eighty Years. Eighty Stories*, produced by Tiffany Ellis, edited by Lauren Ella Renck, posted June 11, 2013, https://americandance-festival.org.

**107** Helen Hall to Mrs. Thorman, June 15, 1993, HSR, Box 57, Folder 15.

**108** *Good News* 1, no. 4, July 1955, HSC.

**109** Graham Hodges, "Lower East Side," in Kenneth T. Jackson, ed., *The Encyclopedia of New York City* (New Haven: Yale University Press; New York: The New-York Historical Society, 1995), 697–8. The entry notes that the neighborhood first became a racially integrated section of the city after World War II, when thousands of Black and Puerto Rican newcomers moved in.

**110** Murray E. Ortoff, *Making New Neighbors in an Old Neighborhood* (New York: Henry Street Settlement), 1958 (mimeographed report), HSC; Miranda J. Martinez, *Power at the Roots: Gentrification, Community Gardens, and the Puerto Ricans of the Lower East Side* (Lanham, Maryland: Lexington Books, 2010), 14.

**111** Robert Halpern, *Fragile Families, Fragile Solutions: A History of Supportive Services for Families in Poverty* (New York: Columbia University Press, 1999), 102–3.

**112** Helen Hall, preface to Larner, *The Addict in the Street*, 26.

**113** Hall, *Unfinished Business*, xv.

**114** Noel A. Cazenave, *Impossible Democracy: The Unlikely Success of the War on Poverty Community Action Programs* (Albany: State University of New York Press, 2007), 21, notes that "children's court and police department statistics showed that youth offenses in the MFY project target area more than doubled from 1951 through 1960, a faster rate than for both all of Manhattan and the city as a whole" (Cazenave is speaking about the Lower East Side); Hall, *Unfinished Business*, 226–30.

**115** "Henry Street Settlement," in David Goldfield, ed., *Encyclopedia of American Urban History* (Thousand Oaks: SAGE Publications, 2006).

**116** Hall, *Unfinished Business*, 108–9.

**117** Hall, *Unfinished Business*, 64.

**118** "Funeral Service for Lieut. Peter Lehman Not Yet Set," *Jewish Telegraphic Agency* newswire, April 12, 1944, *JTA Archive*, www.jta.org.

**119** "About," *Henry Street Settlement*; "Lehmans Dedicate a Youth Center as Memorial to Son Killed in War," *New York Times*, November 29, 1948.

**120** Frank Boyden to Helen Hall, December 6, 1948 (dictated December 2, 1948), HSC.

**121** Helen Hall, Henry Street Settlement press release, January 10, 1964, HSC; Joseph Wershba, "A Poor Boy Who Got Rich Remembers a Settlement House," *New York Post*, November 30, 1961; "The Guttman Family Legacy," *Stella and Charles Guttman Foundation*, accessed October 4, 2019, http://guttmanfoundation.org.

**122** *Arts-for-Living at Henry Street Settlement*, undated [1966], HSC.

**123** Eric C. Schneider, *Vampires, Dragons, and Egyptian Kings: Youth Gangs in Postwar New York* (Princeton: Princeton University Press, 1999), 230, citing Mobilization for Youth, *A Proposal for the Prevention and Control of Delinquency by Expanding Opportunities* (New York: Mobilization for Youth, 1961), 9–10.

**124** Hall, preface to Larner, *The Addict in the Street*, 27; "Ralph Tefferteller," *VCU Libraries Social Welfare History Project*, accessed October 17, 2018, https://socialwelfare.library.vcu.edu.

**125** Larner, *The Addict in the Street*, 16; 43–93.

**126** Ibid., 14.

**127** Robert Fisher and Michael Fabricant, "From Henry Street to Contracted Services: Financing the Settlement House," *Journal of Sociology & Social Welfare* 19, no. 3 (September 1, 2002), 14–15, 25.

**128** Helen Hall and Ruth Tefferteller, "Henry Street Settlement Studies: Pre-Delinquent Gangs," June 4, 1956, 3, HSC.

**129** "A Note on the Inception and Impact of Mobilization for Youth by Helen Hall, director, Henry Street Settlement," March 10, 1967, HSR, Box 80, Folder 4.

**130** "Mobilization for Youth: Its Purposes, Assumptions and Plan of Operation, Revised Edition, November, 1958" with an "introductory note by Helen Hall," HHP, Box 90, Folder 5; Martha F. Davis, *Brutal Need: Lawyers and the Welfare Rights Movement, 1960–1973* (New Haven: Yale University Press, 1995), 27.

**131** Cazenave, *Impossible Democracy*, 21–2; Hall, *Unfinished Business*, 255.

**132** Schneider, *Vampires, Dragons, and Egyptian Kings*, 201.

**133** Cazenave, *Impossible Democracy*, 22.

**134** Ibid.

**135** Hall, *Unfinished Business*, 271–2.

**136** Tamar W. Carroll, "'To Help People Learn to Fight': New York City's Mobilization for Youth and the Origins of the Community Action Programs of the War on Poverty," *The Gotham Center for New York City History*, October 8, 2015, www.gothamcenter.org; "Prepared Statement of Dr. Melvin Herman, Chief of Work Programs, Mobilization for Youth, New York, N.Y.," *Manpower Retraining: Hearings Before the Subcommittee on Employment and Manpower of the Committee on Labor and Public Welfare, United States Senate, Eighty-Eighth*

*Congress, First Session* (Washington, DC: US Government Printing Office, 1963), 137; Schneider, *Vampires, Dragons, and Egyptian Kings*, 214.

137 "New York City in Crisis," *New York Herald Tribune*, June 21, 1965; "Johnson Stumps in City and Asks a 'Great Victory,'" Homer Bigart, *New York Times*, May 29, 1964.

138 "What is Community Action? *Illinois Association of Community Action Agencies, IACAA*, accessed October 1, 2018, www.iacaanet.org; "Interview with Saul Alinsky—Part 7—Organizing the Back of the Yards: Empowering People, Not Elites," *Progress Report*, June 13, 2003.

139 Megan H. Morrissey, "The Life and Career of Helen Hall: Settlement Worker and Social Reformer in Social Work's Second Generation" (PhD diss., University of Minnesota, 1996), 246–7.

140 "Impact Beyond the Neighborhood: Visitors to the Henry Street Settlement 1964-1965-1966, A brief survey . . . With a foreword by Helen Hall, Director," Social Welfare History Archives, Tefferteller Collection, Box 7, no folder.

141 Draft, December 23, 1966, written to appear in *UNH News* of February 7, 1967, HHP, Box 36, Folder 16.

142 "A Note on the Inception and Impact of Mobilization for Youth by Helen Hall, director, Henry Street Settlement," March 10, 1967.

143 Janice Andrews, "Helen Hall (1892–1982): A Second Generation Settlement Leader," *Journal of Sociology & Social Welfare* 19, no. 2 (June 1992): 106.

144 Deborah Beck, interview with the author, April 6, 2015; "East Side Leaders Plan Movement to Settle Strike at Henry Street Settlement," *East Side News*, March 5, 1965; Morrisey, 249.

145 Helen Hall, retirement dinner speech, June 12, 1967, HHP, Box 87, Folder 1.

146 Ibid.

### PART 3: LASTING NEIGHBOR AND STEADY INFLUENCE

1 Newsletter, August 22, 1968, HSR, Box 10, Folder 13; "Groups Participating in Festival on Henry Street," typewritten page, 1968, HSR, Box 10, Folder 13.

2 Hall, *Unfinished Business*, xiv.

3 Deborah Beck, interview with the author, April 6, 2015.

4 Ibid.

5 Morrissey, "The Life and Career of Helen Hall," 253–4.

6 Deborah Beck, interview with the author, July 1, 2013.

7 "In Honor of Founder Bertram M. Beck," *Bertram M. Beck Institute*, accessed August 6, 2014, www.fordham.edu.

8 "Bertram M. Beck," *National Association of Social Workers*, accessed July 1, 2019, naswfoundation.org; Deborah Beck, interview with author, April 6, 2015; Judith Ann Trolander, *Professionalism and Social Change: From the Settlement House Movement to Neighborhood Centers, 1886 to the Present* (New York: Columbia University Press, 1987), 237.

9   Trolander, *Professionalism and Social Change*, 48–50.

10  Bertram Beck, typed manuscript, "Settlements and Community Centers," for *Encyclopedia of Social Work*, 17th edition, HSC, Box 30, Folder 8.

11  Nunez and Sribnick, *The Poor Among Us*, 198, 221.

12  Bertram M. Beck, "Knowledge and Skills in Administration of an Antipoverty Program," reprinted from *Social Work* 11, no. 3 (July 1966): 63, in *Notes from the Ghetto: Papers from the MFY Experience* (New York: Mobilization for Youth, 1966).

13  Minutes, October 14, 1970, HSC; Deborah Beck, interview with author, July 2, 2013.

14  Deborah Beck, interview with author April 6, 2015.

15  Minutes, June 22, 1970, HSC. The name change was not permanent.

16  Rafael Jaquez, interview with the author, June 13, 2019; Henry Street Settlement, *Voices of Henry Street: Portrait of a Community* (New York: Henry Street Settlement, 1993), 28; "About," *Henry Street Settlement*; program, *Banquet and Presentation of the Pioneer Counselor in Training Program, Friday August 22, 1969*, HSR, Box 10, Folder 15; Minutes, November 17, 1975, HSC; "Profile: James H. Robinson, Jr.," private collection.

17  Minutes, July 13, 1970, HSC.

18  "Humans of Henry Street," *Henry Street Settlement*, accessed June 1, 2019, www. henrystreet.org; Rafael Jaquez, interview with the author, June 13, 2019; Minutes, July 13, 1970, HSC.

19  For more on CIP, see "UPS Community Internship Program," *Henry Street Settlement*, accessed October 1, 2018, www.henrystreet.org, and Robert D. Putnam and Lewis M. Feldstein with Don Cohen, *Better Together: Restoring the American Community* (New York: Simon & Schuster, 2003), 206–8.

20  Rafael Jaquez, interview with author, June 13, 2019.

21  Hall, *Unfinished Business*, 119.

22  Meeting for Playhouse Advisory Committee, April 27, 1969, HSC.

23  Cordelia Candelaria, Peter J. Garcia, and Arturo J. Aldama, eds., *Encyclopedia of Latino Popular Culture*, vol. 2 (Westport, Connecticut: Greenwood Publishing Group, 2004), 594; Alberto Sandoval-Sanchez and Nancy Saporta Stembach, *Stages of Life: Transcultural Performance and Identity in U.S. Latina Theater* (Tucson: University of Arizona Press, 2001), 62; Lorca Peress to Danny Kronenfeld, August 21, 1992, HSC.

24  "Mrs. Herbert Luria" to Bertram Beck, November 3, 1965, HSR, Box 42, Folder 7; "Procedures in the School of Dance and Drama," memo, March 4, 1970, HSR, Folder 8, describes how people came to know of the Settlement: "A) Word of mouth particularly stimulated by Alwin Nikolais' local appearances. B) Other schools refer. C) A notice of registration is sent out with catalog. . . . D) Personal contacts. . . . E) Newspaper and radio releases. . . . F) In September, newspaper ads are taken in local papers and in the Times. G) Posters are distributed locally in high-rise apartment buildings, etc. Flyers are distributed under doors in low-income projects. Both posters and flyers are bilingual." The resignations are

described in Betty Young to Bertram Beck, memo, June 12, 1970; Alwin Nikolais to Bertram Beck, letter, n.d.; Alwin Nikolais to the Directors of the Henry Street Settlement, letter, June 5, 1970, Box 42, Folder 8, HSR.

25  Alwin Nikolais to the Directors of the Henry Street Settlement, letter, June 5, 1970, Box 42, Folder 8, HSR; Bertram Beck to Margaret Carlton, memo, June 8, 1970, HSR.

26  Minutes, June 21, 1971, HSC.

27  Memorandum, July 13, 1970, HSR, Box 42, Folder 8; Eleanor Blau, "Something for Everyone at Henry St.," *New York Times*, October 16, 1981.

28  Woodie King Jr., *The Impact of Race: Theatre and Culture* (New York: Applause Theatre & Cinema Books, 2003), 249.

29  Valerie Wingfield, "New Federal Theatre: A Brief History," *New York Public Library*, accessed September 12, 2018, www.nypl.org.

30  "Black Arts Movement," *Amistad Digital Resource*, accessed November 1, 2019, amistadresource.org; *Defending Freedom, Defining Freedom*, exhibition text, National Museum of African American History and Culture, Washington, DC, 2019.

31  King, *The Impact of Race*, 34–5; Karu F. Daniels, "New Federal Theatre Founder Woodie King, Jr. Continues Mission to Tell Untold Stories," *Playbill*, February 21, 2014.

32  Diane Weathers, "Curtains up on Broadway's Newest Star: The Black Producer," *Black Enterprise* 8, no. 5, December 1977, 40.

33  "New Federal Theatre, Inc. Program Statement," undated, HSR, Box 147, Folder 33.

34  Ibid.

35  Daniels, "New Federal Theatre Founder."

36  Ntozake Shange, *for colored girls who have considered suicide / when the rainbow is enuf* (New York: Scribner, 2010), 7–8; Denzel Washington in "Theater Talk: Denzel Washington/Woodie King, Jr.," accessed July 1, 2019, www.youtube.com/watch?v=bBKdduQV2_k.

37  Deborah Beck, interviews with the author, June 11, 2013, and July 2, 2013; Hall, *Unfinished Business*, 120–1; Gabriella Bendiner-Viani, *Contested City: Art and Public History as Mediation at New York's Seward Park Urban Renewal Area* (Iowa City: University of Iowa Press, 2019), xiii.

38  Deborah Beck, interview with the author, April 6, 2015; Hall, *Unfinished Business*, 121.

39  Deborah Beck, interviews with the author, June 11, 2013, and July 2, 2013. The Henry Street board engaged Deborah Beck to help fundraise for the project and, later, oversee it.

40  Deborah Beck, interview with the author, July 2, 2013.

41  "History," *Abrons Arts Center*, accessed July 25, 2019, www.abronsartscenter.org.

42  Ada Louise Huxtable, "Henry Street's New Building—An Urban Triumph," *New York Times*, August 10, 1975.

43  Jonathan Mahler, "How the Fiscal Crisis of the '70s Shaped Today's New York," *New York Times*, May 5, 2017.

44  Nunez and Sribnick, *The Poor Among Us*, 239. Over the course of the 1970s, New
    York City's poverty rate jumped from 14.5 percent to 20.2 percent. The descrip-
    tion of vacant lots is from Charles Kaiser, "Street Fair Tries to Counteract Blight
    on the Lower East Side," *New York Times*, June 1, 1975.

45  Jon Erickson and Charles Wilhelm, eds., *Housing the Homeless* (New Brunswick,
    NJ: Transaction Publishers, 2012), xli.

46  Henry Street Settlement, *Henry Street Settlement's Urban Family Center: The 1st
    Family Shelter in NYC 40th Anniversary*, posted May 32, 2013, www.youtube.com/
    watch?v=lCPMcxNVdPU.

47  Erickson and Wilhelm, *Housing the Homeless*, 30.

48  *Henry Street Settlement 2011 Annual Report*, HSC; Minutes, June 21, 1971, HSC. For
    *An Alternative to Welfare Hotels: A Plan for the Creation of a Temporary Family
    Residence*, Kronenfeld drew, among other sources, upon the ideas of Simeon Golar,
    head of the New York Housing Authority.

49  Nunez and Sribnick, *The Poor Among Us*, 249; Danny Kronenfeld, interview with
    Eileen Condon, April 13, 2018, HSC.

50  Danny Kronenfeld, interview with Eileen Condon, March 23, 2018, HSC.

51  Ed Litvak, "TLD Interview: Verona Middleton-Jeter of the Henry Street
    Settlement," *The Lo-Down: News from the Lower East Side*, August 14, 2009, www.
    thelodownny.com.

52  Eric Pace, "Bertram M. Beck, 82, Leader in the Field of Social Work," *New York
    Times*, April 5, 2000.

53  Deborah Beck, interviews with the author, April 6, 2015, and July 1, 2013.

54  Richard Abrons, *Some of Me in Fact and Fiction* (personal memoir, 2007), 188;
    Minutes, November 28, 1977, HSC.

55  Frank S. Seever, *An Agent of Change: Chicago Commons* (Chicago: Ampersand, Inc.,
    2013), 185.

56  Ibid., 184–5. *Jet* magazine noted in its February 7, 1980, issue, p. 21, that "Dr. Niathan
    Allen, deputy administrator and acting executive director of Henry Street
    Settlement Urban Life Center in New York City, has been elected executive
    director of the 113-year-old social service institution."

57  Blau, "Something for Everyone at Henry St."

58  John Wesley Zeiler, "A Reconsideration of the Arts for Living Center at the Henry
    Street Settlement," 1981, HSM, Box 86, Folder 2.

59  Walter I. Trattner, *From Poor Law to Welfare State: A History of Social Welfare in
    America*, 6th ed. (New York: Free Press, 1998), 362–4.

60  Ibid., 385.

61  Jesse Jackson, "The Number of Working Poor Is Growing," *Philadelphia Inquirer*,
    December 15, 1985.

62  C. Gerald Fraser, "Henry Street Settlement Cuts Arts Programs," *New York Times*,
    October 7, 1982.

63  "New York to Hollywood," *Jet*, January 17, 1983, 55.

**64** Robert W. Snyder, *Crossing Broadway: Washington Heights and the Promise of New York City* (Ithaca: Cornell University Press, 2014), 115–19.

**65** "A Timeline of HIV and AIDS," *HIV.gov*, accessed October 1, 2018, www.aids. gov; AIDS Institute, New York City Department of Health, *The New York State Department of Health AIDS Institute, July 30, 1983–July 30, 2008: 25 Years of Leadership, Service and Compassion* (Albany: AIDS Institute, May 2010), 93.

**66** Diane Grodney, "Programs for Children and Adolescents," in Barbara O. Dane and Carol Levine, eds., *AIDS and the New Orphans: Coping with Death* (Westport, Connecticut: Greenwood Publishing Company, 1994), 136–7; Larraine Ahto, Florence L. Samperi, and Lela Charney, *Reflections: Henry Street Settlement Community Consultation Center 1969–2013* (New York: Larraine Ahto, Florence L. Samperi, Lela Charney, 2019); "Message from the Executive Director 1992–93," HSC. *Reflections* is available in digital form on Henry Street Settlement's website at www.henrystreet.org.

**67** Erickson and Wilhelm, *Housing the Homeless*, xxxix; Edward I. Koch, "Homeless: One Place to Turn," *New York Times*, February 26, 1983.

**68** "Hearing Before the Select Committee on Children, Youth, and Families, House of Representatives, Ninety-Eighth Congress," *Families in Crisis: The Private Sector Response* (Washington, DC: U.S. Government Printing Office, 1983), 61–2.

**69** "Humans of Henry Street."

**70** "About," *Henry Street Settlement*; Ruth Messinger, email exchange with author, August 7, 2019.

**71** Debbie Cox, interview with the author, November 12, 2019; "Humans of Henry Street"; Paul Romita for the New York City Mission Society, *New York City Mission Society* (Charleston: Arcadia Publishing, 2003), n.p.

**72** "From an Article on the Boys Brotherhood Republic by Ralph Lee Goodman, its First Mayor," *Sentinel*, August 11, 1916, accessed October 10, 2019, https://flps. newberry.org/article/5423972_9_1_1456; "Boys Republic Organized By Reformed Crap Shooters," *New York Evening Post*, April 9, 1932; "Boys & Girls Republic," *Henry Street Settlement*, accessed August 4, 2019, www.henrystreet.org.

**73** Henry Street Settlement, *Henry Street's Boys & Girls Republic: What Parents Are Saying*, posted May 7, 2010, www.youtube.com/watch?v=VxHPAxHFjtQ.

**74** Nicole Fogarty, "Deep Roots at the Boys & Girls Republic," April 22, 2016, *Henry Street Settlement*, www.henrystreet.org.

**75** Minutes, November 22, 1982; May 23, 1983; May 21, 1984; September 17, 1984; February 25, 1985; March 18, 1985; April 1, 1985, HSC.

**76** Minutes, April 1, 1985, HSC; Ronald Reagan, speaking at an August 12, 1986 news conference, *Ronald Reagan Presidential Foundation & Institute*, www.reaganfoundation.org.

**77** Minutes, April 1, 1985, HSC; Danny Kronenfeld, interview with the author, June 1, 2013.

78 Richard Abrons, interview with Susan LaRosa, August 7, 2019; "Dinner with Danny: A Very Special Evening," February 20, 2018, *Henry Street Settlement*, www.henrystreet.org.

79 Richard Abrons, interview with Susan LaRosa, August 7, 2019.

80 Eleanor Shakin to Danny Kronenfeld, memo, December 9, 1985, HSR, Box 147, Folder NN.

81 Minutes, February 24, 1986 and September 15, 1986, HSC.

82 Tim Clayton and Phil Craig, *Diana: Story of a Princess* (Great Britain: Hodder & Stoughton, Ltd., 2001), 174–5.

83 These statistics are cited in Andy A. Beveridge, "The Poor in New York City," *Gotham Gazette*, accessed April 15, 2003, www.gothamgazette.com.

84 Min Zhou, *Contemporary Chinese America: Immigration, Ethnicity, and Community Transformation* (Philadelphia: Temple University Press, 2009), 103; Kenneth J. Guest, "From Mott Street to East Broadway: Fuzhounese Immigrants and the Revitalization of New York's Chinatown," *Journal of Chinese Overseas* 7 (2011), 24–5.

85 Vita Iacovone, "9/11: The Great Equalizer," in Yael Danieli and Robert L. Dingman, eds., *On the Ground After September 11: Mental Health Responses and Practical Knowledge Gained* (Binghamton: The Haworth Press, 2005), 174–7.

86 "Henry Street Response to 9/11," *News from Henry Street/Spring 2002*, HSC.

87 "About," *Henry Street Settlement*; News from Henry Street (Winter 2006), www.henrystreet.org, "Humans of Henry Street."

88 Barbara Kancelbaum, interview with the author, July 23, 2019.

89 Susan Dominus describes the arts center and its then-director, Jay Wegman, in "A Love of God, and the Stage," *New York Times*, May 8, 2009; Henry Street Settlement, *Henry Street Settlement Biennial Report 2005–2006*, 2–3, www.henrystreet.org.

90 Diane Cardwell, "With Donations and Grants Down, Social Service Agencies Feel the Pinch," *New York Times*, August 21, 2009.

91 Ibid.

92 Minutes, September 13, 1982 HSC.

93 "Humans of Henry Street," *Henry Street Settlement*, accessed June 1, 2019, www.henrystreet.org.

94 Minutes, February 22, 2010; Nell Porter Brown, "Fighting Need on the Lower East Side," *Harvard Magazine* (March–April 2019), www.harvardmagazine.com; David Garza, interview with the author, July 23, 2019.

95 Brown, "Fighting Need on the Lower East Side."

96 David Garza, interview with the author, July 23, 2019.

97 Peter Edelman, "Poverty in America: Why Can't We End It?" *New York Times*, July 28, 2012. Edelman writes that with many people working at low-wage jobs, and with many households headed by a single parent, it is difficult to make a

living from what is available. "And," he notes, "persistent issues of race and gender mean higher poverty among minorities and families headed by single mothers."

98 David Garza, interview with the author, July 23, 2019.

99 Ibid.

100 "Watch Video: Youth Opportunity Hub Open!" *Henry Street Settlement*, November 16, 2017, www.henrystreet.org; "Lower East Side Youth Opportunity Hub," *Henry Street Settlement*, www.henrystreet.org.

101 Craig T. Peterson, interview with the author, January 24, 2018.

102 "PATHS Infuses Abrons Arts Programming through All Henry Street Programs," *Henry Street Settlement*, July 3, 2019, www.henrystreet.org.

**CONCLUSION**

1 "American Community Survey 2013–2017," *NYU Furman Center*, accessed October 26, 2019, www.furmancenter.org; "American Community Survey 2010–2014," *United States Census Bureau*, December 26, 2018, www.census.gov.

2 Ernest Poole, inscription to Lillian Wald, 1927, Henry Street Guest Book, HSC.

3 "Life Goes on from Forty," 1940, HSR, Box 68, Folder 9.

4 Henry Street Settlement, *Voices of Henry Street*, 76; "Humans of Henry Street"; "Sue Ann Hoahng, Court Attorney, The Civil Court of New York," unpublished profile, HSC; Sue Ann Santos-Hoahng, email exchange with Barbara Kancelbaum, November 15, 2019; "Henry Street Settlement: 120 Years in 4 Minutes," video, 2012.

5 Henry Street Settlement, *Voices of Henry Street*, 46.

6 Wald, *Windows on Henry Street*, 338.

7 Wald, *The House on Henry Street*, 310.

# INDEX

# ABOUT THE AUTHOR

ELLEN M. SNYDER-GRENIER IS A NATIONAL-AWARD-WINNING
curator and writer, and principal of REW & Co. She has directed
research projects, developed physical and digital exhibitions, and written
on the history of New York City—as well the urban centers of Newark
and Philadelphia—with a focus on social justice. The author of an
award-winning history of Brooklyn, Snyder-Grenier is a Fellow of the
New York Academy of History.